# 口译进阶教程：专业交传
Developing Interpreting Competency
Professional Consecutive Interpreting

主　编　梅德明
副主编　张　燕　吴　赟
参编者　侯靖靖　朱　萍　顾秋蓓
　　　　虞文婷　孙珊珊　吴　菲

图书在版编目(CIP)数据

口译进阶教程：专业交传/梅德明主编. —北京：北京大学出版社，2008.12
（21世纪英语专业系列教材）
ISBN 978-7-301-13840-3

Ⅰ.口… Ⅱ.梅… Ⅲ.英语—口译—高等学校—教材 Ⅳ.H315.9

中国版本图书馆 CIP 数据核字(2008)第 067934 号

书　　　名：口译进阶教程：专业交传
著作责任者：梅德明　主编
策　　　划：张　冰　刘　强
责 任 编 辑：高生文
标 准 书 号：ISBN 978-7-301-13840-3/H・2003
出 版 发 行：北京大学出版社
地　　　址：北京市海淀区成府路 205 号　100871
网　　　址：http://www.pup.cn
电 子 邮 箱：zpup@pup.pku.edu.cn
电　　　话：邮购部 62752015　发行部 62750672　编辑部 62767315　出版部 62754962
印　刷　者：北京大学印刷厂
经　销　者：新华书店
　　　　　　787 毫米×1092 毫米　16 开本　17 印张　400 千字
　　　　　　2008 年 12 月第 1 版　2018 年 5 月第 3 次印刷
定　　　价：48.00 元（配有光盘）

未经许可，不得以任何方式复制或抄袭本书之部分或全部内容。
版权所有，侵权必究　举报电话：010－62752024
　　　　　　　　　　电子邮箱：fd@pup.pku.edu.cn

《21世纪英语专业系列教材》编写委员会

(以姓氏笔画排序)
王守仁　王克非　申　丹
刘意青　李　力　胡壮麟
桂诗春　梅德明　程朝翔

# 总　序

北京大学出版社自 2005 年以来已出版《语言与应用语言学知识系列读本》多种,为了配合第十一个五年计划,现又策划陆续出版《21 世纪英语专业系列教材》。这个重大举措势必受到英语专业广大教师和学生的欢迎。

作为英语教师,最让人揪心的莫过于听人说英语不是一个专业,只是一个工具。说这些话的领导和教师的用心是好的,为英语专业的毕业生将来找工作着想,因此要为英语专业的学生多多开设诸如新闻、法律、国际商务、经济、旅游等其他专业的课程。但事与愿违,英语专业的教师们很快发现,学生投入英语学习的时间少了,掌握英语专业课程知识甚微,即使对四个技能的掌握也并不比大学英语学生高明多少,而那个所谓的第二专业在有关专家的眼中只是学到些皮毛而已。

英语专业的路在何方？有没有其他路可走？这是需要我们英语专业教师思索的问题。中央领导关于创新是一个民族的灵魂和要培养创新人才等的指示精神,让我们在层层迷雾中找到了航向。显然,培养学生具有自主学习能力和能进行创造性思维是我们更为重要的战略目标,使英语专业的人才更能适应 21 世纪的需要,迎接 21 世纪的挑战。

如今,北京大学出版社外语部的领导和编辑同志们,也从教材出版的视角探索英语专业的教材问题,从而为贯彻英语专业教学大纲做些有益的工作,为教师们开设大纲中所规定的必修、选修课程提供各种教材。《21 世纪英语专业系列教材》是普通高等教育"十一五"国家级规划教材和国家"十一五"重点出版规划项目《面向新世纪的立体化网络化英语学科建设丛书》的重要组成部分。这套系列教材要体现新世纪英语教学的自主化、协作化、模块化和超文本化,结合外语教材的具体情况,既要解决语言、教学内容、教学方法和教育技术的时代化,也要坚持弘扬以爱国主义为核心的民族精神。因此,今天北京大学出版社在大力提倡专业英语教学改革的基础上,编辑出版各种英语专业技能、英语专业知识和相关专业知识课程的教材,以培养具有创新性思维的和具有实际工作能力的学生,充分体现了时代精神。

北京大学出版社的远见卓识,也反映了英语专业广大师生盼望已久的心愿。由北京大学等全国几十所院校具体组织力量,积极编写相关教材。这就是说，这套教材是由一些高等院校有水平有经验的第一线教师们制定编写大纲，反复讨论，特别是考虑到在不同层次、不同背景学校之间取得平衡，避免了先前的教材或偏难或偏易的弊病。与此同时，一批知名专家教授参与策划和教材审定工作，保证了教材质量。

当然，这套系列教材出版只是初步实现了出版社和编者们的预期目标。为了获得更大效果，希望使用本系列教材的教师和同学不吝指教，及时将意见反馈给我们，使教材更加完善。

航道已经开通，我们有决心乘风破浪，奋勇前进！

胡壮麟

北京大学蓝旗营

# 编者的话

应北京大学出版社的盛情约稿，上海外国语大学英语学院承担了《进阶口译教程》的编写任务。《进阶口译教程》以我国高等院校新设立的本科专业"翻译专业"的学生为主要教学对象，是我国口译教学工作者编写的第一套进阶式系统性教材。之所以称其为《进阶口译教程》，是因为这套教程是按循序渐进、拾阶而上的专业教学原则编写的。这也是我国出版社推出的第一套含一至四册的口译教材。

上海外国语大学英语学院有着持续编写口译教材的良好传统。自1996年以来，我们先后为上海外语教育出版社、人民教育出版社、高等教育出版社、外文出版社、北京大学出版社等全国知名出版机构编写了十几套用于不同教学对象和教学目的的口译教材。这些教材被全国各地近千所高校外语院系和社会培训机构采纳为口译教学的主干教材。

上外英语学院并不满足所取得的成就。这些年来，我们立足教学实践和社会服务，一边从事高校口译教学，打造口译精品课程，一边承担社会口译任务，编写口译精品教材。我们不断总结在教学和服务工作中积累起来的诸多实践经验，将归纳梳理后的心得体会编入口译教材。就这样，我们义无反顾地、一步一个台阶地努力攀登我国口译教学和研究的高峰。多年来的辛勤耕耘和研磨提炼，上外英语学院在口译教材编写方面形成了自己的特色和风格，即"经典性与时代性相结合，典型性与广泛性相结合，专业性和通用性相结合，真实性和参阅性相结合，语言结构与交际功能相结合，专业知识与口译技能相结合"的编写原则，以及"博采众长、精道为重；趋实避虚、剪裁致用；隐括情理，凝练字句"的编写风格。

由于诸多原因，这些年来我国口译教材大多为"单打独斗"类的单卷孤册，只能满足高校单学期或单学年课的口译教学，或各类口译认证考试的短期培训。自2006年起，教育部批准在部分高校试行翻译专业本科教育。我们清楚地意识到，国内现有的教材显然难以满足四年制的翻译专业教学。因此，编写一套适合我国翻译专业本科阶段多学期教学、体系完整的口译教材成了当务之急。这套《进阶口译教程》就是在此背景下应运而生。

《进阶口译教程》根据口译工作的时代要求和职业特点而取材，根据口译教学的目的和学习规律而编写，精取传统口译教材之长，博采现行口译教材之优。根据口译工作双向传递信息的基本要求，《进阶口译教程》将英译汉和汉译英两种口译形式的教学活动贯穿于整个教学过程，以搭建口译平台、组织口译活动为教学手段，以讲解口译知识、传授传译技巧为教学内容，以培养口译能力、提高口译水平为教学目的。

《进阶口译教程》共含四册：第一册为《口译进阶教程：联络陪同》，教授涉外接待和陪同工作所需的口译知识和技能；第二册为《口译进阶教程：通用交传》，教授通用性较强的交传知识和技能；第三册为《口译进阶教程：专业交传》，教授专业性较强的交传知识和技能；第四册为《口译进阶教程：会议同传》，教授有关一般会议的同传基础知识和技能。

我们主张本教程主要以翻译专业二年级和三年级学生为教学对象，每学期用一册。至于一年级和四年级的口译教学，我们建议一年级的教学以强化学生的语言能力为主要目的，四年级的教学应在进一步提高学生口译综合能力的同时，加大口译实习的比重。我们认为，《进阶口译教程》可以作口译教学的主干教材，但是教师应该根据具体的教学对象和教学实际，积极补充教学内容，尤其是要补充一些符合当时国内外形势以及当地社会文化建设和经济建设所需的材料。

对于《进阶口译教程》中存在的纰缪或疏漏之处，编者祈盼使用者不吝赐教。

梅德明<br>
上海外国语大学英语学院<br>
2008 年 3 月 6 日

# 目 录

第 1 单元　广告宣传 Advertising ........................................... 1
　　口译技能　词性转换 ..................................................... 7
　　参考译文 ................................................................... 12

第 2 单元　公共关系 Public Relations ................................... 17
　　口译技能　增词和减词 ................................................. 23
　　参考译文 ................................................................... 28

第 3 单元　投资环境 Investment Environment ....................... 33
　　口译技能　长句处理 ..................................................... 40
　　参考译文 ................................................................... 44

第 4 单元　城市规划 Urban Planning ................................... 51
　　口译技能　句子结构 ..................................................... 57
　　参考译文 ................................................................... 62

第 5 单元　工商管理 Business Administration ....................... 69
　　口译技能　语篇理解(1)：口音和语速 ............................. 75
　　参考译文 ................................................................... 79

第 6 单元　现代物流 Modern Logistics ................................. 85
　　口译技能　语篇理解(2)：逻辑思维 ................................. 91
　　参考译文 ................................................................... 95

第 7 单元　市场营销 Marketing and Sales ............................. 101
　　口译技能　衔接(1) ....................................................... 107
　　参考译文 ................................................................... 111

## 第 8 单元　企业文化 Corporate Culture …… 117
　　口译技能　衔接(2) …… 123
　　参考译文 …… 128

## 第 9 单元　保险业务 Insurance Business …… 135
　　口译技能　司仪口译 …… 141
　　参考译文 …… 145

## 第 10 单元　外贸实务 Foreign Trade …… 151
　　口译技能　记者招待会 …… 157
　　参考译文 …… 162

## 第 11 单元　资本市场 The Capital Market …… 167
　　口译技能　商务口译 …… 173
　　参考译文 …… 177

## 第 12 单元　生命科学 The Biological Science …… 183
　　口译技能　法庭口译 …… 189
　　参考译文 …… 193

## 第 13 单元　信息技术 Information Technology …… 197
　　口译技能　视译 …… 204
　　参考译文 …… 208

## 第 14 单元　法律制度 Law and Legal System …… 215
　　口译技能　模糊表达 …… 220
　　参考译文 …… 224

## 第 15 单元　语言文字 Language and Writing …… 229
　　口译技能　知识习得 …… 235
　　参考译文 …… 239

## 第 16 单元　外交政策 Foreign Policy …… 245
　　口译技能　语言提高 …… 252
　　参考译文 …… 257

# 第 1 单元 广告宣传

 **Advertising**

Unit 1

# 篇章口译

## Passage A (E-C)

### Vocabulary Work

Work on the following words and phrases and write the translated version in the space provided.

| | | | |
|---|---|---|---|
| promotion | media outlet | marketer | target market |
| interactive | evolve | stimulate | revenue |
| the classified section of newspaper | marketing objective | advertising campaign | do-it-yourself advertising |
| professional | advertising agency | | |

### Text Interpreting

**Listen to the tape and interpret the following passage from English into Chinese.**

Do you know what advertising is? Do you know the importance of advertising? And do you know how to manage advertising decisions? Today I'm going to talk about all these questions.

Advertising is a non-personal form of promotion that is always delivered through selected media outlets that, under most circumstances, require the marketer to pay for message placement. Advertising has long been viewed as a method of mass promotion in that a single message can reach a large number of people. But, this mass promotion approach presents problems since many exposed to an advertising message may not be within the marketer's target market, and thus, may be an inefficient use of promotional funds. However, this is changing as new advertising technologies and the emergence of new media outlets offer more options for targeted advertising.

Advertising also has a history of being considered a one-way form of marketing communication where the message receiver is not in position to immediately respond to the message. This too is changing. For example, in the next few years technologies will be readily available to enable a television viewer to click a button to request more details on a product. In fact, it is expected that over the next 10—20 years advertising will move away from a one-way communication model and become one that is highly interactive.

Another characteristic that may change as advertising evolves is the view that advertising does not stimulate immediate demand for the product advertised. That is, customers cannot quickly purchase a product they see advertised. But as more media outlets allow customers to interact with the messages being delivered, the ability of advertising to quickly stimulate demand will improve.

Spending on advertising is huge. ZenithOptimedia, a research firm, estimates that worldwide spending on advertising exceeds $400 billion. This level of spending supports thousands of companies and millions of jobs. In fact, in many countries most media outlets, such as television, radio and newspapers, would not be in business without revenue generated through the sale of advertising.

While worldwide advertising is an important contributor to economic growth, individual marketing organizations differ on the role advertising plays. For some small companies advertising may consist of occasional advertisement and on a very small scale, such as placing small ads in the classified section of a local newspaper. But most organizations, large and small, that rely on marketing to create customer interest are engaged in consistent use of advertising to help meet marketing objectives.

Delivering an effective marketing message through advertising requires many different decisions as the marketer develops their advertising campaign. For small campaigns, that involve little creative effort, one or a few people may handle the bulk of the work. In fact, the Internet has made do-it-yourself advertising an easy-to-manage process and has especially empowered small businesses to manage their advertising decisions. As we will see, not only can small firms handle the creation and placement of advertisements that appear on the Internet, new services have even made it possible for a single person to create advertisements that run on local television.

For larger campaigns the skills needed to make sound advertising decisions can be quite varied and may not be easily handled by a single person. While larger companies manage some advertising activities within the company, they are more likely to rely on the assistance of advertising professionals, such as those found at advertising agencies, to help bring their advertising campaign to market.

Today I made a very brief introduction of advertising, something that we are so familiar with nowadays. Next time I will talk about the main types of advertising. Thank you!

# 篇章口译

## Passage B (C-E)

### Vocabulary Work

Work on the following words and phrases and write the translated version in the space provided.

| 平面广告 | 创作广告 | 创意 | 撰稿人 |
| 美术指导 | 直接反应广告 | 受益点 | 目标受众 |
| 关注点 | 排放问题 | 空气污染控制设备 | 回应 |
| 可信度 | 费用优惠 | | |

### Text Interpreting

**Listen to the tape and interpret the following passage from Chinese into English.**

早上好！

如今，广告已经成为我们生活中非常重要的一部分，我们现在生活在广告的世界中。不论我们喜欢与否，广告都已经侵入了我们的生活。

我知道在座的各位都对平面广告很感兴趣，我也非常高兴能有这个机会与大家一同分享一下我在创作广告方面的一点体验。

在界定什么才是好的平面广告之前，我们先来说一下好的平面广告不应该具备哪些条件。好的广告不应该是为了追求创意而有创意；其设计不应该是为了取悦撰稿人、美术指导甚至客户；其目的也不应该是娱乐或赢得奖项。换句话说，把你们在基础广告学习班中所学的内容或在广告公司中作为实习生所学的内容通通抛开。

好，这些就是好的平面广告不应该具备的条件。那么好的广告又应该具备哪些条件呢？下面我们就来看一下成功的直接反应平面广告的一些共同特点：

首先，它们都强调一个受益点。它们并不是巧妙地隐藏主要卖点，而是相当明确地将其呈现出来，例如"如何才能赢得朋友，并影响他人"，这个标题就非常明确地强调了受益点。

其次，它们都会激起人们的好奇心，使他们想要看下去。此处的关键不是要我们肆无忌惮、毫无节制，而是要求我们去针对目标受众的最主要兴趣点和关注点。例如，"你会犯这些英语错误吗？"这句话就迎合了读者希望避免尴尬、说得正确、写得正确的愿望。

再次，它们都会提供信息和知识。一则成功的广告常常会反映出高层次的知识，以及对产品和产品所解决问题的理解。如"如何应对排放问题——只需传统空气污染控制设备一半的成本"，这一标题之所以会吸引读者，就是因为它有可能提供有用的信息。能为读者提供所需信息的广告通常能赢得更多的读者和更好的回应。

有时，一些所谓的"专业"广告撰稿人会使用一种毫无效果的方法，即将一切事物都归为最简单的共同特色，并假设读者是完全无知的。但这样只会侮辱读者的智力，并损害广告的可信度。

最后，好的平面广告会提供极大的费用优惠。它们会告诉读者购买过程的下一步是什么，并鼓励他们立即购买。提供这样的优惠是极其必要的，至于其中的原因，我会在下一次讲座中为大家解释，谢谢！

# 口译讲评

## Notes on the Text

**Passage A**

1. **under most circumstances, require the marketer to pay for message placement**：译文中可将 marketer 一词作为主语，译成"多数情况下，营销商需要支付广告展示费用"，这样听上去就会很自然。

2. **...since many...may not be within the marketer's target market**：这里若译成"因为很多接收到广告信息的受众也许并不在营销商的目标市场范围里"，听上去会感觉很晦涩，不如意译成"许多接收到广告的受众未必是营销商的目标客户"。

3. **..., may be an inefficient use of promotional funds**：这句也无需拘泥于字面，可以意译为"于是就可能造成促销资金的浪费"。

4. **Advertising also has a history of being considered...**：刻板地追究听到的每个词的意思，绝对是口译中的大忌。譬如这句话中的 history，就完全可以隐含在句中，整句即可译为"广告还一直被认为……"

5. **it is expected that over the next 10—20 years**：遇到这样的句子结构时，中文里常常会根据情况加入适当的主语，如这句就可以译成"人们预期，在未来的 10 到 20 年间"。其他常见的还有：it is generally accepted that...（一般认为；大家公认）、it is believed that...（大家相信；人们相信；据信）、it is claimed that...（有人主张；人们要求）、it is suggested that...（有人建议）等等。

6. **Another characteristic that may change as advertising evolves is the view that advertising does not stimulate immediate demand for the product advertised**：这句话非常长，译员在口译时一定要保持良好的心理素质，切忌慌乱。此外，交传不同于同传，译员可以对句子表达的先后顺序略作调整。这句话调整后即可译为"一般认为，广告不会刺激人们对所宣传商品的即时需求，这一观点也可能会随广告的发展而有所改变"。

7. **ZenithOptimedia**：实力传播公司。它是全球领先的媒体传播公司，在全球 58 个国家设有 161 个办事机构，是全球五大媒体投放公司之一。实力传播于 1996 年进入中国，是中国最早成立的专业媒体代理。自进入中国以来，实力传播每年均稳居中国媒介代理投放量首位。目前旗下有实力媒体和突破传播两大品牌，在上海、北京、广州三地设有办公室，拥有近 700 位员工。

8. **This level of spending supports thousands of companies and millions of jobs**：这句话中的 companies 和 jobs 都是 support 的宾语，但在中文里则需要两个不同的动词来分别修饰 companies 和 jobs，"这样大的花费也养活了成千上万的企业，提供了数以百万计的就业机会"。

9. **... would not be in business without revenue generated through the sale of advertising**：这是个双重否定的句子，可译为"都是依靠广告所得来维持生计的"，亦可译为中文的双重否定句，"若没有广告所得都很难维持生计"。

10. **For some small companies advertising may consist of occasional advertisement**：这里的 consist of 若是生硬地译成"包含"或"由……组成"，整个句子就会显得很拗口，不如灵活地翻译成"一些小公司也许只是偶尔做广告"。

**Passage B**

1. **平面广告**：顾名思义，即两维广告，指的是平面图形，而不是立体图形的广告。平面广告的大发展主要还是在第二次世界大战结束以后。这一时期由于战后经济的迅速复苏以及多种印刷媒体的变革，与商业市场相关的二维空间的设计表现领域得到了极大的扩展，平面广告设计的涵盖面也越来越广。企业和机构的活动越来越多地需要用各种平面广告的方式来传递信息、说明问题。平面广告最重要的设计理念是使人们去接受企业的产品或服务，并告诉人们如何改善现在的生活状况。

2. **在界定什么才是好的平面广告之前**：to define what constitutes good print advertising，这里使用的 constitute 要比 is 形象很多。

3. **好的平面广告不应该具备哪些条件**：若将"条件"一词生硬译出的话，句子就会显得拖沓、不自然，只要将其简简单单地译 what a good print ad should not be 就完全可以了。

4. **直接反应广告**：即任何付费的广告，意在诱发直接的反应，例如在广告中附加一张回执，消费者把该回执剪下寄给制造商即可获得产品的样品、说明书、目录等。它可以采用各种媒介，特别是直接邮递广告（direct mail advertising）和报纸等。

5. **它们并不是巧妙地隐藏主要卖点，而是相当明确地将其呈现出来**：The main selling proposition is not cleverly hidden but is made immediately clear. 这句话的主语不需改变，仍沿用原句中的"它们（这里指成功的直接反应广告）"也可以，译句则为 They make the main selling proposition immediately clear instead of hiding it cleverly.

6. **它们都会激起人们的好奇心，使他们想要看下去**："激起某人的好奇心"除了 arouse curiosity 外，常用的动词还有 excite、provoke 及 stimulate。"使他们想要看下去"可直接译成 invite readership，言简意赅。

7. **此处的关键不是要肆无忌惮、毫无节制**：这里的"肆无忌惮、毫无节制"只需一个 outrageous 就足够了。

8. **就是因为它有可能提供有用的信息**：毫无疑问，这句话译成 because it promises useful information 要比 because it may provide useful information 要好很多。

# 第1单元 广告宣传 Advertising

## 相关词语 Relevant Words and Expressions

分类广告 classified advertisement
广告插页 free-standing inserts
企业广告 corporate advertising
杂志广告 magazine advertisement
招聘广告 recruitment advertising
霓虹灯广告 neon-light advertisement
中国广告节 China Advertising Festival
标准户外广告 standardized outdoor advertising
登广告找房子 advertise for a house
分类图片广告 classified display ads
企业识别广告 corporate identity advertising
别具匠心的广告 a well-designed / an ingenious advertisement
大规模地做广告 advertise extensively
登广告出租房屋 advertise a house for rent
广告极多的报纸 newspaper containing a great deal of advertising
用广告招揽顾客 secure customers by advertising
在报纸上登广告 place an advertisement in a newspaper
购买广告上宣传的商品 buy things from advertisements
大张旗鼓的宣传 thunderous advertisement
报纸上占整版篇幅的广告 full-page newspaper advertisement

## 口译技能 Interpreting Skills

### 词性转换

  英汉两种语言在语法、词汇、文化习惯、表达方式等诸多方面存在众多差异,因此英汉互译时常常需要因势而动,因情制宜,改变表达方式,使译文通顺、流畅、地道。词性转换是其中重要的方法。下面从英汉和汉英口译两方面分述这种方法的具体应用。
  汉语形式较松散,灵活随意,富于弹性,各自为独立小句,如流水,和在一起,一气呵成。英语则句式严谨,缺乏弹性,长句枝干清晰,主次层层链接,每一片叶子的归属都毫无暧昧。在进行英汉口译时,往往有较多的英语名词、介词、形容词或副词转换为汉语动词。如:
  1. *A change of* state from a solid to a liquid form requires heat energy. 从固态变为液态需要热能。

2. They marched on bravely *against* the piercing wind. 他们冒着刺骨的寒风英勇前进。

3. It is a *two-way* street in politics. When you ignore people, you'll be ignored by them. 这是政治上的一种有来必有往的现象,如果你不理睬人们,人们也就不理睬你。

4. Why should we let *in* foreign goods when Americans walk the streets because they can't sell their own goods? 在美国人由于推销不出自己的产品而失业之际,为什么我们还要进口外国货呢?

5. The mayor tried to *Richard Nixon* the tapes of the meeting. 市长极力掩盖真相,抹去会议录音。/ 市长试图像理查德·尼克松那样为掩盖事实真相把会议录音内容抹去。

在上述几个英语句子中,斜体部分的名词、介词、形容词、副词、名词分别都在口译成汉语时转换为动词。而同样英语中的动词在具体情况下,也可以转译为中文中适当的词性。例如:

1. They argue that regimes come and go, that political issues are always transient, that the Olympic spirit is transcendent. 他们说,政权无非是走马灯,政治问题总是朝生夕逝的,只有奥林匹克精神才是永世长存的。

2. In his six consecutive speeches, Nasser indulged in violent attacks on the Baghdad government. 纳赛尔在连续六次的演说中,不断地对巴格达政府进行猛烈的攻击。

3. Hospitals are getting more efficient these days. 近日来,医院的效率越来越高。

4. They returned game and glee. 他们兴高采烈地回来了。

5. It was officially announced that they agreed on a reply to the neighboring country. 官方宣布,他们就给邻国的复信取得了一致意见。

上面几个句子中的斜体部分分别都由动词、形容词、名词、副词转成相应的名词、副词、名词等。由此可见词性转换是应用得极为普遍的一种口译技巧,在汉英口译中同样应用得非常广泛。看以下几个例句:

1. 目前我国各地对各种消费品的需要量大大增加。There is a big increase in number for all kinds of consumer goods in every part of our country.

2. 他们不顾一切困难、挫折,坚持试验。They kept on experimenting in spite of all difficulties and setbacks.

3. 我们要通过加强我们之间的经济、文化、科学、技术交流和人员往来加深了解。We seek a deep-rooted understanding through the multiplication of our economic, cultural, scientific, technical and human ties.

4. 那本书不久就要出版了。That book will be out pretty soon.

5. 该产品的主要特点是工艺精湛,经久耐用。The products of this factory are chiefly characterized by their fine workmanship and durability.

在以上几个句子中,分别有动词和名词转换为名词、介词、形容词、副词和动词的情形。

不难看出,词性转换是英汉及汉英口译中的必备技能之一。在口译实践中,译者必须大胆运用,反复操练,直至可以得心应手,译出自然妥帖的译文。

# 第 1 单元 广告宣传 Advertising

## 翻译练习 Enhancement Practice

### 第一项 Project 1
### 句子精练 Sentences in Focus

**A. Interpret the following sentences from English into Chinese.**

1. If you're running TV and radio commercials, you need to keep them consistent and use the same announcer and music for your commercials.
2. Most advertising spending is directed toward the promotion of specific goods, service or idea, what we have collectively labeled as "product".
3. The only way to know with any accuracy how your advertising strategy is working is to ask the consumer, the opinions of whom can be gathered in several ways.
4. Even though a small business has limited capital and is unable to devote as much money to advertising as a large corporation, it can still develop a highly effective advertising campaign.
5. Before advertising, you need to take a look at each medium, think about your target audience, take a look at your marketing plan and decide which medium will be the most appropriate one.

**B. Interpret the following sentences from Chinese into English.**

1. 去年上半年,中国的广告税收攀升至1700亿元人民币,比前年同期增长了20%。
2. 广告即一种交流,旨在告知潜在消费者关于产品和服务的情况,以及如何使用和获得它们。
3. 在经济持续增长的推动下,中国的广告业蓬勃发展,中国有望在三年内成为仅次于美国的世界第二大广告市场。
4. 如今,大部分广告策略都侧重于实现三大目标:提升公众对企业及其产品的认知度、刺激销售以及树立企业形象。
5. 随着互联网的发展和普及,在线广告也迅速发展起来,它作为一种新型的广告模式,与传统广告在很多方面都有所不同。

### 第二项 Project 2
### 段落口译 Paragraph Interpreting

**A. Interpret the following paragraph from English into Chinese.**

Some of the strongest elements in any advertisement are testimonials, facts, and figures. People love to hear from other people they can relate to who have already taken the risk that they are considering and who have succeeded. Facts and figures support your claims. If your data indicates that the company increases its business by 65% in the first month, the customer gains confidence in your service. It is also important to remember that when you do report facts and figures, never round them off to 60% or $200.00. It's more credible to use figures like 58.6% or $197.60.

**B. Interpret the following paragraph from Chinese into English.**

中国的广告市场于 2005 年 12 月对外开放以来，吸引了许多跨国广告集团，它们有着雄厚的资本实力、科学的管理方法及经验丰富的运作模式，给国内的广告公司带来了更多的机会，也带来了极大的挑战。中国的广告业在持续稳定的经济增长的推动下，必定会有非常灿烂的前景。

第三项 Project 3
篇章口译 Passage Interpreting

**A. Listen to the tape and interpret the following passage from English into Chinese.**

Good afternoon!

Last time I talked about the definition and importance of advertising. Now I'd like to introduce the main types of advertising.

If you ask most people what is meant by "type" of advertising, invariably they will respond by defining it in terms of how it is delivered, such as television ad, radio ad... But in marketing, type of advertising refers to the primary "focus" of the message being sent and falls into one of the following four categories:

The first type is product-oriented advertising. In most cases the goal of product advertising is to clearly promote a specific product to a targeted audience. Marketers can accomplish this in several ways from a low-key approach that simply provides basic information about a product to blatant appeals that try to convince customers to purchase a product that may include direct comparisons between the marketer's product and its competitor's offerings.

However, sometimes marketers intentionally produce product advertising where the target audience cannot readily see a connection to a specific product. Marketers of new products may follow this "teaser" approach in advance of a new product introduction to prepare the market for the product. For instance, one week before the launch of a new product a marketer may air a television advertisement proclaiming "Next week the world will never be the same" but do so without any mention of a product or even the company behind the ad. The goal is to create curiosity in the market and interest of the new product.

The second type is image advertising. Image advertising is undertaken primarily to enhance an organization's perceived importance to a target market. Image advertising does not focus on specific products as much as it presents what an organization has to offer. Image advertising is often used in situations where an organization needs to educate the targeted audience on some issue. For instance, image advertising may be used in situations where a merger has occurred between two companies and the newly formed company has taken on a new name.

Advocacy advertising is the third type. In most cases there is an underlying benefit sought by an organization when they engage in advocacy advertising. For instance, an organization may take a stand on a political issue which they feel could negatively impact the organization and will target advertisements to voice their position on the issue.

The last type is public service advertising. In some countries, not-for-profit organizations are permitted to run advertisements through certain media outlets free-of-charge if the message contained in the ads concerns an issue viewed as for the "greater good" of society. For instance, ads directed at social causes, such as teenage smoking, illegal drug use and mental illness, may run on television, radio and other media without cost to organizations sponsoring the advertisement.

These are the four main categories of advertising. I hope my lecture will be of any help to you. Thank you!

**B. Listen to the tape and interpret the following passage from Chinese into English.**
早上好！

在上一次的讲座中，我说过优惠对于好的平面广告来说极其必要的，现在我就来解释一下其中的原因。

所有的广告都应该提供优惠，因为优惠可以使那些准备购买或至少考虑购买的潜在客户立即做出反应。没有优惠，你就有可能会失去很多潜在客户。

此外，大幅度的优惠还可以扩大读者群，因为人们喜欢能为他们提供优惠的广告，尤其当优惠的内容是一些免费的，而且感觉上价值也挺高的东西。

一些形象广告的作者也许会提出反对，"提供优惠难道不会使广告变得廉价，有损我们的形象吗？毕竟，我们想要的只是意识，而非反应。"但是，提供一本免费的小册子又怎么会削弱广告的力度呢？不会，当然不会！如果你认为引起反应和传达信息无法同时做到的话，那你的整个想法就都是荒谬的、毫无根据的。

那么我们又应该如何设计广告来突出优惠呢？一些图形技术，如粗体的大标题、不拘一格的副标题、优惠券、醒目标出的免费电话号码、星号、旁注等等，都可以使你的广告更加引人注目，从而增加读者群。

也许会有人跳出来反对说："等等，你所说的这些都是成功的直接反应广告的特点，一般广告不会有所不同吗？"也许会。但令一般广告更加有效的方法之一即将它作为直接反应广告来设计。好的广告很少会使用抽象艺术或抽象概念来强迫读者去琢磨广告中的商品。最理想的情形是，让你的读者在看到广告后的 5 秒钟之内就能够确切地明白其中的主题。上述的这些技巧可以使你的广告获得更多反馈，这难道不好吗？

# 参考译文
## Reference Version

**篇章口译 A**

你知道什么是广告吗？你知道广告的重要性吗？你知道如何进行广告决策吗？今天我就要谈论一下这些问题。

广告是一种非个人形式的促销方式，常常通过选定的媒体渠道来进行传播，多数情况下，营销商需要支付广告展示费用。广告一直被视为一种大规模的促销模式，因为它可以将一条信息传达给许许多多的人。但这种大规模的促销模式也有一些问题，许多接收到广告信息的受众未必是营销商的目标客户，于是就可能造成促销资金的浪费。不过，这种情况正在改变，因为新的广告技术和新的媒体渠道的出现为针对性广告提供了更多选择。

广告还一直被认为是一种单向的营销交流方式，信息的接收方无法马上对信息做出反应。这一状况也在改变。譬如，再过几年，技术的发展使得电视观众能够按一个按键就可以了解某一产品的详细信息。事实上，人们预期，在未来的10到20年间，广告将由单向的交流模式转变为一种交互性极强的交流模式。

一般认为，广告不会刺激人们对所宣传商品的即时需求，这一观点也可能会随广告的发展而有所改变。也就是说，消费者无法很快买到广告中的商品，但更多的媒体渠道使得消费者能够与广告信息进行交互，于是，广告迅速刺激需求的能力也会有所提高。

广告需要巨大的投入。据一家市场研究公司——实力传播公司的估计，全球在广告上的花费超过了4000亿美元。这样大的花费也养活了成千上万的企业，提供了数以百万计的就业机会。实际上，许多国家的大部分媒体渠道，如电视、广播、报纸等，都是依靠广告所得来维持生计的。

在全球范围内，广告都是经济增长的重要推动力，然而广告在不同营销机构内所发挥的作用却不尽相同。一些小公司也许只是偶尔做广告，而且规模也很小，譬如在当地报纸上的分类栏目里登小广告。但大部分依靠营销来激发消费者兴趣的公司，无论大小，都是通过不断地做广告来帮助实现营销目标的。

如何通过广告来有效传达营销信息，这需要营销者在开展广告活动时做出许多不同的决策。对于那些对创造性要求不高的小型广告活动来说，一个或几个人即可完成绝大部分工作。事实上，互联网已经使自己动手制作广告变得非常简单，尤其使得小型企业自己就能做出广告决策。正如我们将看到的，不但小公司能够在互联网上创作并安置它们的广告，新的服务甚至使得个人也能够创作出在地方电视台中播放的广告。

对于大型广告活动来说，制定周全的广告决策所需要的技巧可能是多种多样的，也许无法由一个人来轻易完成。当大公司在内部进行广告活动时，有可能会依赖于那些从广告社等地方找来的专业人士的帮助，以将自己的广告活动推向市场。

今天我非常简单地介绍了一下广告这种我们如今非常熟悉的东西。下次我想谈一下广告的主要类型。谢谢大家！

**篇章口译 B**

Good morning!

Nowadays, advertisements have already become a very important part in our life, and we are now living in a world of advertisements. Whether we like them or not, they have poured into our life.

I know that all of you present here are very interested in print advertisements, and I'm very happy to have this opportunity to share with you my own experience in writing advertisements.

To define what constitutes good print advertising, we begin with what a good print ad should not be. A good print ad should not be creative for the sake of being creative; it should not be designed to please copywriters, art directors, or even clients; and its main purpose should not be to entertain or win awards. In other words, ignore most of what you have learned as students in any basic advertising class or as trainees in any ad agencies.

Okay. So that's what a good print ad shouldn't be. As for what a good ad should be, here are some characteristics shared by successful direct response print ads:

Firstly, they all stress a benefit. The main selling proposition is not cleverly hidden but is made immediately clear. For example: The headline "How to Win Friends and Influence People" stresses the benefit explicitly.

Secondly, they all arouse curiosity and invite readership. The key here is not to be outrageous but to address the strongest interests and concerns of your target audience. For example: "Do You Make These Mistakes in English?" appeals to the reader's desire to avoid embarrassment and write and speak properly.

Thirdly, they are informative and knowledgeable. A successful ad usually reflects a high level of knowledge and understanding of the product and the problem it solves. The headline "How to Cope with Emission Problems—at Half the Cost of Conventional Air Pollution Control Devices" lures the reader because it promises useful information. Ads that provide information the reader wants usually get higher readership and better response.

Sometimes an approach which is ineffectively used by some so-called "professional" copywriters, is to reduce everything to the simplest common denominator and assume the reader is completely ignorant. But this can only insult the readers' intelligence and destroy the advertisement's credibility with them.

Finally, good print ads have a strong fee offer. They tell the readers the next step in the buying process and encourage them to take it right now. Such offers are extremely necessary, and I will further explain the reasons behind it next time.

Thank you!

口译练习
第一项 句子精练
A.
1. 如果你同时在电视和广播里做广告,就需要使它们保持一致,使用相同的解说员和音乐。
2. 大部分广告花费的目的都是推介特定的商品、服务或想法,我们将这些统称为"产品"。
3. 若想较为准确地获知你的广告策略究竟如何,唯一的方法就是询问消费者,你可以通过若干种方法来询求消费者的意见。
4. 即使小企业资金有限,无法像大公司那样在广告上投入大量金钱,但它仍然能够有效地进行广告宣传。
5. 做广告前,你需要看一看每种宣传媒介,想一想你的目标受众,考虑一下自己的营销计划,然后再确定最为合适的宣传媒介。

B.
1. In the first half of last year, China's advertising revenue climbed to RMB ¥170 billion, increased by 20% over the same period of the previous year.
2. Advertising is a communication whose purpose is to inform potential customers about products and services and how to use and obtain them.
3. Propelled by the sustained economic growth, China's advertising industry is developing prosperously, and China is expected to become the world's second largest advertising market next to the USA within three years.
4. Today, most advertising strategies focus on achieving three goals: promoting awareness of a business and its product, stimulating sales and establishing a business' image.
5. As a kind of new advertisement mode, online advertisement, which is growing rapidly along with the development and popularization of Internet, differs in many ways from traditional advertisements.

第二项 段落口译
A.
　　广告中一些最有说服力的元素是证书、事实以及数字。如果自己周围有人已经冒过你自己正在考虑的风险,并已经取得成功,那么你会非常乐于听取他们的意见。事实和数字会证实你所说的内容。如果你的数据表明,公司在第一个月内的业务量增长了65%,客户就会对你的服务产生信心。同样重要的是,在报告事实和数字时,千万不要用60%或200美元这样的数,使用58.6%或197.60美元这样确切的数字会更加可信。

B.
　　Since the opening-up of Chinese advertising market to the outside world on December 2005, it has attracted many multi-national advertising groups which, with their capital strength, scientific management methods and experienced operation, have brought more

opportunities as well as great challenges to the domestic advertising companies. Under the impetus from sustainable and steady economic growth, Chinese advertising industry will certainly have a brilliant prospect.

**第三项 篇章口译**

**A.**

下午好！

上次我讲了广告的定义和重要性，今天我要介绍一下广告的主要类别。

如果你问人们广告的"类别"是指什么，大部分人都会依照广告的呈现手段来做答，如电视广告、广播广告等等。但在市场营销中，广告的类型是指被传达信息中的主要"关注点"，并以此分为以下四大类：

第一类是以产品为导向的广告。在多数情况下，产品广告的目标即向目标受众明确地推荐特定产品。营销商可通过若干方式来实现这一点，如通过仅仅提供商品基本信息的低调广告方式，或是通过对广告商品和竞争商品之间的直接对比来极力说服消费者购买某一商品。

然而，有时候营销商也会制作一些产品广告，故意地让目标受众无法立即看到其与产品之间的联系。新产品的营销商在推出新产品之前也许就会采用这种"玩笑式"的广告方法，以使市场为新产品的推出做好准备。譬如，在新产品上市前一周，营销商也许会发布一则电视广告，宣称"下个星期，世界将不再相同"，但在广告中丝毫不提及产品，甚至不提及发布广告的公司。这样做的目的是为了引起市场对这一新产品的好奇心和兴趣。

第二类即形象广告。形象广告的主要目的是提升某一机构在目标市场中的重要性。这类广告并不侧重于具体的产品，而更多的是展示该机构能够提供什么。当某一组织需要告知目标受众什么事情时，常常会使用此类广告。举例来说，当两家公司合并，新成立的公司采用了新名字的时候就有可能会采用形象广告。

倡导型广告是第三类。多数情况下，机构发布倡导型广告的目的是为了寻求潜在的利益。例如，当某机构认为他们对某政治问题的态度可能会给机构带来负面影响时，就会通过倡导型广告来阐明自己的立场。

最后一类是公益广告。在一些国家，如果广告内容关系到社会的"大"利益时，非营利性组织可以免费在某些媒体渠道中发布广告。譬如，针对青少年吸烟、非法使用毒品和精神疾病等社会问题的广告就可以免费在电视、广播及其他媒体上发布。

以上就是广告的四大类别，希望我的讲座能对大家有所帮助。

谢谢！

**B.**

Good morning!

In my last lecture, I said that offers were extremely necessary to good print ads. Now I'd like to tell you why.

All ads should have offers, because the offers generate immediate response from those who are ready to buy or at least thinking about buying. Without an offer, you may run the risk of losing many potential customers.

In addition, strong offers also increase readership, because people like ads that offer them something—especially if it is free and has high perceived value.

Some writers of image advertising may object, "But doesn't making an offer cheapen the ad, and destroy our image? After all, we want awareness, not response." But how does offering a free booklet weaken the rest of the ad? It doesn't, of course. The entire notion that you cannot simultaneously elicit a response and communicate a message is absurd and without foundation.

Then how do we design our ads to emphasize the offer? Graphic techniques such as bold headlines, liberal use of subheads, coupons, toll-free numbers set in large type, asterisks, and marginal notes can make your ads more eye-catching, and thus increase readership.

Some may stand up and object, "Wait a minute. You said these are the characteristics of a successful direct response ad. But isn't general advertising different?" Maybe. But one of the ways to make your general advertising more effective is to design it as a direct response ad. Good advertising rarely uses abstract art or concepts that force the reader to puzzle out what is being sold. Ideally, you should make your readers understand exactly what your proposition is within five seconds of looking at the ad. And the techniques mentioned above will guarantee that your ads will get more response. Isn't that a good thing?

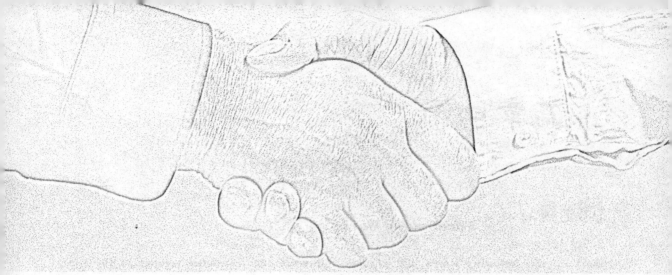

第 2 单元
公共关系

Unit 2 **Public Relations**

# 篇章口译

## Passage A (E-C)

 **Vocabulary Work**

Work on the following words and phrases and write the translated version in the space provided.

| | | | |
|---|---|---|---|
| hurrah | protagonist | eye-watering | blackball |
| purdah | spiel | rainmaker | transmute |
| entre nous | defrock | louche | sine qua non |
| eureka | yarn | hunch | |

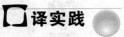 **Text Interpreting**

Listen to the tape and interpret the following passage from English into Chinese.

A writer from a business magazine called me recently for my comments on the hatred all journalists harbor towards PR professionals. I felt horribly inadequate. I do not hate PRs. They sell messages to the media rather than products or services to consumers or companies, but they are still salespeople. And sales are the fundamental activities of business. They deserve a louder hurrah than it gets.

The distrust many journalists feel towards PRs reflects their belief that the only decent story is one the protagonist does not want them to tell. That complicates the job of publicity-hungry business owners, by dictating that a keenness to communicate is interpreted as a symptom of having nothing to say.

To make things easier, here are some tips, offered without the eye-watering fee a financial spin doctor would charge. I may be blackballed from the Royal Society of Small Business Scribblers for disclosing trade secrets. But this is my 99th column and that makes a man feel reckless.

Public company bosses cannot avoid talking to the press if they want to project a positive image to their shareholders. Private entrepreneurs have it easier. You can pop out of purdah to publicize expansion, a deal, or a product whenever you like. If business is going poorly, you can simply ignore calls from reporters. Without such underpinnings as profits warnings or tumbling shares, critical stories are hard to stand up.

The spiel of PR company rainmakers is that PR delivers public esteem more efficiently than advertisements. They claim editorial coverage is cheaper to obtain and is believed more whole-heartedly than advertising copy. The unemphasized downside is unpredictability. A while ago I wrote a short report based on a company press release. The next day the managing director called me. "Thanks for printing our release," he said, "but please don't change the words next time." That is the problem with us journalists. We change the words. As a result, a communiqué innocently titled "Zicco Company Targets Fast-Growing Database Market" can be transmuted into a magazine article headlined "Struggling Zicco Quits Peripherals Market in Disarray".

Broadly, there are two kinds of financial PR consultant. One type is senior and smoothly charming, yet emits disturbing whiffs of brimstone. His duties include phoning journalists to mention, entre nous, that a company boss whose interests conflict with his client's was defrocked as a priest in 1979. The other type is junior and has the bouncy, unfocused eagerness of a red setter puppy.

Business writers are harder to categorize. It is fair to say that few of us are realizing a childhood dream. Tell someone at a dinner party you are a journalist and you provoke flickers of interest. You can quickly quench these by explaining you are a business journalist. To most people that just sounds like a louche accountant. We arrive at our profession by multiple routes.

What unites business journalists is the need to piece together compelling stories from the chaos of commercial life. You are more likely to get the write-up you want if you can present interviewers with a ready-made narrative rather than a jumble of facts, figures and anecdotes. The entrepreneurial success story is, helpfully, a well-developed genre.

Ideally you should either come from a background of lofty privilege or grinding poverty. Royal friends and polo-playing skill guarantee you column inches in many publications. You can make as good a thing of being raised by loving but illiterate traveler folk in a leaky caravan.

If your background is shamingly ordinary, never mind. You can still provide reporters with that sine qua non of the entrepreneur's yarn, the eureka moment. Explain how the revelation of vast untapped demand for monogrammed hearing aids hit you in the bath. A crushing setback, pluckily overcome, is a good plot motif to carry the yarn forward. The order or capital injection that saved your business should materialize, like the Ninth Cavalry, at the last gasp. From there it is an easy canter into recounting your current success and plans for future world domination.

Dealing with a journalist is ultimately just another business transaction, a kind of cashless trading. You pay for exposure by providing information that can be turned into good copy. Critics say corporate PR spending represents a concealed subsidy to the media, that business compromises the objectivity of journalists by spoon-feeding them material. My hunch is that PR is merely a counterweight to the media's strong, commercially driven appetite for bad news. The result would be coverage with the right balance, if for the wrong reasons.

# 篇章口译

## Passage B (C-E)

 **Vocabulary Work**

Work on the following words and phrases and write the translated version in the space provided.

| | | | |
|---|---|---|---|
| 供应商 | 合作者 | 流星危机 | 随机发生 |
| 悄无声息 | 掠夺者危机 | 机密文件 | 崩溃危机 |
| 沟通渠道 | 虚假信息 | 机构重组 | 兼并方 |
| 战术 | | | |

 **Text Interpreting**

Listen to the tape and interpret the following passage from Chinese into English.

有些危机是在某个群体，如客户与公司产生问题时发生的。许多危机可以通过问题管理的办法得以避免。所谓管理问题，你必须在其发展成危机之前就知道这究竟是怎么回事。然后，你才能使有关的群体同你一起寻求共识，找到问题的解决方案。这是公共关系的核心。而有时问题来得太快，而变得十分棘手。

在一起危机中，员工通常会被忽略，尽管事实上他们是受到影响最大的群体之一。一旦公司陷入危机后，他们会被他们的朋友、邻居、供应商和合作者等周围所有人认出来。他们可能在危机处理中发挥相当大的作用。他们应对危机的表现可以对公司的声誉产生重大影响，从而使公司可能从危机中摆脱出来。

事实上危机的类型有几种，比如下面所列举的：

流星危机指的是那些不在预期范围内产生的，其特点是随机发生，悄无声息，往往根本无法预测。之所以如此命名是因为它们似乎从天而降。在大多数流星危机中，公司成为受害者。不仅如此，此番危机的各类观众对公司的信心也处于动荡中。在大家眼里，该公司是无辜还是有罪，是无可责备还是应受责备，这些都取决于该公司作何反应。流星危机的例子包括产品品质篡改或职工意外死亡。

掠夺者危机是指有人将组织内的问题曝光。总的来说，在此类危机中组织是受害者，其结果通常是声誉和信誉受损。那些揭露与公司所声明的立场相矛盾的机密文件的员工就是掠夺者危机的制造者。

崩溃危机是指公司运营失败。这是组织自己造成的。产品责任或者安全事故的发生如果是因为公司政策遭到无视或不走正常程序而选择捷径，就可以视为是一起崩溃危机。

在任何一种类型的危机中，组织都力图达到一些具体的目标，比如：

# 第 2 单元 公共关系 Public Relations

- 向外界呈现和维持正面的公司形象；
- 及时披露准确和最新的信息；
- 保持对外联系；
- 监控沟通渠道,尽早截获虚假信息；
- 维持来自当地人士的支持；
- 顺利渡过危机。

如果沟通顺利的话,那么你永远都不需要问:"我们如何来发布这条坏消息?"你只要采取你以往的沟通方式就行。

正如其他任何沟通计划一样,你需要在一开始就制定目标。比如机构重组,你需要获得员工对重组产生的结果的支持。对兼并方而言,你的目标就是要使重组后的公司迅速进入启动阶段。面对竞争的威胁时你需要下令采取行动。如果你正在创建一个新公司,你的目标就是要员工拥护并体现新的公司形象。如果你正在努力改变公司的文化,你的员工应当去推动变化的发生。战略和战术都从你的目标出发。

# 口译讲评

# *Notes on the Text*

**Passage A**

1. **I do not hate PRs**：根据上下文可以判断这里的 PRs 是指 PR professionals,即公关从业者。

2. **That complicates the job of publicity-hungry business owners, by dictating that a keenness to communicate is interpreted as a symptom of having nothing to say**：publicity-hungry 的字面意思是"对宣传或公众注意如饥似渴的",口译时可化繁为简,如表达为"喜欢曝光的"。另外此句中...is interpreted as...其实是省略了 by journalists,口译时可作增补。整句句子可译为"许多记者之所以不相信公关人士,是因为在记者看来,唯一像样的报道是主人公不愿公之于众的内容。这让那些喜欢曝光的企业老板感到难办,因为按照记者的逻辑,急于沟通是无话可说的症状"。

3. **a financial spin doctor**：这里 spin doctor 是指那些善于公关、为政党出谋划策的媒体顾问或政治顾问。因此该短语可译为"金融媒体顾问"。

4. **public company**：是指那些公开上市的、股东拥有其股权的"上市公司"。public company 不同于 private company（即私有公司）,后者的股票不可以在股市公开交易。

5. **The unemphasized downside is unpredictability**：在口译此句时,应当根据上文作适当增补,可译为"但这番说辞没有提到内容报道的一大弱点,即不可预见性"。

6. **whiffs of brimstone**：brimstone 是指硫黄、暴躁,这里可译为"浮躁气息"。

7. **The other type is junior and has the bouncy, unfocused eagerness of a red setter puppy**：a red setter puppy 是指广受西方人喜爱的爱尔兰雪达犬。这个句子可译为"另一种公关的资历稍浅,精力充沛,干劲十足,但注意力不够集中"。

8. **You can quickly quench these by explaining you are a business journalist**：quench 是止渴或灭火的意思，联系上文，这里可以处理为"但如果你接着告诉人家你是一名商业记者，那么之前的兴趣就会即刻消失"。

9. **You can make as good a thing of being raised by loving but illiterate traveler folk in a leaky caravan**：traveler 除了旅行者的意思外，还可以指吉普赛人。整句可译为"假如你被慈爱但不识字的吉普赛人带大，曾经住在漏风的大篷车里，你可以把这种经历变成一件好事"。

10. **You can still provide reporters with that sine qua non of the entrepreneur's yarn, the eureka moment**：此句可译为"你还是可以向记者提供企业家成功故事中不可缺少的戏剧性素材，即你获得灵感的那一刹那"。

11. **The order or capital injection that saved your business should materialize, like the Ninth Cavalry, at the last gasp**：the Ninth Cavalry，即第九部队。在美国19世纪70年代至80年代，第九部队在美国西部与暴乱的美国印第安人等作战时战绩显著，被认为是最为能战的美国部队之一。

**Passage B**

1. **而有时问题来得太快，而变得十分棘手**：这句话的意思其实是"而有时问题来得太快，以至于没有充分的时间来处理"，可译为 Sometimes, though, issues arise too quickly to manage。

2. **流星危机指的是那些不在预期范围内产生的**：可处理为 Meteor crises are those that cannot be anticipated.

3. **在大家眼里，该公司是无辜还是有罪，是无可责备还是应受责备，这些都取决于该公司作何反应**：此句在口译时适合用被动句式，宜译为 Whether the organization is seen as innocent or guilty, or blameless or culpable, depends on how it responds.

4. **掠夺者危机是指有人将组织内的问题曝光**：这句话按照字面翻译比较困难，可先将原文结构补充完整，即掠夺者危机是指有人将组织内的问题曝光（时所发生的危机）。全句可译为 Predator crises occur when somebody with an issue raises it publicly.

5. **其结果通常是声誉和信誉受损**：可处理为...which usually results in damaged reputation and credibility.

6. **产品责任或者安全事故的发生如果是因为公司政策遭到无视或不走正常程序而选择捷径，就可以视为是一起崩溃危机**：在口译过程中，对于一些无实际意思的词可忽略不译，这句中的"……的发生"可以省去，整句可译为 Product liability or a safety accident can represent breakdown crises if they occurred because a company policy was ignored or a shortcut taken around proper procedures.

7. **对兼并方而言，你的目标就是要使重组后的公司迅速进入启动阶段**：此句宜处理为 For a merger, your goal is for the reshaped company to get off to a fast start.

## 相关词语 Relevant Words and Expressions

滚动 in roll
特写 feature article
宣传 publicity
游说 lobbying
展品 exhibit
招贴 poster
公告牌 bulletin board
排行榜 ranking list
慈善行为 philanthropy
社会参与 community involvement
声望经营 reputation management
危机管理 crisis management
新闻发布 news / press release
意见抽样 opinion sampling
营销公关 marketing public relations
商品的标志 logo
商务沟通方式 business communication style
获得公众的好感 gain goodwill of the public
促销宣传的总预算 total promotion budget
商标的认知度 / 知名度 recognition rate

## 口译技能 Interpreting Skills

### 增词和减词

有人误以为，所谓合乎标准的口译，就是在把一种语言转换为另一种语言的时候，做到"不增、不减、不改"。口译实践告诉我们，由于两种语言表达方式差异，适当的口译往往都是"既增、又减、还改"。这种根据各自语言特点，在具体上下文中适当地"增、减、改"，就是我们所要讨论的口译技巧。

在口译实践中，词量增减是一个事物两个方面，要表达同一个意思，如果英译汉时需要增词，反过来，汉译英时就往往需要减词。词量增减，指是根据原文上下文意思、逻辑关系以及译文语言句法特点和表达习惯，在口译时有时增加原文字面没有出现但实际内容已包含的词，或者减去原文虽有但译文语言表达用不着的词。必须指出的是，词量增减必须防止两个倾向:一是添枝加叶,任意发挥;二是避难就易,肆意裁割。

1. 增词

增词,从理论上说可以增加任何词。根据具体上下文,可增加动词、形容词、名词或别的词类,但在什么时候增加什么样词,才能恰到好处,而不超出一定界限,则需要悉心体会。下面试分析一个译例:

A book, tight shut, is but a block of paper.

译文一:一本书,紧紧合上,只是一叠纸。

译文二:一本书,如果紧紧合上不读,只是一叠纸。

译文三:一本书,如果紧紧合上不读,只是一叠废纸。

译文四:闲置之书只是一叠废纸。

上面同一个英语句子有四个汉语译文,可以体现翻译的不同层次。译文一,与原文似乎丝丝入扣,但却显得支离破碎、关系不清、语意不足;译文二,增加了"如果……不读",意思明白无误,只是觉得"言犹未尽";译文三,又增加了一个"废"字,这可是点睛之举。能否译出这个"废"字,是翻译这个句子的关键,也是判断这个译文优劣的一个重要标准。不读书,不仅是一叠纸,而且是叠废纸。因为如果是叠白纸,还可画出最新最美的图画,只有废纸才是无价值的东西。一个"废"字,说话者语意才得以充分表达。译文三的不足之处,就是行文拖沓累赘;而译文四则简明扼要,笔酣墨浓。

2. 减词

由于两种语言表达习惯不同,口译时如果一字不漏照搬,往往会显得累赘、拖沓、冗杂、或不合行文习惯,甚至产生歧义。采取减词译法可以使译文言简意赅。口译常有以下几种减词情况:

A. 减去代词。例如:

1) We assure you of our prompt attention to this matter.

我们保证立即处理此事。

2) You are kindly requested to let us have your best quotation for the canned fish.

请报鱼罐头最惠价。

B. 减去陈腐或不必要的套语。例如:

We take this opportunity to inform you that we are now in position to make prompt shipment of the merchandise.

兹奉告,该商品可即期装运。(译文比原文大为简明,除减去了 take this opportunity 这一陈腐表达外,还省略了三个代词,并用一个"可"字代替了原文中 in a position 这样繁复的表达方式。)

C. 减去不言而喻或冗杂词语。例如:

1) The price of the products should be set according to the price in the international market. It should be fixed by the two parties at a level that will bring profit to both.

产品价格应该根据国际市场价格,由双方共同商定,须照顾到双方利益。(译文看似没译 at a level,但字里行间却含有其意。)

2) Suitable for men, women and children. 男女老少皆宜。

从以上译例可以看出,减词译法是炼词炼句的一种最重要手段,可以充分显示译文语言优势。减词译法情况同样也十分复杂，往往一个句子中多种情况省略兼而有之，因此很难加以归类，以上编排仅是为了叙述方便。除所列几种情况外，我们可以看出，许多冠词、介词、连词都没有在译文中出现，它们往往都是口译时减词的对象。

# 译练习 *Enhancement Practice*

第一项 Project 1
句子精练 Sentences in Focus

**A. Interpret the following sentences from English into Chinese.**

1. In today's highly competitive environment, the need for effective PR programs cannot be overlooked.
2. Communication between our company and the public is the most important part of our public relations campaign.
3. To build and maintain good reputations, many businesses place heavy emphasis on the coverage they receive in the media.
4. A good public relation plays a vital role in the success of most companies and that role applies to more than just the marketing of goods and services.
5. The communication between an organization and its public ranges from a simple news release to a sophisticated campaign featuring films, speeches and television appearances.

**B. Interpret the following sentences from Chinese into English.**

1. 遭遇公关危机时的处理方式可能会带来截然不同的结果。
2. 关系传播、关系营销、关系管理是当前国际社会科学领域的热门概念。
3. 危机公关能为公关工作赢得美誉，但同时它也是公关工作中最难以把握的。
4. 公关经理是企业信息的制造者、传递者和最终发布者，被誉为企业形象和声誉的守夜人。
5. 如果能够充分预见危机的形成，是可以把危机有效迅速控制并解决的，甚至将危机变成机会。

第二项 Project 2
段落口译 Paragraph Interpreting

**A. Interpret the following paragraph from English into Chinese.**

Some years ago, a senior bank executive in charge of public relations asked me for advice on how to justify the activities of his PR department. I told him bluntly that the survival of his PR department depends largely on the magnanimity of his CEO. I further told him that for his PR department to do well, he must report directly to the CEO as opposed to the senior officer in charge of marketing. This is because in the PR area, a lot of spending has no immediate nor direct returns.

**B. Interpret the following paragraph from Chinese into English.**

即使公司不告诉员工坏消息,员工也会知道。没有一个员工会相信公司发布的所有消息总是那么一片光明。对于真的已经发生的坏消息,在没有权威信息来源的情况下,他们会通过小道消息打听到,而且更为有效。他们可能从媒体了解到情况。况且,因特网提供了新的信息来源,可以通过它发现许多细节。

第三项 Project 3
篇章口译 Passage Interpreting

**A. Listen to the tape and interpret the following passage from English into Chinese.**

Business is booming for the public relations (PR) industry on both sides of the Atlantic; the top 30 agencies saw increases of around 17% in the US and by 10.5% in the UK this year compared with last year.

PR's own reputation has emerged from the shadows as the industry itself has become more professional. It is increasingly being seen as the guardian of both brand and corporate reputation, especially in an environment that is becoming more fragmented across a very diverse number of media platforms.

The very nature of this diversity is adding to the strength of the PR industry, as the astonishing growth of social community sites, citizen journalism and, most of all, "the blogosphere" (the weblogging environment) provide a hotbed of opinion in which reputation can rapidly be consumed. Only PR can hope to interact at the deep levels needed to influence online opinion. It is here that practitioners have told us that PR needs to develop its talents.

In these days of increased globalization, corporate reputation is at the top of everyone's "shopping list". It is in this discipline that the industry has seen most growth and expects to see continuing growth in the future. In terms of vertical markets, healthcare has been identified by several of the industry spokespeople as the fastest-growing sector; however, the public sector, particularly in the light of the new labor leadership, the environment and corporate social responsibility (CSR) are all emerging as growth areas for PR.

The overriding concern of the industry is the skills shortage. Almost all agencies are hiring, a trend that is itself indicative of growth, and some are looking outside the PR industry to bring in new skills.

In the past, there has been a relatively clear distinction between PR and other marketing disciplines, but this is changing. The giant marketing communications companies, such as CPP and Sinicom, have always numbered PR and communications agencies among their holdings. These are now rising to greater prominence within the groups, although not yet rivaling the mighty advertising agency networks that occupy pride of place.

Nonetheless, the number of newcomers to the scene is growing, mainly through acquisitions, largely in the PR field. Companies such as Herth and Cime, and the world-leading SOL, which are PR centered, are able to compete with the CPP and Sinicom networks on a global scale in order to manage clients' corporate and brand reputations.

Even these companies have rivals; other service groups are also taking an interest in the PR market. Last year saw strategic acquisitions made by a leading global financial consultancy and by leading information-services companies. PR is becoming hot. It is also becoming global.

Although there are many thousands of small agencies and individual consultants serving very local markets, larger agencies are forging partnerships across the globe to meet demand from clients that themselves are extending their global reach. Yet it is not enough to simply market goods and services in individual territories; there must be a deeper understanding of those cultures for PR to be effective.

**B. Listen to the tape and interpret the following passage from Chinese into English.**

在过去的20年中,中国的公共关系行业在规模和业务范围方面的发展显著。当中国刚开始出现公关这一行时,宣传的都是关于工厂开业。比如会召开新闻发布会、邀请媒体出席、邀请重要的政府官员并在人民日报上登上一张照片。现在工厂开业宣传只是我们做的一小部分。我们是要帮助公司打造一个完整的故事。

现在在中国运营的中外公司都迅速地意识到建立品牌意识的重要性,鉴于此,公关公司面临的服务需求增加了。

然而,尽管公关行业增长迅速,中国的公关领域还有待成熟。随着中国媒体业的发展变化,公关业面临着一系列的阻碍。另外,中国本土的机构正挣扎着走出远比其经验丰富的国际合作者和对手的阴影。但是,随着传统广告形式在走下坡路,创新的公关解决方案在未来几年中对中外企业来说都是日益重要的工具。

运用传统媒体如电视、广播或印刷品做广告一度是公司宣传开支的主要去向,现在公关被放在了越来越重要的位置。公关作为一种营销工具与广告在许多方面不同。广告是组织和客户直接沟通的形式,是明确的信息发送者。相比之下,公关通过第三方来操作,通常是记者来报道话题。

一方面公关比传统媒体如电视、广播或印刷品广告更难操控,公司却日益将公关视为到达目标受众的更为可信、有效的方法。消费者越来越以鄙视的眼光来看待直接广告,或者对公司而言更糟的是,消费者对广告根本不屑一顾。结果就是,公司不得不改变其自我宣传的方式,并找到与消费者直接产生联系的方法。

在中国,大量的出版物、电视和广播频道使得做传统的直接广告成本很高,且效率很低。中国的媒体形式太多,因此向目标受众做广告变得过于昂贵。如此,在中国市场做品牌必须采用以公关为主的方式进行。

# 参考译文
## Reference Version

**篇章口译 A**

最近,一位商业杂志撰稿人给我打来电话,说到所有记者都不喜欢公关专业人士,让我谈谈对此的看法。我觉得自己不够资格:我并不厌恶搞公共关系的人。他们向媒体卖消息,而不是向消费者或企业卖产品或卖服务,但他们依然是销售人员。而销售是商业的基本行为,它得到的欢呼声应该更热烈些。

许多记者之所以不相信公关人士,是因为在记者看来,唯一像样的报道是主人公不愿公之于众的内容。这让那些喜欢曝光的企业老板感到难办,因为按照记者的逻辑,急于沟通是无话可说的症状。

下面我给大家提供一些贴士。与那些金融界媒体顾问不同,我不会为此收取巨额费用。也许,我会因为泄露业内诀窍而被"皇家小企业撰稿人协会"除名。不过,这是我第99篇专栏,我感到胆子特别大。

如果上市公司要让股东对公司有个好印象,公司老板就不可避免地要与媒体打交道。在这方面,私有公司可以轻松些。你可以随时撩开面纱,对外公布公司的拓展、交易或者产品。如果生意不好,你可以不理记者的电话。只要没有盈利警告或股价暴跌这样的事实,批评性的报道本身难以立足。

按照公关公司的说法,与广告相比,公关能以更高效率为企业赢得公众的尊敬。他们称,内容报道花费更低,而且比广告文案更能赢得信任。但这番说辞没有提到内容报道的一大弱点,即不可预见性。就在前不久,我以某家公司的新闻发布为依据撰写了一篇简短的新闻。第二天,该公司的总经理给我打来电话。他说:"非常感谢你刊载我公司的新闻稿,但下次请勿改动其中的文字。"这就是我们记者的问题:我们会改动原文。其结果是,如果一篇新闻发布的原名为"Zicco公司拟打入快速发展的数据库市场",经过记者一改,杂志上的标题成了"Zicco公司境况不佳,仓皇退出外围设备市场"。

广义上讲,有两类商业公关顾问。一种属于资深级的,很能打动人心,但浑身散发着令人不安的浮躁气息。他的职责包括给记者打电话,神秘兮兮地告诉他们,与他的客户存在利害冲突的某公司老板在1979年被免去牧师资格。另一种公关的资历稍浅,精力充沛,干劲十足,但注意力不够集中。

商业记者较难归类。公平地讲,我们中几乎无人是在实现儿时的梦想。如果你在宴会上告诉某人你是个记者,你会引起他人的兴趣。但如果你接着告诉人家你是一名商业记者,那么之前的兴趣就会即刻消失。在多数人看来,商业记者听起来和品性不端的会计师差不多。我们成为商业记者的道路不尽相同。

商业记者的共同点,就是要从纷繁混乱的商业生活中,提炼出引人入胜的报道。如果企业能向采访者提供现成的故事,而非一大堆事实、数据和轶事,那就更有可能看到自己希望的报道。好的地方是,企业家成功故事是一种发展较为成熟的体裁。

理想情况下,企业家应该出身高贵,享有特权或者出身贫寒。如果你有皇室朋友,还擅长打马球，那么你在许多出版物上占的专栏空间就牢不可破。假如你被慈爱但不识字的吉普赛人带大，曾经住在漏风的大篷车里，你可以把这种经历变成一件好事。

如果你的背景平凡得令人汗颜，那也没什么关系。你还是可以向记者提供企业家成功故事中不可缺少的戏剧性素材，即你获得灵感的那一刹那。你可以解释一下，你是如何在洗澡时突然想到刻字的助听器还有许多市场潜力可挖。如果你的公司曾遭受过一次毁灭性的打击，但你的勇气让公司度过了难关，那么这个情节也很不错，能推动故事的发展。如果你的公司曾濒临破产，但终于得到一份订单或注资，让公司柳暗花明，这样的细节要放在高潮部分。以此为基础，记者就能轻而易举地叙述你现在的成功和主导国际市场的未来计划。

归根结底，和记者打交道是一种商业往来，一种无现金的交易。你为了得到媒体曝光而向记者提供信息，让记者写成一篇好故事。批评者称，企业的公关经费是对媒体的隐性补贴，理由是企业向记者"喂"资料，损害了记者的客观性。我的感觉是，公关只是一个平衡块，平衡媒体由商业利益驱动的对负面新闻的贪欲。结果就是恰到好处的新闻报道，即使其初衷有问题。

**篇章口译 B**

  Some crises arise when a public like customers, have an issue with the company. Many crises can be averted through the practice of issues management. To manage an issue, you must know what it is before it boils over into a crisis. Then, you can engage the interested public groups to find common ground and identify solutions. This is the heart of public relations. Sometimes, though, issues arise too quickly to manage.

  Employees are often a neglected audience during a crisis, despite the fact that they represent one of the most affected of all groups. They will be identified with the company in crisis by everyone from friends and neighbors to vendors and partners. They may well have a part to play in handling the crisis. And how they behave could have an impact on the reputation with which the company emerges from the crisis.

  There are, in fact, several types of crises, such as the following:

  Meteor crises are those that cannot be anticipated. They are random, senseless, and impossible to predict. In most meteor crises—so named because they seem to fall from the sky, the company is a victim. Still, the confidence various audiences have in the organization is at risk. Whether the organization is seen as innocent or guilty, or blameless or culpable, depends on how it responds. Examples of meter crises include a product tampering or an accidental fatality on the job.

  Predator crises occur when somebody with an issue raises it publicly. Generally, the organization is a victim in a predator crisis, which usually results in damaged reputation and credibility. An employee disclosing confidential documents that contradict the company's stated position is a predator crisis.

  Breakdown crises represent a failure of the company to perform. It is something the organization does to itself. Product liability or a safety accident can represent breakdown crises if they occurred because a company policy was ignored or a shortcut taken around proper procedures.

In any crisis, organizations strive to achieve specific objectives, such as:
- Present and maintain a positive image of the company.
- Present timely, accurate, and up-to-date information.
- Remain accessible.
- Monitor communication channels to catch misinformation early.
- Maintain constituent support.
- Survive the crisis.

As in any other communication plan, you need to begin with a goal. For example, in a reorganization, you will seek employee support for the outcomes you have established. For a merger, your goal is for the reshaped company to get off to a fast start. You will issue a call to action when faced with a competitive threat. If you are launching a new identity, your goal is for employees to embrace and reflect that new image. And if you're trying to affect a change to the company's culture, your employees should drive that change. Strategies and tactics both flow from your goals.

If you are communicating well, you need never ask: "How do we communicate this bad news?" You simply communicate the way you always do.

**口译练习**

**第一项 句子精练**

**A.**
1. 在今天高度竞争的环境里,有效的公关计划却是忽略不得的。
2. 我们公司和公众之间的沟通是我们公共关系活动中最重要的部分。
3. 为了建立和维护良好的声誉,许多企业非常重视媒体对其的报道。
4. 良好的公共关系对大多数企业的成功而言起到很大的作用,并且其作用不仅限于产品和服务的营销。
5. 组织与公众沟通的方式从简单的新闻发布到复杂的公关活动如制作电影、做演讲和上电视。

**B.**
1. Different methods to handle crisis of public relations may bring entirely different results.
2. The relation communication, marketing and management are the popular conceptions in the international social scientific fields at present.
3. Crisis public relations can win fine reputation for the public relations work, but at the same time it is also the most difficult to control.
4. PR manager is the producer, transmitter and final promulgator of the corporate information, who is considered as a watchman of the image and reputation of a company.

5. Crisis can be efficiently managed and resolved, even manipulated as an opportunity, if it is well prepared for.

## 第二项 段落口译

**A.**

好几年前,一名主管公关部门的银行高级执行员问我,要怎样证明给人家看,公关部的工作不是可有可无的?我直截了当回答:他的部门的存活率很大程度上取决于他的执行总裁有多大量。我进一步告诉他,公关部门要有所作为,就得直接向总裁而不是负责行销的主管汇报。理由是公关领域里有很多花费是没有直接或马上看得到回报的。

**B.**

Employees will find out about bad news even if the company doesn't share it with them. No employee believes all the news from the company will be rosy all the time. As for the bad news that does occur, they will hear it through that grapevine that is so much more effective when there is no authoritative source of information. They may hear it from the media. And the Internet has spawned a new source of information for employees to find details online.

## 第三项 篇章口译

**A.**

在大西洋的两边,公共关系产业的发展如火如荼。与去年相比,今年排名前30名的公关机构的业务增长在美国达到17%,在英国达到10.5%。

随着公关行业的运作愈加职业化,其本身的声誉也已经从阴影中走出来。公关越来越被视为是品牌和公司声誉的守护人,特别是当媒体平台变得多元,商业环境日趋分裂化。

多元化的本质促进了公关行业的发展。社会团体、新闻传播以及最突出的"博客世界",即网上日志的环境成长速度惊人,为意见的表达提供了温床,在这样的情况下,声誉可以迅速成为消费的对象。因此,只有公关才有望在深层次参与影响网上意见的表达。在这里,公关从业者告诉我们公关行业需要培养专业的人才。

在如今日趋全球化的时代,公司声誉被列于所有人的购物单之首。在这样的风气下,该行业增长迅猛,并有望保持持续发展。就垂直市场而言,一些行业发言人认为医疗服务是发展最快的部分;然而,公有部门,尤其在新的劳工部领导人的管理下,其运作环境和公司社会责任都成为了公关行业的增长领域。

公关行业的首要问题是具有行业技能人才的短缺。几乎所有的公关机构的工作仅在招聘,这种趋势本身说明了该行业在增长。有些机构在公关行业之外寻找人才,并将新的技能带进本行业。

过去,公关和其他营销领域的界限划分相对清晰,但这种情况在发生变化。市场传播巨头,如CPP和Sinicom都将公关和传播机构列于持有股中。现在,它们的地位更显突出,尽管还未能与占据头号交椅的广告机构网络相匹敌。

然而,新来者越来越多,主要是通过公关领域的兼并。例如Herth公司和Cime公司,与以公关业务为主的世界行业翘楚 SOL 公司有能力与 CPP 和 Sinicom 网络在全球范围内竞争,为了能管理客户的公司和品牌声誉。

甚至这些公司也有对手;其他的服务集团也对公关市场蠢蠢欲动。去年,一流的全球金融咨询公司和信息服务公司都进行了战略兼并。公关正变得热门起来,其运作也日趋全球化。

尽管有数千家小机构和个体咨询公司为当地市场提供服务,大型机构正在全球建立合作,以满足那些正在走向国际的客户的需求。然而,仅仅在区域内独立营销产品和服务是不够的:公关行业应该对相关的文化有更深层次的了解,从而使运营更有效地满足客户的需要。

**B.**

In the 20-plus years since, the public relations industry in China has grown markedly in size and scope. When PR first started in China, it was all about factory openings. You would do a press release, get media out there, invite key government officials, and try to get a picture in the *People's Daily*. Now factory openings are a very small part of what we do. We help companies create their entire story.

As both Chinese and foreign firms operating in the country rapidly realize the importance of cultivating greater brand awareness, PR firms are seeing a greater demand for their services.

However, even with the industry's rapid growth, China's public relations sector is far from mature and, with the country's shifting media landscape, it faces a number of hurdles. In addition, local Chinese agencies are struggling to emerge from the shadows of their vastly more experienced international partners and rivals. But with traditional advertising forms on the decline, innovative public relations solutions are going to become an increasingly important tool for both Chinese and foreign firms in the coming years.

Whereas direct advertising in traditional media such as TV, radio or print publications once dominated firms' promotional spending, PR is becoming increasingly important. As a marketing tool, PR is different from advertising in a number of ways. Advertising is a form of direct communication between an organization and consumers, with a very clear sender. By contrast, PR operates through a third party, usually a journalist, talking about a topic.

While PR is more difficult to control than traditional TV, radio or print media advertising, firms increasingly see it as a more credible and effective way to reach their target audience. Consumers are increasingly viewing direct advertising in a cynical light, or, worse still for firms, are not viewing the ads at all. Consequently, firms have to change the way they promote themselves and to find ways of linking directly with consumers.

In China, the large number of publications, TV and radio channels make traditional direct advertising both costly and ineffective. In China, there are simply too many media forms, so advertising to reach the target group would be prohibitively expensive. Thus, brands have had to adopt a more PR-based approach to the Chinese market.

# 第 3 单元 投资环境

## Unit 3 Investment Environment

# 篇章口译

## Passage A (E-C)

### Vocabulary Work

Work on the following words and phrases and write the translated version in the space provided.

| | |
|---|---|
| the New York Stock Exchange | NASDAQ |
| aviation | marine insurance |
| brokering | derivatives trading |
| Over the Counter market | regime |
| corporate tax rate | Chancellor of the Exchequer |
| box-ticking | onerous |
| Big Bang | the London Stock Exchange |
| springboard | |

### Text Interpreting

Listen to the tape and interpret the following passage from English into Chinese.

Ladies and gentlemen, I am delighted to be able to join you at this press conference on the exciting Boao Forum for Asia International Capital Conference.

London has 3.5 trillion under management, more than any other market in the world and lists more companies in any one year than the New York Stock Exchange, NASDAQ and Hong Kong combined. And with 34% of global currency trading, London is the most international and most liquid of all the world's financial centers. Within the City of London, 90% of the world's trade in metals takes place, 25% of the world's aviation and marine insurance and almost 50% of all ship brokering. And in the ever expanding area of derivatives trading, London has 43% of the Over the Counter market.

Openness of market entry and competition are prime factors in London's success. But there are others.

First, the fiscal environment. The UK has a particularly generous regime for foreign nationals working in the UK in that they are not taxed on income arising outside the UK. Then, just recently, corporate tax rates were reduced. Our new Chancellor of the Exchequer has also announced his intention of continuing to simplify the tax regime.

Secondly, the independence which the present Prime Minister gave to the Bank of England ten years ago when he was Chancellor of the Exchequer, with its focus on monetary policy, has also helped to ensure a stable and successful macro-economy.

Thirdly, one of the most important success factors has been the regulatory environment. Our Government created a single, business-friendly regulator for all financial services: the Financial Services Authority. The FSA adopts a principled, risk-based approach. This is very different from the line-by-line rules-based approach, with its box-ticking mentality. The UK model reduces the cost to global businesses of complying with detailed onerous regulations. By adopting this business-friendly approach, the FSA has given the UK-based financial services a framework within which businesses can innovate and prosper.

The result of this open market access and the favorable regulatory environment means that foreign financial companies have flocked to London. Today, 20 years after "Big Bang", roughly 50% of City firms are foreign owned and there are 200,000 professionals from overseas in the UK financial services sector. Almost 50% of office property in the City is owned by foreign financial institutions, with German pension funds owning almost a quarter.

All this adds up to one thing: a successful and expanding market which is ideal for Chinese companies raising capital.

To conclude, we warmly welcome the increasing number of Chinese companies establishing themselves in the UK, a number of which are making it the headquarters for their European operations. Apart from London being the world's leading international financial centre and the UK being a low-tax economy, Chinese companies appreciate the strength of our Research & Development and also our design and marketing expertise. With 1% of the world's population, we produce 5.5% of the world's R&D. Setting up a business in the UK is very easy: it takes, on average, only 18 hours. And we have a fast and efficient visa service and visa offices in 12 Chinese cities. At the beginning of last year there were 220 mainland companies in Britain. Now there are over 340. At the beginning of this year there were 27 companies listed on the London Stock Exchange. Now there are 68. The message is clear. We are an open economy which welcomes companies from all parts of the world. The UK is not only a good place to invest but a good springboard for global growth.

# 篇章口译

## Passage B (C-E)

### Vocabulary Work

Work on the following words and phrases and write the translated version in the space provided.

| | | | |
|---|---|---|---|
| 商品展览会暨投资洽谈会 | 商务部 | 中国经济贸易总商会 | 源远流长 |
| 棕榈油 | 相互投资 | "走出去"战略 | 对华实际投资 |
| 双赢合作 | 中国对外贸易中心 | 世界旅游组织 | 东盟国家 |
| 经济互补性 | 平等互利、共同发展 | | |

### Text Interpreting

**Listen to the tape and interpret the following passage from Chinese into English.**

女士们、先生们：

今天，第四届"马来西亚2007中国进出口商品展览会暨投资洽谈会"隆重开幕了。我谨代表中国商务部对出席展会开幕式的各位贵宾和朋友表示热烈欢迎。同时，也向马来西亚中国经济贸易总商会对展会的大力支持表示衷心感谢。

中国和马来西亚是友好近邻，两国传统友谊源远流长。中马建交33年来，两国经贸合作持续快速发展。中国海关统计，去年两国贸易额达371亿美元，今年将超过450亿美元。中马两国互为重要贸易伙伴。中国已成为马来西亚棕榈油的最大出口市场和电子产品第四大出口市场。

在双边贸易快速增长的同时，两国之间的相互投资也取得较大发展。截至去年9月底，马来西亚对华实际投资已超过45亿美元。随着中国经济实力的不断增强和"走出去"战略的实施，已有越来越多的中国企业到马来西亚开展投资合作。

为推动中国与马来西亚以及东盟各国之间的友好往来，发展双边贸易关系，中国商务部在马来西亚政府和工商界的大力支持下，举办了中国商品展览会。展会从2004年至今已成功举办三届，也已在中国和马来西亚两国的企业界树立起良好的形象。本次展会参展企业超过200家，将有8000多名买家到会。我相信，本次展会一定会对中国和马来西亚的经贸合作起到积极推动作用。

女士们、先生们，

中国改革开放近三十年来，经济保持了较快的增长速度。开放的具有活力的中国经济，正在为世界经济的发展注入新的动力。据世界旅游组织预计，两年后中国每年将有5000多万旅游者走出国门。东盟国家与中国地理位置邻近，经济互补性强，中国巨大的市场将为包

括马来西亚在内的所有东盟国家提供更广阔的市场和更丰富的商机。

女士们、先生们，

进一步加强中马友好合作，符合两国根本利益。扩大中马互利经贸合作将为中国和马来西亚的友好关系注入更多的实质性内容，为两国人民创造更多的福祉。我们愿与马来西亚方面共同努力，在"平等互利、共同发展"的原则基础上开展多种形式的互利合作，不断开创两国经贸合作的新局面。

最后，预祝本次展览洽谈会取得圆满成功！

# 口译讲评

# Notes on the Text

**Passage A**

1. **London has 3.5 trillion under management, more than any other market in the world and lists more companies in any one year than the New York Stock Exchange, NASDAQ and Hong Kong combined**：listed more companies 在这里是指公司上市，而 the New York Stock Exchange、NASDAQ 和 Hong Kong 指的是世界著名的三大证券交易所。

2. **the Over the Counter market**：即店头市场，亦称"柜台市场"、"场外市场"，是指在证券交易所之外的某一固定场所，专供未上市的证券或不足以成交批量的证券进行交易的市场。该市场因买卖双方一般都通过电话、电报协商完成交易，故又称之为电话市场。店头市场是一个广泛而又复杂的市场，其证券交易量远远超过证券交易所交易量。

3. **The UK has a particularly generous regime for foreign nationals working in the UK in that they are not taxed on income arising outside the UK**：regime 在这里指的是"制度"，in that 引导的是一个表示原因的从句，在译为汉语时，相关的逻辑连词可省略，全句可以译为"英国对在这里工作的海外人士实施极其大方的税收制度，对于从英国以外的地区所获得的收入，他们可以免于缴纳所得税。"

4. **Secondly, the independence which the present Prime Minister gave to the Bank of England ten years ago when he was Chancellor of the Exchequer, with its focus on monetary policy, has also helped to ensure a stable and successful macro-economy**：这是一句典型的长句，翻译时可作多次切分，形成多个独立小句，以符合口译时汉语的流畅表达习惯，如句眼的 independence 一词可以单独成句。整句话可以译为"第二是独立。这是现任首相在10年前任财政大臣的时候授予英格兰银行的权利，货币政策是其重点，帮助宏观经济保证稳定和成功运行。"

5. **Our Government created a single, business-friendly regulator for all financial services**：the Financial Services Authority：the Financial Services Authority，即 FSA，为英国金融服务管理局，于1997年10月由证券投资委员会（Securities and Investments Board, SIB）改制而成，是一个独立的非政府组织，作为英国金融市场统一的监管机构，它行使法定职责，直接向财政部负责。其宗旨是对金融服务行业进行监管，以保持高效、有序、廉洁的金融

市场,并帮助中小消费者取得公平交易机会。

6. **This is very different from the line-by-line rules-based approach, with its box-ticking mentality**:line-by-line 的意思是"级对级",box-ticking 的意思是"逐项核查"。
7. **By adopting this business-friendly approach, the FSA has given the UK-based financial services a framework within which businesses can innovate and prosper**:关系从句的翻译可以采用后置复指的方法,使得句意自然、充分。整句可译为:"通过使用这种商业友好型的办法,英国金融服务管理局为英国本土的金融服务机构提供了一个框架,有了这个框架,商业活动就能够不断创新,取得成功。"
8. **Big Bang**:即创举大爆炸式改革。这个短语原本是用来描述宇宙形成过程的。在宇宙漫长的发展过程中,发生在 100 亿到 150 亿年前的宇宙大爆炸起了决定性的作用,从而促动了宇宙的形成。但现在这个短语多用于金融方面,并且特指伦敦证券交易所于 1986 年 10 月进行的较大规模的交易体制改革。此次改革取消了中介人的固定回扣,证券交易市场完全依靠电脑所传送信息的速度而定。这在证券交易史上无疑是一次巨大的革命。继 1986 年的"创举大爆炸式改革"之后,伦敦证券交易所又于 1997 年 10 月 20 日进行了第二次规模宏大的股票交易改革,这在金融史上称为 Big Bang II,其中心是建立了以市场为中心的股票交易自动报价系统(Stock Exchange Automatic Quotation System)。

**Passage B**

1. **中国和马来西亚是友好近邻,两国传统友谊源远流长**:这句话翻译时要注意分清主次,前半句"中国和马来西亚是友好近邻"可以用 as 短语引导,这样一来,整个句子宜用 China and Malaysia 作为主语;全句可译为 As friendly close neighbors, China and Malaysia have enjoyed a time-honored friendship.
2. **随着中国经济实力的不断增强和"走出去"战略的实施,已有越来越多的中国企业到马来西亚开展投资合作**:"走出去"战略可以翻译为"going global" strategy。实施"走出去"战略,是党中央从我国经济发展全局做出的重大决策,对拓展国民经济发展空间和促进共同发展都具有十分重要的意义。它既可以补充我国需要的资源,又可以带动商品和劳务出口,还可以培育我国的跨国公司和知名品牌。同时,企业到境外投资办厂,促进了东道国经济发展和就业,实现了我国产品市场多元化和原产地多元化,有利于缓解贸易摩擦。
3. **为推动中国与马来西亚以及东盟各国之间的友好往来,发展双边贸易关系,中国商务部在马来西亚政府和工商界的大力支持下,举办了中国商品展览会**:要注意这句话中相关专有名词的翻译,如"东盟各国"译为 ASEAN countries,"中国商务部"译为 Ministry of Commerce,"中国商品展览会"译为 the Chinese Import and Export Commodities Exhibition。
4. **中国改革开放近三十年来,经济保持了较快的增长速度**:此类句子在政治经济类讲话中经常出现,译者平时可细心收集与积累,以保证现场翻译时可以快速准确地给出相关译文,China's economy has maintained a comparatively fast growth rate since the adoption of its reform and opening up 30 years ago.
5. **开放而具有活力的中国经济,正在为世界经济发展注入新的动力**:"注入新的动力"可以用短语 pump new vitality and momentum into...

6. 据世界旅游组织预计,到2010年中国每年将有5000多万旅游者走出国门:"走出国门"在这里比较地道的翻译处理可以理解为"the outbound travel",整句话可以译为 World Tourism Organization forecasted that by the year 2010 over 50 million Chinese tourists will join the outbound travel.

7. 我们愿与马来西亚方面共同努力,在"平等互利、共同发展"的原则基础上开展多种形式的互利合作,不断开创两国经贸合作的新局面:这句中文长句在转译时要注意均衡再现原文的重心和层次,译者可逐层推开,给出条理清晰的译文,可参考译为 China is willing to work with Malaysia and conduct mutually beneficial cooperation in a variety of fields and incessantly attain new progress in the bilateral trade and economic cooperation of the two countries on the basis of the principle of "Equality, Mutual Benefit and Common Development".

# 相关词语 Relevant Words and Expressions

投资热 investment fever
总投资 gross investment
边际投资 marginal investment
分散投资 investment diversification
计划投资 intended / plan / planned investment
投资意向 investment proposal
投资总额 total amount of investment; aggregate investment
衍生产品 derivative instrument
优等投资 prime investment
不动产投资 real estate investment
收购与兼并 merger and acquisition
投资周转率 investment turnover
一揽子投资 package / packaged investment
招标投标制 the system of public bidding for projects
投资风险机制 risk mechanism for investment
证券组合投资 portfolio investment
危险／风险投资 risk investment
风险资本 venture capital
国内私人投资总额 gross private domestic investment
外国／外商直接投资 FDI [foreign direct investment]
用多余资金投资;顺应需要的投资 leeway investment

# 口译技能
## Interpreting Skills

### 长句处理

口译过程中，译员经常会遭遇长句。如何处理长句，也就相应地成为口译的一个难点问题。

英语中长句较多，句中修饰语多且长，句式结构复杂，所以英译汉时，不能照样克隆复制，而是得根据汉语语法的特点，灵活处理。切分就是一种常用的方法，即是将长句分解为若干小句。它常包括单词分译、短语分译和句子分译等三种情况。看几个句子：

1. We recognize that China's long-term modernization program understandably and necessarily emphasizes economic growth. 我们认识到，中国的长期现代化计划以发展经济为重点，这是可以理解的，也是必要的。这句话中的两个副词 understandably and necessarily 都被拆分出来，这样既突出了重点，又使语言自然流畅。

2. The military is forbidden to kill the vessel, a relatively easy task. 军方被禁止击毁这艘潜艇，虽然要击毁它并不怎么费事。这句话中的名词短语 a relatively easy task 被分出来译为短句，使得句意更为清晰。

3. But another round of war in the region clearly would put strains on international relations. 但是，如果该地区再次发生战争，显然会使国际关系处于紧张状态。这句简单句在翻译时增添了逻辑关系，使得容量沉重的简单句模式变为两个独立分句，更加符合汉语的表达习惯。

4. The recruitment of Chinese labor was not universally accepted in racially conscious 19th century America and some white workers were unsettled by their appearance in large numbers. 在种族意识十分强的19世纪的美国，招募中国劳工的做法并非普遍为人接受。由于工地上大批出现中国劳工，某些白人工人感到心绪不宁。这句话是由连词 and 处连缀的两个顺接式的被动语态。中文表达中，不太习惯用被动句，这时通常就要根据句意进行切分，并将句中若干成分的词性做适当转换，使得长句翻译时显得更为充分。

一般说来，英语句子因较为绵长复杂，往往需要切分为小的流水句，但有时根据具体情况，也需要进行合并。例如：

1. She is intelligent, ambitious and hard-working. She is also good at solving problems. 她很有才智、雄心勃勃、工作努力，还善于解决问题。在这句话中，两句合一，翻译显得干净利落。

汉英口译时，遇到较长的句子，要注意随时断句，在一句之中，注意要做到主次分明，结构清晰。例如：

2. 他为这家杂志写了两篇稿子，一篇本期即将发表，另一篇将在下期刊载。He has written two articles for the journal, one to be published in this issue, the other to come out in the next.

# 第3单元 投资环境 Investment Environment

3. 这些艺术品丰富多彩,栩栩如生,而且别出心裁,具有鲜明的民族特色和地方色彩。Colorful, lifelike and original, these works of art had distinctive national and local characteristics.
4. 他是一位天才的语言学家,同样精通法、德、英多种语言。A gifted linguist, he was equally at home in French, German and English.

这几个中文原句无一例外,都如流水般随句意而下,而英文翻译都增加了相应的层级结构,使得译文显得充分而自然。

总体而言,在口译中,遇到长句,译者要进行适当的切分、合并或是增补语法构架,这既是出于句法的需要,也是为了修饰上的需要,使得译文不至于生硬晦涩,翻译腔十足,反而能理顺句意,突出重点。

## 译练习 *Enhancement Practice*

第一项 Project 1
句子精练 Sentences in Focus

**A. Interpret the following sentences from English into Chinese.**

1. There are many examples of new financial instruments and new areas of business that have been created in New York in recent years.
2. The UK has the most open attitude to mergers & acquisitions of any major country with the UK accounting for $367 billion, or about 9%, of total global M&A.
3. The Summit, which takes place in London next June, will introduce many Chinese companies to the financial services available in London, the world's largest financial centre.
4. Many of the products now on sale throughout the Muslim world were invented, developed and marketed from London, which has helped it develop into the leading centre for Islamic Finance.
5. Most major US investment banks locate their headquarters for Europe, Africa, the Middle East and South Asia in London, and it's interesting as well that big EU players also choose London as a focus for investment banking activity—it really is the bridge between Europe and the global financial markets.

**B. Interpret the following sentences from Chinese into English.**

1. 我国是由56个民族共同组成的多民族大家庭,民族用品独具特色,饮食文化源远流长。
2. 随着西部大开发战略和各项民族政策的贯彻实施,广大西部地区经济社会取得了快速发展。
3. 马来西亚经济快速增长,投资环境优越,中国政府积极支持和鼓励有实力的中国企业到马投资,开展双赢合作。
4. 中国国内生产总值从1978年的2165亿美元,增长到今年的2.6万亿美元,增长了11倍,人均GDP达到2000美元。

5. 近年来,一大批蕴含民族文化内涵、具有鲜明民族特色的产品不断推陈出新,极大地繁荣了市场,丰富了人民物质文化生活。

第二项 Project 2
段落口译 Paragraph Interpreting

**A. Interpret the following paragraph from English into Chinese.**

　　We have a very open and advanced economy. Some of the most advanced users in the world for all ICT services are based in the City of London, a global financial centre. The UK was rated as the best environment for e-commerce among major markets in a recent survey. We are a leading market in mobile communications, in digital television, and in other areas. A recent survey shows that about 40% of America's and Japan's massive investments in to Europe go to one single country out of the 25 nations that make up the EU—to Britain.

**B. Interpret the following paragraph from Chinese into English.**

　　马来西亚和香港都是亚太近海富饶流域的门户地区,是依靠贸易、外资和旅游业繁荣的外向型经济实体。去年,马来西亚是香港的第九大贸易伙伴,双边贸易额高达90亿美元。我们也同时成马来西亚的第五大贸易伙伴。过去五年来,两地的经济一直呈稳步增长态势,年增长率超过7%。

第三项 Project 3
篇章口译 Passage Interpreting

**A. Listen to the tape and interpret the following passage from English into Chinese.**
Distinguished guests, ladies and gentlemen,

　　I am delighted to have the opportunity to address you at the opening of the 7th China Beijing International High-tech Expo.

　　In the last two years I have been living and working in Beijing. I have witnessed tremendous advances across China particularly in hi-tech manufacturing sectors, in science and research.

　　Britain is well placed to enable China to develop even faster in these areas, and in a way that is sustainable over the long term. Hi-tech manufacturing industries are global and they matter to us all. The China market has been a lifeline for the global industry over the last three years. And British markets, companies and research institutions are ideally positioned to make a strong contribution to China's success in hi-tech sectors such as Information and Communications Technology, biotechnology and many more.

　　As China grows world class companies and these go out into international markets, many are attracted to Britain. We now have over 300 Chinese companies operating profitably and successfully in Britain.

We are the world's fifth largest trading nation, and probably the most international in orientation-so a great place for Chinese companies wishing to develop international competitiveness. We are the second largest investor overseas. We are the leading European investor in China, with 3,400 joint ventures and nearly US $20 billion in contractual investment.

Crucially, Britain is also the second largest recipient of inward investment in the world. That means the best companies from around the world choose Britain to base their investments in Europe, and to help in their global research effort.

How can all this help Chinese companies?

First, we have learnt that investment overseas—the "going global" policy in China—brings enormous benefits to the parent company and to its own home economy over the short and long term. We have the longest experience as a country in helping new investors to succeed with profit.

Second, we know how important it is to choose the right country to invest in on the basis of objective criteria. The most important criterion is the judgment of international business, and international business has shown clearly its own preference for Britain as the location of choice in Europe.

Finally let me remind you of the fundamental reasons why Britain is the best performing economy in Europe by far and a natural choice for Chinese companies when they seek a location in Europe. These are:

- a light, transparent regulatory framework giving certainty to business;
- a stable political and industrial climate;
- low taxes;
- the English language;
- a multi-racial, multi-cultural society with established ethnic populations including 150,000 Chinese;
- one of the most flexible labor markets in the world;
- easy access to world-class science and technology and high value skills in areas from marketing to research.

Our Trade & Investment teams in China stand ready to help you take advantage of all this. I encourage you to take a minute today to speak with our team about what we have to offer.

**B. Listen to the tape and interpret the following passage from Chinese into English.**

尊敬的各位来宾、女士们、先生们、朋友们：

我谨代表商务部，对首届中国宁夏清真食品民族用品节暨宁夏投资贸易洽谈会隆重召开表示热烈祝贺！

宁夏是我国最大的少数民族聚居区之一，在发展清真食品、民族用品方面优势非常突出，潜力非常巨大。通过大家的共同努力，宁夏的清真牛羊肉等一批具有回族民族特色的品牌已成功走向国际市场。民族经济的发展有力地带动了农民脱贫致富,推动了地区经济、社会的快速发展。

当今世界,经济全球化趋势日益明显,各个民族、地区、国家之间在经济、文化等领域的交流十分活跃。清真食品、民族用品也跨越了民族、地区、国家界限,不断融合、创新、发展。面对这一历史性机遇,我们要根据少数民族的生活、文化特点,加大资金投入力度,在保持民族特色的基础上,不断创新,打造国际国内知名品牌,进一步拓展和繁荣具有民族特色的清真食品和民族用品市场,丰富世界各国人民生活,为推动构建和谐社会做出应有的贡献。

宁夏不仅拥有丰富的自然资源,而且拥有一批具有较强竞争力的特色产业,这里的商机无限,广大客商到这里开展投资合作前景非常广阔。

我相信,在党中央国务院正确领导下,只要我们坚持科学发展观,牢牢把握各民族共同团结奋斗、共同发展的主题,紧紧抓住西部大开发的历史机遇,充分利用投资贸易洽谈会平台,进一步扩大对内、对外开放,宁夏的经济和社会发展必将不断跃上新台阶。

预祝首届中国宁夏清真食品民族用品节暨宁夏投资贸易洽谈会取得圆满成功!

# 参考译文

## Reference Version

**篇章口译 A**

女士们、先生们,我很高兴能和大家一起,参加博鳌亚洲论坛国际资本大会今天的记者招待会。

伦敦管理着全球 3.5 万亿英镑的资金,比世界上其他任何市场的都多,每年在伦敦上市的公司数量比在纽约证券交易所、纳斯达克和香港上市的总和还多。伦敦占了全球 34% 的货币贸易额,是最国际化、流动最快的全球金融中心。在伦敦城,进行着全球 90% 的金属交易、全球 25% 的航空和海上保险和近 50% 的全球船舶交易。而在不断扩大着的衍生贸易领域,伦敦占了全球店头市场份额的 43%。

对市场准入和竞争的开放,是英国成功的主要因素。不过也还存在着其他因素。

第一是财政环境。英国对在这里工作的海外人士实施极其大方的税收制度,对于从英国以外的地区所获得的收入,他们可以免于缴纳所得税。而且,英国最近还降低了企业税的税率。我们新上任的财政大臣也宣布了他进一步简化税收政策的打算。

第二是独立。这是现任首相在 10 年前任财政大臣的时候授予英格兰银行的权利,货币政策是其重点,帮助宏观经济保证稳定和成功运行。

第三个也是制胜的关键因素之一,即制度环境。我们的政府为所有的金融服务创造了一个单一、商业友好型的调解员——英国金融服务管理局。英国金融服务管理局采取了以规避风险为基础的办法。这种办法不同于"级对级"以制度为基础、逐项核查的办法。英国的这种模式减少了全球商业因为要遵循繁琐的规则而需要付出的成本。通过使用这种商业友好型的办法,英国金融服务管理局为英国本土的金融服务机构提供了一个框架,有了这个框架,商业活动就能够不断创新,取得成功。

# 第3单元 投资环境 Investment Environment

开放市场准入和有利的制度环境所带来的结果就是国外金融公司大量涌入伦敦。在"大爆炸式改革创举"过去20年之后的今天,金融城内大约50%的企业都为外资所有,英国金融服务领域内有200,000名从业人员来自海外。而且金融城内50%左右的办公资产也都为外国金融机构所有,其中德国的养老基金几乎就占了1/4。

所有的这些举措都达到了一个目的:成功和不断扩大的市场——一个中国公司可以投注资本的理想市场。

最后,我们欢迎越来越多的中国公司来英国建立分公司,同时也希望其中一些公司把自己在欧洲的总部设在英国。除了能享受到伦敦作为世界主要金融中心的便利和英国的低税收经济政策之外,中国公司还能利用到我们的研发实力,以及我们在设计和营销上的专业知识。我们的人口占世界的1%,而研发成果占世界的5.5%。在英国建立公司是很简单的,平均来说,只需18个小时。而且,我们还提供快捷、高效的签证服务,英国在中国的12个城市设立了签证办事处。去年年初的时候,有220家中国的公司在英国设立分公司,而现在这个数字已经增加到了340。今年年初,有27家中国公司在伦敦证券交易所挂牌上市,现在达到了68家。信息是如此地清晰。我们所实施的开放型经济欢迎来自世界各地的公司。英国不仅是投资的好地点,也是迈向全球发展的良好起点。

**篇章口译 B**

Ladies and gentlemen,

The 2007 Malaysia's Chinese Import and Export Commodities Exhibition & Investment Conference, the fourth session of its kind, is officially opened today. On behalf of China's Ministry of Commerce, I would like to extend a warm welcome to all the distinguished guests and friends present at the opening ceremony. I would also like to express our sincere gratitude to the Malaysia-China Chamber of Commerce for their great support to the exhibition.

As friendly close neighbors, China and Malaysia have enjoyed a time-honored friendship. The China-Malaysia trade and economic cooperation has seen rapid development since the two countries established diplomatic ties 33 years ago. According to statistics from China's Customs, their trade totaled USD $37.1 billion last year, and it is expected to surpass USD $45 billion this year. China and Malaysia are important trading partners of each other. China has become Malaysia's largest export market of palm oil and the fourth largest export market of the latter's electronic products.

With the rapid development of bilateral trade, the two-way investment between China and Malaysia has also made tremendous progress. By the end of last September, Malaysia's actual investment in China has exceeded USD $4.5 billion. With China's continuous increase of economic strength and the implementation of the "going global" strategy, more and more Chinese enterprises start investing in and cooperating with Malaysia.

Aiming at boosting the friendly exchanges between China and Malaysia and other ASEAN countries, as well as promoting the bilateral trade relations, Ministry of

Commerce hosted, with energetic support from the Malaysian government and industrial and commercial circles, the Chinese Import and Export Commodities Exhibition. Such an exhibition has been held successfully for three times since 2004, and a good image has been set up for both Chinese and Malaysian enterprises. This year, the number of enterprise exhibitors has exceeded 200, and over 8,000 buyers are expected to be present at the exhibition. I am confident that this exhibition will surely play an active role in boosting China-Malaysia trade and economic cooperation.

Ladies and gentlemen,

China's economy has maintained a comparatively fast growth rate since the adoption of its reform and opening up 30 years ago. China's open and robust economy has pumped new vitality and momentum into the development of world economy. World Tourism Organization forecasted that in just two years over 50 million Chinese tourists will join the outbound travel. China and ASEAN countries are close neighbors and are highly economically complementary. China's tremendous market will provide an even wider market and more business opportunities for Malaysia and other ASEAN countries.

Ladies and gentlemen,

It is in the fundamental interests of both countries to further strengthen China-Malaysia friendly cooperation. Expanding the mutually beneficial trade and economic cooperation between our two countries will input more substantial contents to China-Malaysia friendly relations and bring about more benefits to the two peoples. China is willing to work with Malaysia and conduct mutually beneficial cooperation in a variety of fields and incessantly attain new progress in the bilateral trade and economic cooperation of the two countries on the basis of the principle of "Equality, Mutual Benefit and Common Development".

In conclusion, I wish the Exhibition & Investment Conference every success.

## 口译练习
### 第一项 句子精练
A.
1. 有许多例证可以证明,近些年来,在伦敦建立起了新的金融工具和新的商业领域。
2. 与任何大国比起来,英国对并购持最开放的姿态,本年度的全球并购资金中占约9%,计有3670亿美元。
3. 峰会将于6月在伦敦举行,届时将向伦敦——全球最大金融中心的金融服务行业介绍众多的中国公司。
4. 目前在穆斯林世界出售的许多产品都是在伦敦发明、开发和销售过的,这也帮助伦敦发展成了伊斯兰金融世界的主要中心。
5. 绝大多数的美国主要投资银行都把他们在欧洲、非洲、中东和南亚的总部设在了伦敦,有趣的是,欧共体主要成员也把伦敦作为银行投资活动的主要地点,它实际已成为欧洲和全球金融市场的桥梁。

# 第 3 单元 投资环境 Investment Environment

**B.**

1. The Chinese nation is a big family composed of 56 nationalities, featured by distinctive ethnic articles and a time-honored dietary culture.
2. In recent years, with the implementation of the Strategy of Developing Western China and policies towards ethnic minorities, most Chinese western regions have witnessed rapid economic and social development.
3. The Chinese government encourages and supports competitive Chinese enterprises to make investment in and conduct win-win cooperation with Malaysia, a nation with a fast economic growth and an investment-friendly environment.
4. China's GDP had increased by 11 times from USD $216.5 billion in 1978 to USD $2.6 trillion this year, and the GDP per capita reached USD $2,000.
5. A batch of new articles with ethnic culture and distinctive ethnic characteristics have been brought forth to the public, thus the market has been greatly thrived and the material and cultural life of the local people has been extremely improved.

## 第二项 段落口译

**A.**

我们有非常开放和先进的经济模式。伦敦金融区是全球金融中心,拥有世界上所有信息与通信技术服务领域内的一些最高端用户。在最近一份调查中,英国在电子商务这类主要市场的经济环境方面名列榜首。我们的移动通信、数字电视以及其他领域内的市场都是首屈一指的。一份最近的调查显示,在美国和日本对欧盟共25个国家的投资中,仅进入了英国一个国家的巨额投资就大约占了40%。

**B.**

As gateways to rich hinterlands in the Asia-Pacific region, Hong Kong and Malaysia both are externally-oriented economies thriving much on trade, foreign investment and tourism. Last year, Malaysia was Hong Kong's ninth largest trading partner, with total bilateral trade amounting to US$9 billion. Reciprocally, we were the fifth largest trading partner to Malaysia. Indeed, we have witnessed sustained growth of trade between our two economies in the past five years with an annual increase of more than 7%.

## 第三项 篇章口译

**A.**

尊敬的来宾们,女士们、先生们:

我很高兴能有机会在第七届中国北京国际科技产业博览会的开幕式上发言。

两年来,我一直在北京生活、工作,见证了整个中国的巨大进步,尤其在高科技制造和科研领域取得了世界瞩目的成就。

英国深具优势,能帮助中国在这些领域发展得更快,且在长期内保持一定发展速度。高科技制造业是全球性的产业,对我们所有人都至关重要。最近三年来,中国市场已经成为了世界工业的生命线。而英国的市场、公司和研究机构极具优势,能大大推动中国在诸如信息与通信技术、生物技术乃至更多的高科技领域内获得成功。

中国正在出现很多世界级公司,它们正在走出国门,走向国际市场,其中有许多公司都选择英国进一步发展。英国现在有300多家运营顺利、收益良好的中国公司。

英国是世界第五大贸易国,也可能是最国际化的一个,因此对那些希望参与国际竞争的中国公司而言,英国是理想的地点。我们是全球第二大对外投资国。我们是欧洲在中国投资最多的国家,有3400家合资企业和将近200亿美元的合同性投资。

重要的是,英国还是世界上第二大吸引外资的国家。这意味着全世界最好的公司都把英国作为他们在欧洲的投资基地,为其全球研究工作助上一臂之力。

这一切对中国公司会有怎样的帮助呢?

首先,我们知道中国政府的"走出去"政策鼓励海外投资,这在短期和长期内不仅会给母公司,还会给中国经济本身带来巨大的利益。英国在帮助新投资者成功盈利方面拥有最为丰富的经验。

其次,我们知道根据客观标准来选择正确投资国的重要性。最重要的标准是对国际商务的判断,而国际商务已经很明显地显示出,英国是人们在欧洲进行投资的首选地点。

最后,请允许我来提醒各位英国之所以能成为目前欧洲表现最佳的经济体,以及成为中国公司在欧洲投资首选地的七条根本原因。他们是:

- 轻松透明的规章制度,为商业提供确定性;
- 稳定的政治和产业气候;
- 低税率;
- 英语环境;
- 多民族、多文化社会,拥有确定的种族人口,包括大约15万华人;
- 全世界最灵活变通的劳工市场之一;
- 可轻易获得从销售到研究领域内的世界级科技和高价值技能。

我们在中国的贸易与投资团队随时准备帮助您利用这些优势。我建议大家今天能抽空与我们的团队沟通一下,了解我们所提供的服务。

**B.**

Distinguished Guests, Ladies and Gentlemen, Dear Friends,

On Behalf of the Ministry of Commerce, I would like to extend my warm congratulations to the opening of the First Islamic Food and Articles Fair, Ningxia, China and Ningxia Fair for Investment and Trade.

Ningxia, one of the biggest minority areas in China, has a remarkable superiority and great potential in the development of Islamic food and ethnic articles. With the joint efforts from all parties, a number of brands of Ningxia Islamic beef and mutton with Hui nationality features have successfully gained reputation in the international market. The development of national economy has helped the local farmers to get rid of poverty and become rich, and driven the development of regional economy and local community.

# 第 3 单元　投资环境　Investment Environment

　　In the present world, economic globalization is an increasingly prominent trend, and there have been quite active communications in such areas as economy and culture among nationalities, regions and countries. Islamic food and articles are getting to integrate, innovate and develop regardless of boundaries across nations and regions. Faced with this historic opportunity, we should increase fund investment based on the life and culture of ethnic minorities. On the one hand, we should always innovate and create brands famous at home and abroad, and on the other hand, we cannot forget to keep the original ethnic flavor. Therefore, the market of Islamic food and articles can be expanded and thrived, the lives of people in the world hopefully improved, and ultimately due contributions devoted to the construction of a harmonious society.

　　Ningxia has abundant natural resources and a number of special industries with strong competitiveness as well. There are enormous business opportunities here, and will be an extensive prospect for traders to invest and develop business.

　　I believe that under the leadership of CPC Central Committee and the State Council, as long as we insist on the Scientific Development Concept, adhere to the theme of unity, striving and common development of all the nationalities, seize the historic opportunity of Development of Western China, and take full advantage of the platform of the Fair for Trade and Investment to further open up to the domestic and international market, Ningxia is sure to make splendid progress in its economic and social development.

　　I wish the First Islamic Food and Articles Fair, Ningxia, China and Ningxia Fair for Investment and Trade a complete success!

# Unit 4　Urban Planning

## 第 4 单元　城市规划

# 篇章口译

## Passage A (E-C)

### Vocabulary Work

Work on the following words and phrases and write the translated version in the space provided.

| | | | |
|---|---|---|---|
| accommodate | equivalent | viability | fiscal stability |
| livability | fulfilling | ill suited to | cutting-edge |
| messy | amenity | facilitate | conserve |
| a fine grain mix of | civic engagement | incorporate | |

### Text Interpreting

**Listen to the tape and interpret the following passage from English into Chinese.**

Since 1987, I have spent summers in Beijing working on urban design issues and projects with graduate students from MIT and Tsinghua University. Over those 17 years I have seen tremendous changes in this great city, and other urban centers in China, as investment has poured in along with the people and the cars.

We have just seen the beginning of these transformations. The urban population of China is doubling every 20 years, so that by 2050 there will be 600 million more people living in cities. To accommodate them will require building the equivalent of 50 more urban areas the size of Shanghai.

These new and expanded cities will shape the economic viability and image of China in the world. Their success will depend upon:

• Their competitiveness for economic activity with other cities and regions in the world;

• How well they are managed and governed;

• Their fiscal stability;

• Their livability as three-dimensional places that offer not only survival but also the opportunity for a more fulfilling life.

The way that cities achieve these goals in the future will be different than in the past. For much of the 20th century, the vision of a competitive, efficient city was one with standardized, separated land uses, accessed by ever-widening roads and highways, where the poor were isolated from the rich, and there was little place for local tradition and culture.

We are now learning that this model, which requires vast amounts of land and resources, is inefficient, inequitable, and very costly to maintain. More importantly, it is ill suited to an information economy where uniqueness, diversity and culture are becoming more and more economically valuable.

If we scan what are considered to be the progressive cities and cutting-edge projects in the world today, emphasis is being placed on qualities that are opposite the 20th century ideal. Cities and private developers are focusing on making places that are less standard, more messy, more integrated, with more amenities, serving a wider range of people, that facilitate (in a word) livability—the day to day quality of life in cities.

Livability has emerged as a priority not because planners say it's a good thing, but because information firms and the creative, entrepreneurial people, who work for them, have many choices where they can invest their money and time. In that global market for talent and jobs, cities that are more distinctive and offer a higher quality of experience for a greater number of people have a competitive advantage. And so, we find that cities are acting to enhance their livability by:

- Limiting the impact of the car;
- Striving for creativity in architecture and public places;
- Conserving and developing local cultural heritage;
- Promoting a fine grain mix of activities for diverse kinds of people; and
- Building on civic engagement where residents can help to shape the environment in unique ways.

Bank and government investments that enhance livability can yield some of the highest returns because:

- They affect people at a level they can appreciate, directly enhancing their homes, businesses, and daily life;
- They can redress some of the inequalities of poverty—such as poor transportation and lack of recreational opportunities;

A good environment is increasingly critical to attracting leading private firms, and jobs necessary to sustain the city; thus livability can benefit both competitiveness and fiscal stability.

I would like to applaud the China Development Bank and the World Bank for convening this conference, which I see as a first step in that direction. Banks can have a powerful influence on the quality of city making, simply by defining livability as an important consideration. But to operationalize these concerns will require research into ways that livability can be incorporated into standard economic development projects and how to measure success.

# 篇章口译

## Passage B (C-E)

### Vocabulary Work

Work on the following words and phrases and write the translated version in the space provided.

| | | | |
|---|---|---|---|
| 专家委员会 | 土地和生态规划 | 双重视角 | 地形条件 |
| 可耕地 | 居住密集地区 | 冲积平原 | 内陆江河流域 |
| 生物多样性 | 利益方 | 枢纽港口 | 储备库 |
| 高性能运输网络 | 填海造地 | | |

### Text Interpreting

Listen to the tape and interpret the following passage from Chinese into English.

近来，中国国家开发银行专家委员会副主席王先生向我告知有关举办一场题为"中国的城市规划未来"研讨会的计划。王先生友好地问我是否可以中国大城市土地和生态规划的双重视角参与这一重要活动。

尽管中国幅员辽阔，占地面积约933万平方公里，但很大一部分土地由于地形条件、气候条件恶劣以及交通不便等原因，并不适合人们生活居住。约125万平方公里为可耕地，占世界可耕地总量的8%不到，然而中国现有人口却占世界人口总量的约21%。

居住密集地区主要集中在东部沿海省区广大的冲积平原及部分内陆江河流域。这些地区的城市发展压力正迅速上升，需要更为有效地使用土地——在区域、次区域和各级地区进行基础设施规划，并制订和及时执行相关的发展计划。与此紧密相关的问题涉及城市化直接或间接对内地主要城镇的生态环境所造成的影响。在这些关键领域的主要顾虑涉及对城市和农村高质量用水的保护和供应、空气质量标准、多种土壤的可持续使用、对具有生物多样性土地及海洋区域的保护以及对供公众娱乐的自然乡村和沿海地区的保护和管理。

我曾多年在香港特别行政区工作，在该地区约700万人口居住在面积仅1000平方公里之地。从我多年从事的工作来看，我清楚地意识到需要一个框架性的规划和发展进程。在此框架下，各主要"利益方"能在资源允许和其他限制的范围内协调各种努力。在此方面，我有幸连续35年参与一个规划进程的创建和应用工作。这一进程在1973年建立了第一个全港发展战略，该战略迄今为止相继更新了好几次。此外，我很荣幸地承担起创建港口机场发展战略(PADS)的工作，并作为项目经理负责香港大型新城中的一座。

尽管香港很小，它却是中国南部广大内陆的枢纽港口、金融中心、专业技能和技术创新的储备库以及文化和旅游中心。在过去50年间，香港不得不应对越来越大的城市化压力，

# 第4单元 城市规划 Urban Planning

包括对更好的住房、就业机会、公共设施、高性能运输网络以及其他主要的基础设施和改善的环境条件的需求。总的来说,通过填海造地、将所选农村区域重新分区以及重新开发城市等方式,为城市发展提供了新的土地,从而满足了上述需求。

总而言之,新的城市开发必须建设成为密度越来越高,并拥有高性能运输系统和其他基础设施。此外,具有独特的生物多样性的区域被单独分隔开来,以作为科学兴趣和海洋公园的特别区域。所有这些都要求对一连串的计划和执行项目进行细致协调的准备。

## 口译讲评

## Notes on the Text

**Passage A**

1. **as investment has poured in along with the people and the cars**:可以译为"随着投资的大量涌入,人口和车辆的不断增加"。

2. **For much of the 20th century, the vision of a competitive, efficient city was one with standardized, separated land uses**:separated land uses 是指根据土地不同的目的而进行分类使用。

3. **We are now learning that this model, which requires vast amounts of land and resources, is inefficient, inequitable, and very costly to maintain**:在口译 this model 时,宜根据上文提到的内容稍作补充和解释,可译为"这种城市发展的模式"。

4. **emphasis is being placed on qualities that are opposite the 20th century ideal**:quality 作集合名词(单数形式出现)时有质量、品质之意,为复数形式时可译为"特征"。这里根据上半句提到的"如果对我们所认为的发展中城市和当前世界的前沿项目进行审视",可以推出讨论的是城市建设的问题,因此 quality 可补充处理为"城市建设特征"。

5. **but because information firms and the creative, entrepreneurial people, who work for them, have many choices where they can invest their money and time**:试比较"而是因为信息公司以及为这些公司工作的、具有创造力和创业精神的人拥有许多把金钱和时间投入何处的选择"与"而是因为信息公司以及为这些公司工作的、具有创造力和创业精神的人拥有许多选择,他们可以决定把金钱和时间投入何处",后者运用了顺译的技巧。

6. **They affect people at a level they can appreciate, directly enhancing their homes, businesses, and daily life**:试比较直译"它们会在人们产生感激之情的情况下影响人们,直接改善人们的住房、业务和日常生活"与意译"它们能够给人们带来好处并产生积极的影响,直接改善人们的住房、业务和日常生活",后者通顺易懂。

7. **attracting leading private firms, and jobs necessary to sustain the city**:试比较"吸引一流私营企业和就业机会"与"吸引一流私营企业、创造就业机会",口译时作适当增补,可以使译文听上去更地道。

8. **But to operationalize these concerns will require research into ways that livability can be incorporated into standard economic development projects and how to measure success**:在

口译此长句时,关键是怎样处理好 require research into ways that livability can be incorporated into standard economic development projects and how to measure success。针对这种英语中常见的从句部分较长的句式,可以采用断句加增补的译法。整句话可处理为"但是要使这些问题得到实际解决,我们还需要进行研究,找出如何把适居性和标准经济发展项目相结合以及如何衡量成功的方法"。

**Passage B**

1. **中国国家开发银行**:China Development Bank（CDB）。国家开发银行为中国三大政策性银行之一,为国务院直属的具有国家信用的开发性金融机构,负责为国家基础设施、基础产业、支柱产业、高新技术产业的发展和国家重大项目的建设提供政策性金融支持。

2. **但很大一部分土地由于地形条件、气候条件恶劣以及交通不便等原因,并不适合人们生活居住**:此句可用顺译的方法,可处理为 a high proportion comprises land which, by reason of difficult topography, adverse climatic conditions and limited access, is inhospitable to human habitation。注意译文将"地形条件、气候条件恶劣以及交通不便"的结构转化为简洁易懂的"恶劣的地形条件、气候条件以及不便的交通"。

3. **居住密集地区主要集中在东部沿海省区广大的冲积平原及部分内陆江河流域**:此句宜译为 Intensively settled areas are generally confined to extensive alluvial plains in the eastern coastal provinces and also to certain inland river basins。

4. **在这些关键领域的主要顾虑涉及对城市和农村高质量用水的保护和供应、空气质量标准、多种土壤的可持续使用、对具有生物多样性土地及海洋区域的保护以及对供公众娱乐的自然乡村和沿海地区的保护和管理**:遇到口译多项列举内容时,根据英语的表达习惯,可采用结构如 such issues/matters/fields/areas as＋具体的列举项目。整句可译为 Key areas of concern relate to such matters as the conservation and supply of water of acceptable quality for both urban and rural uses; standards of air quality; the sustainable use of versatile soils; the protection of land and marine areas with high biodiversity values; and the reservation and management of scenic rural and coastal areas for public enjoyment。

5. **利益方**:即利益相关者,在英语中可对应的词是 stakeholder。

6. 英语中表示(地方、地区的)中心的词有 center、hub、node、pivot 等。

7. **在过去50年间,香港不得不应对越来越大的城市化压力,包括对更好的住房、就业机会、公共设施、高性能运输网络以及其他主要的基础设施和改善的环境条件的需求**:译好此句关键在处理好……城市化压力与后文列举项目的关系。所列举的项目是城市化压力的来源。整句可译为 Over the past 50 years, Hong Kong has had to cope with increasing pressures of urbanization generated by demands for better housing, employment opportunities, community facilities, high capacity transport networks, other key infrastructure services and improved environmental conditions。

8. **总的来说,通过填海造地、将所选农村区域重新分区以及重新开发城市等方式,为城市发展提供了新的土地,从而满足了上述需求**:此句的逻辑关系是——填海造地、将所选农村区域重新分区以及重新开发城市→为城市发展提供了新的土地→满足了上述需求,口译时可考虑使用如 through, by means of 等连接词来连接句子。整句宜译为 Overall, these needs have been met through the provision of new land for urban use by such means as the reclamation of areas of sea bed; the rezoning of selected rural areas; and the redevelopment of obsolete parts of the city.

## 相关词语  Relevant Words and Expressions

城市化 urbanization
建筑群 edifices
郊区化 suburbanization
城市边缘 urban fringes
城市复苏 urban revitalization
城市结构 urban fabric
城市形体 urban form
景观节点 landscape node
旧城改造 urban redevelopment
特大城市 megalopolis
交通分界面 transportation interface
控制性详规 regulatory detailed planning
城市整体布局 over-all urban layout
城市总体规划 urban comprehensive planning
地理信息系统 GIS [geography information system]
交通瓶颈地段 traffic bottleneck
交通枢纽城市 traffic point city
城市道路横断面 urban road cross-section
城市中心商业区 CBD [central business district]
城市管理信息系统 urban management information system

## 口译技能

# Interpreting Skills

### 句子结构

中英两种语言之间的巨大差异决定了翻译的艰巨性和复杂性。王力先生曾总结说,"汉语里多用意合法,联结成分并非必要;西方多用形合法,联结成分在大多数情况下是不可少的。"汉语是一种高语境语言,无时态,无词语屈折变化,无前缀后缀,意义之间的联系多建立在词语和短语语序和语境中,而且含义往往内含,隐在上下文中,无明确连接词。句与句之间的衔接主要靠语义,通过读者的理解来承前启后。总体说来,汉语形式较松散、灵活随意,富于弹性,断句没有严格明确的界限,各独立小句如流水,一气呵成,连绵而下。而英语则是一种低语境语言,富含屈折变化、时态变化、单复数变化,意义之间的联系必须由连接词清楚明白地表达。在英语中,逻辑连接词至关重要。他们承接意义,抚顺句与句间的联系,指明作者思维方向。总体说来,英语句式严谨,弹性较小。长句多如大树,枝干清明,主次层层链接,每一片叶子的位置都十分明确。两种语言的天壤之别使得完全的机器翻译异常困难。

中英这两种语言在句子结构上的巨大差异要求译员在口译时要特别留心,采取恰当的翻译手法,进行适当的转换和处理。如在英语关系从句的口译时,译员可以顺应原句特点,采取不同的翻译策略。看以下例句:

1. Space and oceans are the New World which scientists are trying to explore. 太空和海洋是科学家们努力探索的新领域。
2. Pollution is a pressing problem which we must deal with. 污染是我们必须解决的一个迫切问题。
3. This type of meter is called a multimeter, which is used to measure electricity. 这种仪表称为万用表,用来测量电。
4. Galileo was a famous Italian scientist by whom the Copernican theory was further proved correct. 伽利略是意大利著名的科学家,他进一步证明了哥白尼学说是正确的。
5. The periodical physical examination must be given to a patient who has recuperated from hepatitis. 肝炎患者虽然痊愈,但仍须对其进行定期的健康检查。
6. They are striving for the ideal which is close to the heart of every Chinese and for which, in the past, many Chinese have laid their lives. 他们正努力去实现那个理想,那个每一个中国人珍藏于心中的理想,那个许许多多中国人曾为之献出了生命的理想。

在以上六句话中,关系从句的口译分别采用了不同方法,相应译为前置定语、简单句、后置顺接句、后置复指先行词、让步状语从句以及重复中心词。

除了关系从句,句子成分之间的转换在口译过程中是屡见不鲜的。再看以下三个例句:

1. You can always tell the somebodies from the nobodies at a cocktail party. The somebodies come late. 在鸡尾酒会上人们常常可以看出大人物和无名小卒来。那些迟到的就是大人物。不难看出,这句话在翻译时,主语转换为表语;谓语转换为主语。
2. Cheerful, efficient and warm-hearted, they will do everything to make your journey smooth and comfortable. 他们乐观、能干、热情,总是想方设法使你一路上顺利舒适。在这句话中,状语转换为了谓语。
3. Heat is constantly produced by the body as a result of muscular and cellular activity. 由于肌肉和细胞活动的结果,身体不断地产生热。英语被动句式翻译时,常常转换为汉语主动句式。

汉英口译时,句子结构也是译员要考虑的重心所在。与英汉口译不同的是,译员要尤为注意分清主从。请看以下例句:

1. 到处你都可以看见人们穿着节日服装,满脸笑容。Everywhere you can see people in their holiday dresses, their faces shining with smiles.
2. 数以千计的船民被淹死,其中许多是小孩。Thousands of boat people were drowned, many of them children.
3. 他端着枪,走进那间黑屋子。He entered the dark room, gun in hand.
4. 你必须告诉我真实情况,既不夸大,也不缩小。You must give me a true account, with nothing added and nothing removed.
5. 错误与挫折教训了我们,使我们变得聪明起来,我们的事情就办得好一些。Taught by mistakes and setbacks, we have become wiser and can handle out problem better.
6. 这些艺术品丰富多彩,栩栩如生,而且别出心裁,具有鲜明的民族特色和地方色彩。Colorful, lifelike and original, these works of art had distinctive national and local characteristics.
7. 中国不做超级大国,现在不做,将来也不做。China will not be a superpower, not either today or even in future.

以上例句的翻译分别选用了名词性结构、过去分词结构、形容词短语等结构模式来凸现句子中主句与从句之间的联系。作为"形合"的语言,英语特别要求建立起层次分明而严谨的译文,译者在口译过程要对语言之间的差异有相当的敏感度,对语言之间的转换也有相当的创建能力。

总而言之,无论英汉还是汉英口译,译员都必须充分意识到句子结构在口译过程中的重要性,要根据具体语境和句式要求,采取恰当的翻译策略,进行信息转换和输出。

## 译练习 Enhancement Practice

第一项 Project 1
句子精练 Sentences in Focus

**A. Interpret the following sentences from English into Chinese.**

1. The long-term costs of a poor urban image can be exceedingly high.
2. When you look at the traditional streets and buildings of your community, don't think of them as bricks and mortar, think of them as stories.
3. The story of Beijing, for example, is about the courtyard—from the humblest house to the great Imperial Palace.
4. The more stakeholders that are involved with development decisions, the more diverse and unique the city will become, and in an information economy, the more competitive it will be.
5. Leading edge cities are now seeking a finer grain mix of the old and the new, like the

Xintiandi project in Shanghai, where historic houses have been converted into human-scaled shops and restaurants.

**B. Interpret the following sentences from Chinese into English.**
1. 在新的形势下,人居环境科学发展要明确在"五大原则"之上,要增加"五大统筹"。
2. 随着大小洋山港、石油化工区的建设以及杭州湾大通道建设的开展,"南上海"呼之欲出。
3. 在过去十年中,我有机会在中国和其他一些国家参与许多以规划和发展为主题的会议和项目。
4. 驾驭城市变化的规律,谋求城市朝着更适宜人类和平友善地相融、相处以及生活质量不断提升并可持续发展的环境变化,是人类面临的重要命题。
5. 持续、较快的城市化,正在彻底改变中国延续了数千年的以农耕经济和农村社会为主体的社会结构,这是一个历史性的变迁,是一个不可逆的过程,是中国走向现代化社会的必然结果。

第二项 Project 2
段落口译 Paragraph Interpreting

**A. Interpret the following paragraph from English into Chinese.**

There is a tremendous desire now in China not only to modernize outdated infrastructure, but also to make symbols of a new society. In an information age, much of our world is driven by visual images and symbols, and new urban icons—such as Pudong in Shanghai—are important to the identity of the city, even the nation. So, sometimes it really is worth getting rid of the old stuff to make way for something different. The challenge is: when you seek to make a new image, be sure it is of greater value than what you already have. And just because something is different doesn't make it worthwhile.

**B. Interpret the following paragraph from Chinese into English.**

近十年以来,我有机会在中国和其他一些国家参与许多以规划和发展为主题的会议和项目。同样,这些经历充实了我的以下看法,即考虑到有文化、经济和社会的差异,因此经过仔细安排的、现实的规划与开发系统是必要的,在这些系统下,公共和私营机构能各尽所能地参与到其中,从而从整体上提高了整个社会的生活水平。

第三项 Project 3
篇章口译 Passage Interpreting

**A. Listen to the tape and interpret the following passage from English into Chinese.**

The theme of World Habitat Day this year, "Cities—Engines of Rural Development", was chosen to remind development policy-makers at every level not to think of "urban" and "rural" as separate entities, but rather as parts of an economic and social whole.

Cities interact with rural areas in many ways. Migrants living and working in cities send money to families in rural areas. Cities absorb excess rural populations, and offer markets for farm produce and other rural products. They provide services and amenities—such as universities and hospitals—that may not be available or feasible in rural areas. Cities are also the locus of most global investment, raising demand for goods, labor and other inputs from rural areas.

In the next 25 years, virtually all population growth will take place in the world's cities, mostly in the cities of developing countries. The fastest growing cities will be secondary and market towns, which are especially close to rural areas. This growth can help to improve rural life and ease the problems associated with mega-cities. But to do so, it will need to be well-managed, with significant investments in communication, transport channels and other infrastructure, and with concerted efforts to ensure that all people have access to adequate services.

As stated in the Istanbul Charter of the Habitat II of UN, "Urban and rural developments are correlated. In addition to improving the living environments in urban areas, we should make great efforts to increase appropriate infrastructures, public service establishments and employment opportunities in rural areas so as to enhance the attraction of countryside. We should develop unified residential networks to reduce the rural-to-urban migrations. Due attention should be given to the medium and small sized cities and towns."

Take China for example. The main difficulties of the urban and rural development of China lie in the "three issues concerning agriculture, countryside and farmer". Yet from the view of sciences of human settlements, the problems lie both within and beyond the "three issues", and some problems must be solved in short term while the others in long term. The core of the solutions to the "three issues" is the coordinated development of urban and rural areas as a whole. Therefore, we need to examine the path of urbanization from the angle of coordinated development of urban and rural areas, and we need to gradually establish the institution of coordinated urban and rural development by the way of constituting relevant policies and undertaking institutional reforms.

While there are obvious differences between urban and rural development that require different interventions, ultimately sustainable development cannot and should not focus exclusively on one or the other. On this World Habitat Day, let us recognize that cities have a crucial contribution to make to rural development, and let us pursue development in a comprehensive way that reflects that understanding.

**B. Listen to the tape and interpret the following passage from Chinese into English.**

中国未来城市化进程的速度有多快？20年后城市化地区的规模将多大？是规划未来中国的城市体系时遇到的首要问题。

中国城市人口的比例（城市化率）从1978年的17.9%提高到2003年的40.5%，平均每年提高0.88个百分点。城市化进程是逐渐加速的，从1978至1995这17年，城市化率平均每年提高0.65个百分点，1995至2003这八年平均每年提高1.44个百分点。2003年以来，我国城市化进程加速更快。过去305年城市化水平的提高是在旧户籍制度的阻遏下实现的,这种户籍制度产生于上世纪50年代建立计划经济的时期,在1959—1961的全国性大饥荒之后被极大地强化,它严格限制农村人口成为城市永久居民的自由。新一届政府提出改革户籍制度,今后没有了制度因素的限制,中国的城市化进程势必加速。假设2010年以前我国的城市化率平均每年提高1.5个百分点,2011至2020平均每年提高1.6个百分点,那么2020年的城市化率将达到67%。

要估计2020年的城镇人口规模,除了预测城市化率之外,还要依据全国的人口预测。上世纪80年代,专业机构对中国人口的预测认为,即使长期坚持当时力度的计划生育政策,也要到2040年才能达到人口增长的顶峰,顶峰时的人口数量将达到16亿。现在看来情况要比20年前的预测乐观了许多。

对未来中国总人口持乐观预测的理由是,城市化对控制人口增长的作用比计划生育政策的作用更大。大量农村居民进入城市后,生育率明显降低。假设目前人口自然增长率已降低到平均为5‰,2011—2020期间降低到平均为4‰,可以比较有把握地认为,到了2020年代,中国的人口增长就能够到达顶峰,顶峰时的人口可能最多在14亿上下。

持续、较快的城市化,正在彻底改变中国延续了数千年的以农耕经济和农村社会为主体的社会结构,这是一个历史性的变迁,是一个不可逆过程,是中国走向现代化社会的必然结果。

# 参考译文
## Reference Version

**篇章口译 A**

自1987年以来,我已经在北京度过了几个夏天,与来自麻省理工学院和清华大学的研究生一起研究有关城市设计的问题和项目。在这17年里,随着投资的大量涌入,人口和车辆的不断增加,这个伟大的城市以及中国的其他中心城市都发生了巨大的变化。

我们所看到的仅仅只是这些变革的开始。中国的城市人口每20年就翻一番,那么到2050年,将新增6亿城市人口。为了容纳他们,我们需要建造面积相当于50个上海那么大的城区。

这些新建与扩建的城市将促进中国的经济活力和塑造中国的全球形象。它们的成功将依赖于以下几点:

- 与世界其他城市和地区相比,它们的经济活动是否具有竞争性;
- 如何对它们进行更好的管理和治理;
- 它们的财政是否稳定;
- 城市的适居性如何,不仅仅提供生存空间,同时也提供令人满意的生活机会。

未来的城市要达到这些目标的方式将和过去有所不同。在20世纪的大部分时间里,人们认为一个具有竞争力、高效率的城市通常是这样的城市:对土地实行标准化的分类使用,城市间拥有宽阔的马路和高速公路,在这些城市里,穷人通常与富人分开居住,当地传统和文化发展的空间非常狭小。

我们现在认识到,这种要求有大量土地和资源的城市发展模型是低效的、不公平的,且维护的成本相当高。更重要的是,它与一个具有独特性、多元性和文化越来越具有经济价值的信息经济不相匹配。

如果对我们所认为的发展中城市和当前世界的前沿项目进行审视,我们会发现现在我们所强调的城市建设特征与20世纪的理想模型截然相反。城市和私人开发商注重将地区开发成为不太标准、更混杂、更综合性的社区,它能提供更多的福利设施,同时服务于更大范围的居民,从而促进该地区的(用一个词表达就是)适居性——就是指在城市中的每天生活质量。

适居性已成为规划者优先考虑的问题,并不是因为规划者们说它是一个好东西,而是因为信息公司以及为这些公司工作的、具有创造力和创业精神的人拥有许多把金钱和时间投入何处的选择。在全球人才和就业市场中,那些更加与众不同、为更多的人提供更高质量体验的城市才具有竞争优势。因此,我们发现城市正在通过以下方式加强它们的适居性:

- 减少汽车的影响;
- 努力追求建筑领域和公共场所建设的创造性;
- 保护并发展当地文化遗产;
- 促进为各类居民提供丰富多彩的活动;
- 建立市民参与系统,使居民能以其独特的方式帮助塑造环境。

银行和政府对强化适居性进行的投资会获得某些最大的回报,理由是:

- 能够给人们带来好处并产生积极的影响,直接改善人们的住房、业务和日常生活;
- 能够弥补因贫困而带来的不平等——例如交通不便和缺乏娱乐设施。

一个好的环境对于吸引一流私营企业、创造就业机会以支持城市的可持续发展来说越来越重要,因此说,适居性有利于提高城市的竞争力和促进财政稳定。

我非常赞赏中国国家开发银行和世界银行召开此次会议。我认为这是朝着那个方向发展的第一步。银行只需通过把适居性确定为一个重要因素,就可以对城市建设质量产生强大的影响。但是要使这些问题得到实际解决,我们还需要进行研究,找出如何把适居性和标准经济发展项目相结合以及如何衡量成功的方法。

**篇章口译 B**

Recently, I was advised by Mr. Wang, Vice Chairman of the Expert Committee, China Development Bank of proposals for a symposium on "Planning the Future of Cities in China." Mr. Wang kindly requested whether I would be prepared to participate in this important matter viewed from the dual perspectives of land and ecology planning for big cities in China.

While China covers a very large land mass of about 9.33 million square kilometers, a high proportion comprises land which, by reason of difficult topography, adverse climatic conditions and limited access, is inhospitable to human habitation. Approximately 1.25 million square kilometers comprise arable farmland, equivalent to just under 8% of the world's stock of such land. Against that proportion, however, China now has almost 21% of the global population.

Intensively settled areas are generally confined to extensive alluvial plains in the eastern coastal provinces and also to certain inland river basins. Pressures of urban growth in such areas are escalating rapidly, creating a need for more effective land use—infrastructure planning at regional, sub-regional and district levels and also the formulation and timely implementation of associated development programs. A closely associated matter relates to the effects that urbanization is directly and indirectly having on the ecological conditions within the hinterlands of major towns and cities. Key areas of concern relate to such matters as the conservation and supply and of water of acceptable quality for both urban and rural uses; standards of air quality; the sustainable use of versatile soils; the protection of land and marine areas with high biodiversity values; and the reservation and management of scenic rural and coastal areas for public enjoyment.

From the work I have undertaken over many years in the Hong Kong Special Administrative Region, with a current population of almost 7 million people living within a territory of only about 1000 kilometers, I am acutely aware of the need for a planning and development process that provides a framework within which various key "stakeholders" can coordinate their efforts within limits set by resource availability and other constraints. In that connection, I have been fortunate to have been involved for about 35 years in the setting up and application of a planning process that resulted in the creation in 1973 of the first territorial development strategy that was subsequently updated several times to the present. I was also privileged to be given the task of producing a Port and Airport Development Strategy (PADS) and taking charge as Project Manager for one of Hong Kong's large new towns.

While Hong Kong is only a small place, it serves an extensive hinterland in South China as a hub port; a centre of finance; a reservoir of professional expertise and technical innovation; and a cultural and tourist node. Over the past 50 years, Hong Kong has had to cope with increasing pressures of urbanization generated by demands for better housing, employment opportunities, community facilities, high capacity transport networks, other key infrastructure services and improved environmental conditions. Overall, these needs have been met through the provision of new land for urban use by such means as the reclamation of areas of sea bed; the rezoning of selected rural areas; and the redevelopment of obsolete parts of the city.

Overall, it has been necessary for new urban development to be constructed at increasingly higher densities and provided with high capacity transport systems and other infrastructure. Additionally, areas of unique biodiversity have been set aside as Special Areas of Scientific Interest and Marine Parks. All this has required the carefully coordinated preparation of a hierarchy of plans and implementation programs.

## 第 4 单元　城市规划　Urban Planning

**口译练习**

第一项　句子精练

A.
1. 不良城市形象的长期成本极其高昂。
2. 当你看到社区里的传统街道和建筑时，不要把它们仅仅看成是砖块和水泥，而要把它们当做故事一样来品味。
3. 举例来说，北京的故事是关于院落——从最简陋的民房到宏伟的紫禁城。
4. 介入发展决策的利益方越多，城市就将变得愈发多样化和具有独特性，在信息经济中将更具竞争力。
5. 主流前沿城市当前正在寻求一种使新旧建筑更为融合的模型，如上海的新天地项目，历史性建筑在那里被改造成商店与餐厅。

B.
1. Concerning the development of Sciences of Human Settlements under new circumstances, "Five Balances" should be taken into consideration seriously besides the "Five Principles".
2. A Southern Shanghai is coming forth with the construction of the large and small Yangshan ports, the development of the petrochemical district, and the commencement of the Hangzhou Bay Thoroughfare.
3. In the past decade, I have had opportunities to participate in various conferences and projects in both China and other countries, relating to major planning and development issues.
4. How to master the law governing the changes of cities, and make efforts to develop the cities in a way that leads to better livability which enables the human race to live in peace and amiability, improved living standard, and sustainable development are important issues facing mankind.
5. Sustainable and rapid urbanization is changing China's millennium-long social structure dominated by rural farming economy and rural society. This is a historical transformation and an irreversible process, and is the inevitable result of China's modernization.

第二项　段落口译

A.
　　中国目前有一种强烈的愿望，即不仅要使落后的基础设施现代化，同时也要创造一个新的社会形象。在信息时代，我们的世界大多受视觉形象和标志的推动，新的城市标志，如上海的浦东，对于一个城市甚至整个国家的形象来说都十分重要。所以，有时确实应摆脱一些旧事物，从而为一些与众不同的新事物让路。但挑战在于：当你寻求创建一种新的形象时，你必须确定这种新的形象比你的现有形象更有价值。仅仅因为这个东西有些不同并不能说明它有价值。

**B.**

Over the past ten years, I have had opportunities to participate in various conferences and projects in both China and other countries, relating to major planning and development issues. Again, such experiences have reinforced my perceptions that—allowing for cultural, economic and social differences—there need to be carefully structured and practical systems of planning and development within which both public and private bodies can participate to their mutual advantage in order to achieve improved standards of living for the community in general.

## 第三项 篇章口译

**A.**

今年世界人居日的主题是:"城市——农村发展的动力",我们之所以选择这一主题是为了提请所有各级的发展决策者不要将"城市"和"农村"作为单独的实体,而是作为经济和社会整体的组成部分。

城市在许多方面与农村相辅相成。在城市里生活和工作的移栖者向其农村地区的家人汇款。城市吸收过剩的农村人口,并为农产品和其他农村产品提供市场。城市提供农村地区所没有或可能无法提供的各种服务和设施,例如大学和医院。城市还是多数全球投资的中心,增强对来自农村地区的商品、劳力和其他投入的需求。

在今后的25年里,几乎所有人口增长都将出现在世界各城市里,而发展中国家的城市居多。特别靠近农村地区的中等集市城镇将成为增长最快的城市。这种增长将有助于改进农村生活并缓减特大城市引起的问题。但要做到这一点,就需要进行良好的管理,对通讯运输渠道和其他基础设施进行重大的投资,并同心协力确保所有人都取得足够的服务。

联合国"人居二"会议发表的《伊斯坦布尔宣言》指出:"城市和乡村的发展是相互联系的。除改善城市生活环境外,我们还应努力为农村地区增加适当的基础设施、公共服务设施和就业机会,以增强它们的吸引力;开发统一的住区网点,从而尽量减少农村人口向城市流动。中、小城镇应给予关注。"

以中国为例。中国城乡发展的难点是"三农"问题。从人居环境科学的观念看,这既有"三农"之内的问题,也有"三农"之外的问题,既有在近期要解决的问题,也有在长期要解决的问题,而解决"三农"问题的核心就是城乡整体协调发展。为此,我们需要从城乡整体协调发展的角度,审视城市化道路;制定有关政策,进行制度改革,逐步向城乡整体协调发展的制度过渡。

尽管城市和农村发展之间有明显的差别,因而需要采取不同的方法,而最终可持续发展不能也不应该完全偏重于一方,而忽视另一方面。值此世界人居日之际,让我们认识到,城市可以对农村发展做出关键的贡献,让我们以反映这种思维的全面方式来追求发展。

**B.**

At what speed will China's urbanization make headway, and what will be the size of urbanized areas in twenty years? These are the primary questions encountered in planning

China's future urban system.

The proportion of China's urban population (urbanization rate) increased from 17.9% in 1978 to 40.5% in 2003, up 0.88% on average per year. The urbanization is a gradually accelerated process. Over the 17 years from 1978 to 1995, China's urbanization grew at an average annual rate of 0.65%, and over the 8 years from 1995 to 2003, at 1.44%. The last few years since 2003 witnessed still greater acceleration of China's urbanization. For the past 30 years, the increase of the urbanization level was realized under the restriction of the old household registration system, which came into being in the 1950s when the planned economy was taking shape, and was greatly strengthened after the nationwide famine from 1959 to 1961. Such a system deprived the rural population of the opportunity to become permanent urban residents. The newly elected government decided to reform the old household registration system. Therefore, free from the institutional restrictions, China's urbanization will grow at a speed faster than the present rate. Suppose China's urbanization grew by 1.5% annually before 2010, and 1.6% from 2011 to 2020, by 2020, the urbanization rate will reach 67%.

To predict China's urban population in 2020, it is necessary to estimate the whole nation's population growth rate as well as the urbanization rate. In the 1980s, according to the prediction of some specialized agencies, given the long-term implementation of the family planning policy, China's population would not reach the peak of 1.6 billion until 2040. Now the situation seems much more optimistic than the prediction made twenty years ago.

Sustainable and rapid urbanization is changing China's millennia-long social structure dominated by rural farming economy and rural society. This is a historical transformation and an irreversible process, and is the inevitable result of China's modernization.

The reason for an optimistic prediction toward China's population growth in the future is that the urbanization will play a larger role than the family planning policy in controlling the population growth. After a large number of rural population entered the city, their birth rate decreased significantly. Given that the present natural population growth rate has decreased to an average of 5‰, and 4‰ from 2011 to 2020, we can say for sure that by the 2020s, China's population will reach the peak of at most 1.4 billion.

工商管理

第 5 单元

# Unit 5 Business Administration

# 篇章口译

## Passage A (E-C)

### Vocabulary Work

Work on the following words and phrases and write the translated version in the space provided.

| | | | |
|---|---|---|---|
| infrastructure | building block | meritocracy | gargantuan |
| laissez-faire | anonymity | vis-à-vis | regimentation |
| entrepreneurship | parochialism | expurgate | utilitarian |
| disseminate | pervasiveness | convergence | |

### Text Interpreting

Listen to the tape and interpret the following passage from English into Chinese.

Dear Participants,

Today I'll talk about American management. The American style of management is like any other—it may have its weaknesses, but it also has strengths that need to be emphasized. I'll touch upon three aspects. What makes America American? What makes American firms American? What makes American managers American?

What makes America American? There are three major characteristics that separate the United States from other nations. The first is the often-over-looked sound infrastructure for conducting business. The fundamental building blocks, such as the well-developed internet, efficient telephone system, postal system, and other basic utilities are in place for sound economy. The next distinctively American societal characteristic is a strong commitment to the philosophy of meritocracy. The third important national-level characteristic is the gargantuan size of the American economy. This trait, apparently, helps kindle the spirit of meritocracy and laissez-faire by affording suppliers, distributors, and other players a certain anonymity vis-à-vis each other. However, what I want to mention here is that size comes with its disadvantages. Ironically, the source of the US's strength—its vast internal resources—is turning out to be its Achilles' heel in an increasingly globalized economy.

What makes American firms American? American firms possess the requisite qualities for high performance: efficiency, an orientation toward performance, dislike for red-tape, and a rational outlook on strategic planning. Several problems, however, blot an otherwise verdant landscape; an overemphasis on scientific/rational strategic planning and overlooking the artistic, diplomatic, and humanistic aspect of business, a short-term orientation of American managers with money (in the form of stock market valuation, quarterly profits, or even personal advancement) as a prime motivator, and regimentation and style over substance, such as corporate dress, documentation formats and office decor.

What makes American managers American? The personal traits of American managers mentioned most often by the international managers are industriousness, entrepreneurship, impatience, pragmatism, aggressiveness, materialism, informality and parochialism. These traits fit well with the smoothly functioning business system of a land that enshrines the gambling game of laissez-faire; most likely they have led to a corporate style characterized by directness, speed, professionalism and a mentality geared toward matching customer's needs. Yet a gloomier way to view these traits is as increasingly irrelevant attributes of a bygone frontier society. And some of the negatives can never be expurgated because they form the woof and warp of the American cultural fabric. Perhaps the materialistic, utilitarian bent of the United States was best captured in Oscar Wilde's comments on the American Man, "He thinks that civilization began with the introduction of steam and looks with contempt upon all the centuries that had no hot-water apparatuses in their houses. The ruin and decay of time has no pathos in his eyes.... His one desire is to get the whole of Europe into thorough repair...."

For all its faults and weaknesses, American business still forms a key model for much of the world. The individualistic American style may be more palatable than any style involving tremendous self-sacrifice. An important force in disseminating the American style of management is the role of the US as the world's largest manufacturer of contemporary culture. Also to be blamed or credited is the establishment of MBA programs and multinational corporations overseas. Partly because of the pervasiveness of American culture, managerial education, and multinational corporations, the younger business people in Japan and the Pacific Rim are relaxing more, while Europeans and members of other industrializing nations are working harder. There is also an increasing convergence, however slow, to a style marked by increased rationalization, impatience and mobility, and informality.

Managers the world over must carefully scrutinize the American problems. Some uniquely American "problems" in an international context perhaps are not problems so much as misunderstandings stemming from cultural differences. The Chinese have a saying that when the water drains out, the rocks are revealed. The ebbing of American competitiveness is starting to show up the pearls as well as the rocks in the American style of management.

Thank you.

# 篇章口译

## Passage B (C-E)

 **Vocabulary Work**

Work on the following words and phrases and write the translated version in the space provided.

| | | | |
|---|---|---|---|
| 经济全球化 | 推动力量 | 互利合作 | 相互依存 |
| 合作共赢 | 外商直接投资 | 外商投资企业 | 研发中心 |
| 涉外经济管理体制 | 知识产权保护 | 参与者 | 推动者 |
| 经济技术合作 | 经营经验 | 携手努力 | |

 **Text Interpreting**

Listen to the tape and interpret the following passage from Chinese into English.

尊敬的各位贵宾，女士们、先生们：

晚上好！在这个美好的夜晚，我很高兴同大家在这里相聚，参加《财富》全球论坛的开幕式。首先，我谨代表中国政府，并以我个人的名义，对各位朋友的到来表示诚挚的欢迎！向论坛主办方美国时代华纳集团表示衷心的祝贺！

这次论坛确定以"中国和新的亚洲世纪"为主题，充分表达了大家对中国和亚洲发展前景的关注，表达了大家对中国及亚洲的发展对全球经济增长所发挥的作用的关注。这也充分说明，在经济全球化趋势深入发展的条件下，中国及亚洲的发展正在成为世界经济发展新的推动力量，世界经济发展也将给中国及亚洲发展带来新的重要机遇。世界各国经济互利合作、相互依存的加深，必将给全球经济增长创造更加美好的前景。

中国的发展同亚洲及世界的发展紧密相关。中国的发展已经并将继续为亚洲及世界各国带来合作共赢的机遇。截至去年底，中国累计实际利用外商直接投资额达到5621亿美元，批准外商投资企业50多万个，并形成了年进口5600多亿美元的大市场。目前，绝大多数国家和地区都有企业来华投资，《财富》500强企业中已有400多家在华投资，外商投资在华设立的研发中心达700多家。随着中国的不断发展，中国同世界各国和各类企业的合作必将进一步扩大。

中国将继续稳步开放市场，创新引进外资的形式，完善有关鼓励和保护外商投资的法律法规，改革涉外经济管理体制，加强知识产权保护，努力为中国的对外经贸合作和外国来华投资提供一切便利，创造更好的环境。

在座各位大企业的领导人，是国际经济活动的重要参与者和推动者。长期以来，你们中的许多人及你们的企业，积极推动和开展与中国的经济技术合作，为中国经济的持续发展和中国有关产业技术水平的提高作出了重要贡献。

实践证明,这种互利合作对双方都有利。我们欢迎各位继续扩大在中国的投资和贸易,加强同中国企业的经济技术合作。我相信,你们一定能够发挥各自的企业优势和丰富的经营经验,在推动国际经济技术合作、促进地区及世界经济发展方面发挥重要作用。让我们携手努力,为维护世界和平、促进共同发展作出更大的贡献。

最后,我预祝北京《财富》全球论坛取得圆满成功!谢谢大家!

# 口译讲评

# Notes on the Text

**Passage A**

1. **This trait, apparently, helps kindle the spirit of meritocracy and laissez-faire by affording suppliers, distributors, and other players a certain anonymity vis-à-vis each other**:此句的意思是"正是这一特点引发了精英管理和自由放任的经营理念,供应商、分销商和其他商人彼此之间可以公平竞争,没有特权",其中 anonymity vis-à-vis each other 是指"他们在面对面时彼此之间是匿名的、不熟悉的",意即不像在小地方因为彼此认识或有关系而使业务往来不能完全公平公正行事。

2. **Achilles' heel**:阿基里斯的脚踵,致命的弱点,唯一的弱点。源自希腊神话故事,阿基里斯出生后被他母亲握脚踵倒提着在冥河水中浸过,所以除未浸过水的脚踵外,浑身刀枪不入。在特洛伊战役中,他被特洛伊城的巴里斯王子(Paris)一箭射中脚踵而阵亡。后人即以 Achilles' heel 表示"致命伤"。

3. **they form the woof and warp of the American cultural fabric**:他们是美国文化的有机组成部分。the woof and warp 指纺织品的纬纱和经纱,引申为一种结构的基石或组织机构的基础,例如:The Constitution and the Declaration of Independence are the warp and woof of the American nation(《宪法》和《独立宣言》是美国的立国之本)。

4. **Oscar Wilde**:奥斯卡·王尔德(1854—1900)是19世纪英国最伟大的艺术家之一,以其剧作、诗歌、童话、艺术评论和小说闻名于世。著名的作品包括剧作 Lady Windermere's Fan,The Importance of Being Earnest,小说 The Picture of Dorian Gray,童话 The Happy Prince 等。

5. **For all its faults and weaknesses, American business still forms a key model for much of the world**:尽管有种种缺点和不足之处,美国的商业管理模式对世界来说还是一种典范。

6. **Also to be blamed or credited is the establishment of MBA programs and multinational corporations overseas**:翻译此句时可以采用添词法,例如"另一个应受谴责或表扬的(美国管理模式)传播者是 MBA 项目和进驻海外的跨国公司"。

7. **the Pacific Rim**:这是政治地理概念,指"环太平洋圈的国家和地区"。

8. **Some uniquely American "problems" in an international context perhaps are not problems so much as misunderstandings stemming from cultural differences**:翻译此句时注意 not so

much...as 的结构,例如可以译成"有些美国特有的'问题'与其说是问题,还不如说是因为各国文化不同而产生的误解"。

**Passage B**

1. **《财富》全球论坛**:the *Fortune* Global Forum。1995年开始创办的《财富》全球论坛由美国时代华纳集团所属的《财富》杂志主办,旨在探讨世界工商业发展中大家共同关心的问题。每年在世界上选一个最具有经济活力的地方举行一次。第一届在新加坡,上海、香港和北京均举办过《财富》论坛。

2. **时代华纳集团**:the Time Warner Inc. AOL。时代华纳集团是由美国在线公司AOL与时代华纳2000年宣布合并而组成的媒体巨人,是全球最大的媒体、通讯、娱乐、网络公司之一,在100多个国家拥有自己的子公司。

3. **世界各国经济互利合作、相互依存的加深,必将给全球经济增长创造更加美好的前景**:翻译此句时可以将"加深"转为形容词置于句首,例如:Continued mutually beneficial economic cooperation and rising interdependence among the world's countries will usher in an even better future for global economy in development.

4. **中国的发展已经并将继续为亚洲及世界各国带来合作共赢的机遇**:"已经并将继续"表明中国的"一贯"做法,可以用 as always 表示:A developing China will, as always, generate cooperation opportunities with win-win results for other countries in Asia and the world over.

5. **《财富》500强企业中已有400多家在华投资**:Over 400 firms out of the *Fortune* 500 have invested in China.

6. **改革涉外经济管理体制,加强知识产权保护**:表示"改革"和"加强"的词语很多,最常用有 reform 和 strengthen,这里选择了 revamp 和 step up:revamp foreign economic management and step up protection of intellectual property rights

7. **我们欢迎各位继续扩大在中国的投资和贸易,加强同中国企业的经济技术合作**:此句中"继续"的处理也可以采用词性转译法,将动词转为形容词,例如:We look forward to continued expansion of your investment in China and your still closer economic and technological cooperation with Chinese enterprises.

## Relevant Words and Expressions

  定价机制 pricing mechanism
  民族企业 domestic enterprise
  有序竞争 orderly competition
  中国名牌 Chinese brand name
  中小型企业 small and medium-sized enterprises
  生产资料市场 market for factors of production
  外国直接投资 FDI [foreign direct investment]

跨国企业/公司 MNE/MNC [multinational enterprise / company]
公司合并与收购 corporate merger and acquisition
借鉴国外发展经验 draw on the experience of other countries in development
全面提高开放水平 improve opening-up in all respects
社会主义初级阶段 the primary stage of socialism
适应新的发展要求 meet new requirements of development
全面协调可持续发展 comprehensive, balanced and sustainable development
加快转变经济发展方式 accelerate transformation of the mode of economic development
推动产业结构优化升级 promote upgrading of the industrial structure
推进各方面体制改革创新 promote institutional reform and innovation in various sectors
引入竞争机制，深化垄断企业改革 deepen the reform of monopoly industries by introducing competition
鼓励、支持、引导非公有制经济发展 encourage, support and guide the development of the non-public sectors
公有制为主体、多种所有制经济共同发展 public ownership is dominant and different economic sectors develop side by side

# 口译技能

## Interpreting Skills

### 语篇理解(1)：口音和语速

口译是一个复杂的交际过程，其基本要素包含输入、解译、输出。译员的信息输入主要通过"听入"，视译有时作为一种辅助手段。口译通过"听"获取信息，经过分析理解原话要表达的本意，在此基础上选择使用合适的词汇、语域、语气和语体，将其译成目的语。所以听懂理解原文是口译的关键第一步。而理解困难除了词汇、专业术语、议题内容、背景知识方面的原因，还有可能是说话人异乎寻常的快语速或怪僻的口音或语调造成的。在口译时，原文的输入仅发生一次，译员对说话者的发言没有控制权，对说话者的口音、语速、节奏、长短必须被动接受。这对译员的听力能力提出了很高的要求。

从口音来说，译员不能期待总听"标准"、"规范"的英语，何况业界对何为标准英语也有不同界定。英语是世界性的大语种，译员不但要翻译英美人讲话，还要翻译加拿大人、澳大利亚人、新西兰人的讲话。这些人的语音、语调、用词习惯已有很大的差别。更何况译员还要翻译许多非英语民族的人的英语发言或讲话，很多情况下他们所说的英语不同程度地带有自己母语的烙印。

在语速方面，讲话快一方面可能是个人说话习惯，另一方面有可能是讲话人用讲稿发言造成的。如果是即兴发言，讲话人需要构思内容、寻找恰当的词语来表达，发言时会有正常的停顿、赘词、重复等，口译跟上速度不成问题。如果发言者以较快的速度念讲稿就会对译员造成很大的困难，所以口译界一般要求讲稿需事先发给译员。有时即使手头有讲稿，在同声传译时还是会发生不能同步的情况，尤其是中译英，由于语言体系本身的原因，英语译文会比中文长，所需时间多一些，此时译员可适当加快语速，但不可过快，重要的是保持节奏，把主要意思翻译过去，保证内容完整。

当口译中发生没听清或听懂一个单词、句子、甚至是一段话的情况时，译员必须保持冷静，不要慌张。口译不是字词的对译，而是信息的传达。个别词漏听或不熟悉，并不一定影响对整段话的理解，所以，此时关键是保持冷静，继续往下听，经常可以根据上下文得出整段话的含义和关键信息所在。因此，对个别未听懂的部分，可以省略或采取模糊处理的方法，比如说一些与上下文关联的话。但如果遇到关键的信息没有听懂，影响口译的正确性和连贯性时，则可请讲话人解释一下，再进行口译。当然此类情形只可偶尔为之，应尽量根据自己对口译任务和讲话人背景的了解，结合上下文进行合理的猜测。

总之，听入不是被动的，而是一个主动行为，它的认知模式包含三个层次的技巧：吸收声音信息、分析、记忆。译员在平时训练时，既要精听，也要泛听。精听指注意听、辨析英语中的重音、语音、语调、节奏、词序、连读、易混淆的辅音、易混淆的词、同音异义的词等。泛听一方面指随时随地利用一切可能的机会随意听以增加语感，提高自己的反应能力，另一方面指有意识地多听一些不同口音的英语，熟悉不同人的发音习惯，使自己更好地适应非英语民族人的讲话。最后，听力的训练应从大处着眼，从整体意思着眼，抓住重点，抓住语言单位间的逻辑意义，抓住整段话的含义和精神，因为口译的最终目的是传达信息、传达意义，而不是字、词或句法的完全对等。

## 口译练习 Enhancement Practice

### 第一项 Project 1
句子精练 Sentences in Focus

A. Interpret the following sentences from English into Chinese.

1. Unless there is a steep fall in oil and food prices soon, there is a strong possibility of stagflation in the US next year.
2. Food inflation used to be seen as a problem mainly for developing countries. Now the bite is being felt in the heart of Europe.
3. One variable commonly used to measure where and how fast internationalization is taking place is the increase in total foreign direct investment.
4. The best outcome would be a symmetric slowdown in global economic growth—enough to take pressure off global inflation, but not big enough to do any damage.
5. Economies of scale to reduce unit costs are always a management goal. One means of achieving them is to globalize product lines to reduce development, production, and inventory costs.

## 第5单元 工商管理 Business Administration

**B. Interpret the following sentences from Chinese into English.**
1. 大部分公司由三组人员组成：股东、管理层和职员。由董事长领衔的董事会是公司的最高决策层。
2. 如果有顾客投诉，售货员首先必须道歉，即使他/她此时对状况一无所知，先道歉然后再着手解决问题。
3. 公司使用"猎头公司"的好处在于公司可以省却组织登广告、挑选、面谈合适应聘者这个既费钱又费时的过程。
4. 管理风格通常根据国家文化的不同而有变化，文化决定经理人如何被培训，如何领导他人，如何处理工作。
5. 如果执行总裁们愿意作出一定的让步，为股东创造最大利益，置公司利益于个人权力欲望之上，成功的合并是可能的。

第二项 Project 2
段落口译 Paragraph Interpreting

**A. Interpret the following paragraph from English into Chinese.**
  Competitiveness refers to the company's ability to maintain and gain market share in its industry. It is related to company effectiveness, which is determined by whether the company satisfies the needs of stakeholders. Important stakeholders include stockholders, who want a return on their investment; customers, who want a high-quality product or service; and employees, who desire interesting work and reasonable compensation for their service. The community, which wants the company to contribute to activities and projects and minimize pollution of the environment, is also an important stakeholder. Companies that do not meet stakeholders' needs are unlikely to have a competitive advantage over other firms in their industry.

**B. Interpret the following paragraph from Chinese into English.**
  最近这几年，不管是哪个行业。不管是大公司还是小公司，管理者和研发人员做成了以前想都不敢想的事，或者说他们正在被迫做以前想都没有想过要做的事情。每个管理者都在为他们的公司设计如何在新的环境中蓬勃发展或者至少如何生存下来的战略。如果不主动创新，就会被竞争对手超越。

第三项 Project 3
篇章口译 Passage Interpreting

**A. Listen to the tape and interpret the following passage from English into Chinese.**
  In a vast curtained room in Xi'an in western China, rows of dark, pony-tailed heads are silently bowed, fingers moving quickly and expertly. They might be in any Chinese factory—except that they are not assembling shoes, nor soldering circuit boards, but sitting at computer terminals processing medical-claim forms from New York and car-loan

applications from Detroit and marking examinations for high-school students in Melbourne, Australia.

The worldwide market for offshore spending on IT services for Western companies is growing in double digits. The market for business process outsourcing (BPO), which encompasses processing bills and credit-card applications to managing entire human-resources operations is expanding even faster.

India has captured the bulk of this work. But China has plenty of potential. Its workers are well educated in basic computing and mathematics. They are disciplined and readily trained, making them better at tedious jobs than most Indians are. This suits the BPO business. These are repetitive, rules-based tasks. This business needs millions of low-cost workers, and China has them. India used to be cheaper, but salaries for graduates, engineers and programmers have been climbing fast and staff turnover at IT companies can reach 30—40% a year. Throw in China's superior infrastructure, tax breaks and strong support from the state, plus the desire of multinational companies to spread risk away from India, and it is clear why many large companies are turning to China. IBM, Hewlett-Packard, Microsoft and Siemens have been in China for several years and all are busily adding staff.

Yet China is still five to ten years behind India in IT. It has two big disadvantages. First, although many Chinese can read English, they speak and write it badly. That's a problem in services that require frequent communication with overseas offices. It looks bad if the employees cannot talk to their counterparts elsewhere. People confuse language competence with technical ability. Second, few Chinese engineering and computer graduates are as good as their qualifications suggest. While they often have a more solid grasp of theory than their European counterparts, few leave university able to apply it to real-life problems, such as developing software. It is as if they can describe a hacksaw and how it works perfectly, but have no idea of how to build a door with it. Meanwhile, fears about piracy of intellectual property—more rampant in China than India—will constrain growth. Though foreign companies in China say that copying sophisticated IT processes is difficult and can be thwarted by relatively simple safeguards, the perception that sensitive business information is at risk is likely to slow development.

All this suggests that, for the moment, China is likely to capture an increasing share of low-level BPO tasks, such as data entry, form processing and software testing, while India continues to dominate higher-value functions, such as research and design, which require greater creativity and language skills. However, this will change as more western firms demand support in China and domestic opportunities grow.

**B. Listen to the tape and interpret the following passage from Chinese into English.**

要在今天的竞争环境中蓬勃发展,企业必须应对几大挑战。首先,企业要提供价值。传统上,价值的概念属于金融学和会计学所考虑的范畴,然而,我认为如何管理人力资源对企业的长期发展非常关键,甚至关系到企业的生存。价值的定义不仅包括利润,还包括员工的发展、他们的满意度、额外的就业机会、对环境的保护和对社区项目的支持。

人力资源管理的各方面,包括企业与环境的关系,人力资源的获取、发展和补偿问题,以及工作的设计和评估都有助于企业迎接竞争挑战并创造价值。企业所面临的挑战可以分为四类:

一、国际挑战。企业越来越体会到要生存就必须应对来自全球范围企业的竞争。一方面要保护自己的国内市场不被外来竞争者蚕食,另一方面必须扩展业务走向国际市场。

二、质量挑战。今日世界成功的关键在于向客户提供高质量的产品和服务。不能以合理的成本为客户提供高质量产品的企业会输给竞争对手。

三、社会挑战。合理运用多元化的劳动力以及合理合法地运作企业。符合道德规范、有责任性的企业将获益良多。

四、高绩效工作体系的挑战。利用新技术能使企业具有竞争优势,比如计算机辅助生产、虚拟现实、因特网等。新技术的运用有助于员工以更聪明的方式工作,从而向客户提供更高质量的产品和服务。而从新技术中获利最多的企业往往有人力管理措施来支持使用新技术。因此工作设计、培训项目、报酬体系需要重新配置完善以支持员工使用新技术。

我相信,要创造并维持价值,企业必须成功应对这些挑战,而应对挑战的关键就是一支有积极性、受过良好培训、尽心尽责的员工队伍。

# 参考译文

## Reference Version

**篇章口译 A**

各位与会者:

今天我将谈谈美国的管理。如同任何其他事物一样,美国的管理风格有它的不足之处,也有值得赞赏的优点。我想谈三个方面的情况:美国的特点、美国公司的特点和美国经理人的特点。

美国有三个与其他国家不同的特点。首先,美国有非常好的基础设施,有利于业务经营,这一点往往被美国人自己忽视。健康经济发展需要的基本构成要素都已到位,包括完备的因特网、高效的电话、邮政系统和其他各种设施等。第二,崇尚精英管理是美国社会一大特征。第三,美国经济规模巨大。正是这一特点引发了精英管理和自由放任的经营理念,供应商、分销商和其他商人彼此之间可以公平竞争,没有特权。当然,我也要强调一点,规模大也有弊端。具有讽刺意味的是:巨大的内部资源作为美国的力量源泉却在经济全球化程度越来越高的今天成了其致命的弱点。

美国企业的特点是什么?美国企业拥有企业高效运作所需的所有特质:效率高,重视业绩,不喜欢繁文缛节,理性,注重战略计划。然而,存在着的几个问题也玷污了这幅美丽的绿野图:一、过于强调理性的战略计划,忽视了商业运作艺术性、技巧性、人性化的一面;二、其管理人追求短期目标,金钱成了他们的动力,像股票的市值、季度利润、个人的升职等;三、过分注重管理形式和风格而忽视了管理实质,比如在公司着装、文件格式、办公室装潢等方面的严格要求。

美国经理人的特点是什么?国际经理人经常提到的有关美国经理人有这么一些特点:工作勤奋,富有企业家精神,容易急躁,务实,有冲劲,注重实利,不拘礼节,比较狭隘。这些特质很适合美国运作自如的商业体系,它崇尚放任自由的经营模式;而经理人倡导的企业风格就是直截了当、高效率、专业化、尽力满足客户需求。但是比较悲观的看法是经理人的这些特质是当年开疆辟土时所需的,已跟现代社会脱节。而某些负面的东西已成了美国文化的有机组成部分,无法被抹去了。王尔德对美国人的评价惟妙惟肖地刻画出了美国人的这种物质主义、功利主义倾向:"美国人认为人类文明始于蒸汽机的发明,任何没有家庭热水系统的年代都令人鄙视。时代的衰败对他来说不算什么,他的一大愿望是对整个欧洲进行彻底的修缮……"

尽管有种种缺点和不足之处,美国的商业管理模式对世界来说还是一种典范。美国的这种个人主义的方式或许比其他需要巨大自我牺牲的模式更受人欢迎。而美国作为现代文化最大创造者的角色在传播美国管理模式方面起了重要作用。另一个应受谴责或表扬的传播者是MBA项目和进驻海外的跨国公司。在某种程度上,正由于美国文化、管理教育和跨国公司的普遍存在,日本和太平洋地区的年轻商务人士开始稍有松懈,而欧洲和其他工业国家的人们开始勤勉起来。而管理风格也在缓慢地趋同:更理性化、耐心减少、流动增加、不拘小节。

全世界的管理者应该仔细甄别美国所存在的问题,有些美国特有的"问题"与其说是问题,还不如说是因为各国文化不同而产生的误解。中国人有句话叫"水落石出",随着美国竞争力的减弱,美国管理模式中好的和不好的方方面面都开始呈现出来了。

谢谢大家。

## 篇章口译 B

Distinguished Guests, Ladies and Gentlemen,

Good evening! It is a great pleasure for me to join all of you here at the opening ceremony of the *Fortune* Global Forum on this pleasant evening. Let me begin by extending, on behalf of the Chinese government and also in my own name, my warm welcome to all of you and my sincere congratulations to the sponsor of the Forum, the Time Warner Inc. of the United States.

The theme of the Forum, "China and the New Asian Century", gives full expression to the widespread interest in the prospects of development in China and Asia as a whole, as well as in the impact of their development on global economic growth. It also shows that with surging economic globalization, China and Asia are quickly becoming a new growth engine for the world while the global boom is also generating more important opportunities for China and Asia. Continued mutually beneficial economic cooperation and rising interdependence among the world's countries will usher in an even better future for global economy in development.

China and the rest of Asia and the world at large are closely related when it comes to development. A developing China will, as always, generate cooperation opportunities with win-win results for other countries in Asia and the world over. By the end of last year, China had attracted a total of $562.1 billion in FDI, approved the establishment in China of more than 500,000 foreign-funded enterprises and created a huge import market of some $560 billion annually. At present, most countries and regions have had enterprises with investment in China, and over 400 firms out of the *Fortune* 500 have invested in China. The number of R&D centers set up by foreign investors in China has exceeded 700. As China becomes more developed, its cooperation with the other countries and their corporations of various types is bound to increase in scale.

China will keep opening up its market, find new ways of using foreign capital, improve laws and regulations for encouraging and protecting foreign investors, revamp foreign economic management, step up protection of intellectual property rights, and work still harder to help foreign investors and create an even better environment for trade and economic cooperation between China and the rest of the world.

All of you are important corporate leaders participating and promoting international economic activities. Many of you and the companies you represent have been vigorously involved for years in pushing economic and technological cooperation with China and made significant contribution to China's sustained economic growth and technological upgrading in certain industries.

Facts have proved that such cooperation serves our mutual interests. We look forward to continued expansion of your investment in China and your still closer economic and technological cooperation with Chinese enterprises. I believe that you will give greater scope to the advantages of your companies and your rich managerial expertise and play a critical role in facilitating international economic and technological cooperation and promoting economic development in regions and globally. Let us join hands and work together to contribute a greater share to world peace and common development.

May I conclude my remarks by wishing the Fortune Global Forum in Beijing a complete success. Thank you.

**口译练习**
第一项 句子精练
**A.**
1. 除非油价和食品价格马上大幅下降，否则美国经济明年出现滞胀的可能性很大。
2. 食物通胀过去主要被看成是发展中国家的一个问题。现在欧洲的中心地区也感到这一棘手的问题。
3. 通常用外国直接投资总额的增长这一变量来测量国际化在何地发生，并以何种速度发展。
4. 最好的结果是全球经济有条不紊地放慢速度，其速度足以消除全球通胀的压力，但不足以造成任何破坏。

5. 以规模效应来降低单位成本一直是管理目标之一。达到规模效应的一种方法就是将生产线全球化,从而降低开发、生产和库存成本。

B.
1. Most companies are made up of three groups of people: the shareholders, the management and the workforce. The Board of Directors, headed by the Chairperson or President is at the top of the company hierarchy, responsible for policy decisions.
2. If a customer has a complaint, the first thing the sales assistant does is to apologize, even if he or she knows nothing about the circumstances. Then they go on to sort the problem out.
3. The advantages for a company to use the services of a "headhunters firm" are that it does not have to organize the costly and time-consuming process of advertising, selecting and interviewing suitable applicants.
4. The styles of management often vary according to national culture, which can determine how managers are trained, how they lead people and how they approach their jobs.
5. A successful merger is possible if CEOs are willing to make the necessary comprises to bring about the most advantages for their shareholders, and put the company's interests before their personal desires for powers.

## 第二项 段落口译
A.
　　竞争力指的是公司保持和获取本行业市场份额的能力。竞争力与公司的效率相关联,而效率高低取决于公司是否能够满足利益相关者的要求。重要的利益相关者包括几个方面:要求获得投资回报的股票持有者,希望得到高质量的产品和服务的客户,想工作有趣又能得到合理报酬的员工。另外,社区也是重要的利益相关者,它们期待公司能对社区活动和项目有所支助,同时把对环境的污染降到最低。不能满足利益相关者需求的企业不可能在其行业具备竞争优势。

B.
　　In recent years, entrepreneurs and innovators from all different types of businesses, large or small have been able to do things they have never dreamed possible before, or that they are being forced to do things they have never dreamed necessary before. Each is figuring out a strategy for his or her company to thrive or at least survive in this new environment. If they do not drive the innovation, their competitors will use it to drive over them.

## 第三项 篇章口译
A.
　　中国西部城市西安,一个宽敞的挂着窗帘的房间里,一排排黑色头发扎成马尾辫的脑袋静悄悄地低着,手指灵巧地动着。她们或许在任何一个中国的工厂里,但是她们不是在做鞋,也不是在焊接集成板电路,而是在电脑终端前处理纽约的医疗索赔表格、底特律的购车贷款申请或是批改澳大利亚墨尔本中学生的考卷。

为西方公司提供IT服务的离岸外包业务额在以两位数的速度递增,而业务流程外包(BPO)市场更是发展迅猛,从处理票据、信用卡申请到管理整个人力资源的运作,它无所不包。

目前印度占有了大部分的市场,但是中国很有潜力。它的工人有很好的计算机和数学基础。他们有纪律、受过培训,比大多数印度工人更适应劳累的工作。这些素质很适合业务流程外包这一行,BPO做的就是重复性强的、有规可依的工作。它需要成千上万的低成本工人,而这正是中国所能够提供的。印度过去成本比较低廉,但是现在毕业生、工程师、编程员的工资飞速上涨,而且员工的离职率每年高达30%—40%。再加上中国优良的基础设施、优惠的税收政策、国家的大力支持、跨国公司又有从印度规避风险的需求,因而许多跨国公司纷纷转向中国,像IBM、惠普、微软、西门子等公司已经在中国多年,现在更是在扩充人手。

但是中国的IT产业仍然落后于印度5至10年。中国有两大不利因素。第一,中国人的英语水平不高。虽然他们能阅读英语,但是说和写的能力都不够,这在需要和海外客户沟通的服务业是个问题,如果员工不能和在别处的客户流利交流,情况会很糟糕,因为人们往往把语言能力和技术水平挂钩。第二,中国工程或计算机专业的毕业生水平不尽如人意。虽然他们的理论基础比欧洲的毕业生扎实,但很少人能将理论应用于实际来解决问题,像软件编程之类的。就如同他们能清楚地描述一把弓锯的形状和功能,却无法用它来做一扇门。

同时对知识产权侵权问题(这一点中国的现状不如印度)的担忧也会阻碍发展。虽然在中国的外国公司认为要拷贝复杂的IT程序并不容易,而且要防范也不难,但是对敏感的业务信息有外泄可能的顾虑还是会影响发展速度的。

所有这一切都说明,在目前阶段,中国在低层次的BPO中占有更高的份额,诸如数据输入、表格处理、软件测试等,而印度继续占领高价值的一端,包括研发和设计,这要求具有更好的创意和更强的语言能力。当然,随着更多的西方公司需要在中国获得支持和中国国内企业需求的增加,这种现状会随之改变。

**B.**

To grow and thrive in today's competitive environment, organizations must deal with several major challenges. They must provide value. Traditionally, the concept of value has been considered a function of finance or accounting. However, I believe that how human resources are managed is crucial to the long-term value of a company and ultimately to its survival. The definition of value includes not only profits but also employment growth and satisfaction, additional employment opportunities, protection of the environment, and contribution to community programs.

All aspects of human resource management—including how companies interact with the environment, acquire, develop, and compensate human resources, and design and measure work—can help companies meet their competitive challenges and create value. Meeting challenges is necessary to create value and to gain a competitive advantage. The challenges organizations face today can be grouped into four categories:

The global challenge. Increasingly, organizations are finding that they must compete with organizations around the world in order to survive. Companies must both defend their domestic markets from foreign competitors and broaden their scope to encompass global markets.

The quality challenge. Key to the success in today's world is providing customers with high-quality products and services. Companies that cannot give customers high quality at a reasonable cost risk losing out to competitors.

The social challenge. Utilize a diverse work force and operate in an ethical and legal manner. Businesses will benefit by behaving ethically and responsibly.

The high-performance work system challenge. Using new technologies such as computer-aided manufacturing, virtual reality and the Internet can provide companies with an edge in competition. New technologies can result in employees' working in smarter ways as well as providing higher-quality products and services to customers. However, companies that have seen the greatest gains from new technology have human resources practices that support the use of technology. The design of work, training programs, and reward systems often need to be reconfigured to support employees' use of technology.

I believe that organizations must successfully deal with these challenges to create and maintain value, and the key to facing these challenges is a motivated, well-trained, and committed work force.

第 6 单元

现代物流

Unit 6 **Modern Logistics**

# 篇章口译

## Passage A (E-C)

### 词汇预习  Vocabulary Work

Work on the following words and phrases and write the translated version in the space provided.

| | |
|---|---|
| overland transport | supply chain management |
| optimal delivery performance | tailor-made industry solution |
| standardised service | competitive edge |
| acquisition | express |
| freight service | part and full load |
| value-added service | product and service portfolio |
| top-flight | co-packing |
| price labelling | billing |
| order processing | |

###   Text Interpreting

**Listen to the tape and interpret the following passage from English into Chinese.**

Upon the questions you have raised concerning logistics, I think the best way to answer these question is to share with you our experience with the DHL operation. DHL is the global market leader in international express, overland transport and air freight. It is also the world's number one in ocean freight and contract logistics. DHL offers a full range of customised solutions—from express document shipping to supply chain management. We transport shipments rapidly, safely and on time all over the world. The basis for this is our comprehensive network, combining air and ground transport for optimal delivery performance. On the one hand, this gives us worldwide reach, and on the other, a strong local presence and unique understanding of local markets and customers.

In the logistics area, globalisation is creating ever more complex supply chains. Again, DHL's combination of global reach and local knowledge is a key competitive edge. We also offer a wide range of standardised services as well as tailor-made industry solutions. This is the only way to deliver to the high standards that our global customers are demanding. DHL's international network links more than 220 countries and territories worldwide. Around 285,000 employees are dedicated to providing fast and reliable services that exceed customers' expectations in 120,000 destinations in all continents.

With the acquisition of Exel, Deutsche Post World Net further strengthened its logistics power. As a result, DHL is now operating with two new logistics brands: DHL Exel Supply Chain and DHL Global Forwarding. To cover all of your service needs, the new DHL operates under five specialist divisions.

DHL Express is the result of the consolidation of the former DHL Worldwide Express business and the Deutsche Post Euro Express parcels business and offers express, parcel and freight services. DHL Express is the perfect partner for all your worldwide express and parcel needs. Our network covers over 4,000 offices and more than 120,000 destinations worldwide.

DHL Freight offers international and national transport solutions for part and full load in Europe. We move goods by road, rail and a combination of the two. DHL Freight covers the former DHL's non-documents and non-parcels business as well as the former Danzas Eurocargo road transport business.

DHL Global Forwarding is the market leader in air and ocean freight and a project logistics services provider operating worldwide. A range of value-added services rounds off the product and service portfolio, giving an excellent market position and providing our customers with a unique service dimension worldwide.

DHL-Sinotrans was founded in Beijing. The joint venture combined DHL's leading expertise in the global air express industry and Sinotrans' unrivalled local knowledge in the China foreign trade transport market. DHL-Sinotrans has developed a comprehensive service network covering 318 cities throughout China, with 50 joint venture offices. DHL-Sinotrans' business performance has grown almost 60-fold at an astonishing average rate of 40% in the past decade. The company has secured the leadership position in the China air express industry.

Regardless of whether you operate in the healthcare, technology, aerospace, automotive, industrial or retail, consumer, fashion sectors, we can handle all of your complex, global logistics tasks: DHL Exel Supply Chain provides you with customised, IT-based solutions along the entire supply chain.

As well as core procurement logistics, warehousing and sales logistics operations, we offer top-flight value-added services such as finishing, co-packing, price labelling, billing, order processing—all the way to sales promotion and financial services.

Our task as a global logistics provider is to network the world. Our aim is to provide excellent service quality to our customers at attractive prices, in the most environment-friendly way possible, embracing our social responsibilities.

Increasingly, the challenges that global companies must address to be profitable longer-term are intertwined with the challenges that broader society must address to improve quality of life. We believe commitment to good corporate citizenship is a fundamental part of achieving sustained value creation for both society and our company, and thus to ensuring the future of the work that we do.

# 篇章口译

## Passage B (C-E)

 **Vocabulary Work**

Work on the following words and phrases and write the translated version in the space provided.

| 政府物流服务部门 | 采购 | 仓库 | 运输队 |
| 预支账目 | 用户 | 承办商 | 非政府机构 |
| 物料 | 挑选货源 | 招标 | 公务合约 |
| 物业管理 | 停车收费表 | 废物处理设施 | |

 **Text Interpreting**

Listen to the tape and interpret the following passage from Chinese into English.

接下来我们来谈谈政府物流服务部门。政府物流服务部门为政府各决策局和部门提供物流支援服务，其中包括采购和物料供应、运输和车辆管理以及印刷服务。政府物流服务部门是政府的中央采购代理。

政府的采购政策，首重经济效益，目的是取得最物有所值的货品和服务，帮助推行政府的计划和工作。我们也致力于为所有参与竞投政府采购合约的本地及海外供应商和服务承办商提供公平的竞争环境。换言之，政府是透过明确、公开和公平竞争的程序，批出货品和服务供应的合约，既不偏袒，也不歧视。

政府物流服务部门拥有现代化的仓库和运输队，并库存多种必需品及管制表格。这个部门先通过一个预支账目支取款项缴付该等物品的费用，待用户从该部门提取物品时才向该用户收回费用。该部门也通过大批采购合约，为政府部门及许多非政府机构采购各式各样常用物品，包括文具及清洁用品。使用部门可在有需要时根据大批采购合约，直接向承办商提取所需物品，并从本身的账目拨款支付购货费用。这个物流服务部同时也是签订合约的一方，并在整段合约期内提供合约管理服务。

此外，政府物流服务部还为各部门及小部分非政府机构采购特定使用的物料和设备。使用部门从自己的账目拨款支付购货费用，但是需借助政府物流服务部门在挑选货源、招标、洽谈及合约管理方面的专业特长。政府物流服务部门代为采购的货品种类繁多。

政府物流服务部门除就公务合约的招标程序及合约管理事宜提供一般指引及技术上的意见外，还备存一套认可的工程承包商名册，以及工程承包商表现评核报告制度，必要时还要协助审核承包商的财政能力。

此外,政府的采购服务还包括财务和管理方面的顾问服务及其他类型的服务合约。政府招标承投的服务合约很多,比较典型的有清洁工作、物业管理、停车收费表管理,以及交通和废物处理设施的操作。

# 口译讲评

## Notes on the Text

**Passage A**

1. **DHL is the global market leader in international express, overland transport and air freight. It is also the world's number one in ocean freight and contract logistics**:这两句主语相同,在译为汉语时可以合并为一个句子。第二句根据上下文需增译"提供商"一词,便于理解。全句译文为:DHL是全球快递、洲际运输和航空货运的领导者,也是全球第一的海运和合同物流提供商。

2. **DHL offers a full range of customised solutions—from express document shipping to supply chain management**:DHL为客户提供从文件快递到供应链管理的全套物流解决方案。顺译时,也可译为DHL为客户提供全套的物流解决方案,从文件快递到供应链管理。但前者更符合汉语表达习惯。

3. **We transport shipments rapidly, safely and on time all over the world**:我们在全球快速、安全和及时的运送货物。这句句子较短,所以译时,将副词放在动词词组之前比较符合表达习惯。

4. **The basis for this is our comprehensive network, combining air and ground transport for optimal delivery performance**:这其中的基础是我们广泛的网络,结合空中和地面的运输方式以达到最优化的递送效率。for optimal delivery performance 这里作断句处理,用"以达到……"来表达可以较好地体现其中的逻辑关系。

5. **this gives us worldwide reach**:这使我们的服务可以遍及世界每一角落。而之后的DHL's combination of global reach and local knowledge 则可以译为"DHL 全球触角和对本土市场了解的结合"。

6. **With the acquisition of Exel…**:结合下文,可以看出这里的 with 表示的是时间,可以译为"完成对 Exel 的并购之后"。

7. **DHL-Sinotrans' business performance has grown almost 60-fold at an astonishing average rate of 40% in the past decade**:过去10年里,公司业务年平均增长率为40%,跃升了60倍之多。这句要注意译时的先后顺序,涉及逻辑关系。

8. **Our task as a global logistics provider is to network the world**:作为一家全球物流服务提供商,我们的任务即是网络联结全世界。这里 network 被活用为动词,翻译时需要增译"联结"一词。

**Passage B**

1. 政府的采购政策,首重经济效益,目的是取得最物有所值的货品和服务,帮助推行政府的计划和工作：The procurement policy of the Government is to obtain goods and services at the best value for money in support of the Government's programmes and activities. "首重经济效益"在口译中可以省略,因为下文已经充分表明这层意思。另外,汉语中两个动词"取得"、"帮助"在英语用了一个动词,一个介词词组,很好地表达了逻辑关系。

2. 我们亦致力为所有参与竞投政府采购合约的本地及海外供应商和服务承办商提供公平的竞争环境：We are committed to providing equal opportunities for domestic and foreign suppliers and service providers, participating or competing in Government procurement. 因为"海外供应商和服务承办商"的定语较长,所以可以采用从句或分词结构的形式放在句尾。"公平的竞争环境"依据英文表达习惯译为 equal opportunities。

3. 既无偏袒,也无歧视：No favours. No discrimination. 这里采用词性转换的形式,使句子简洁明了,而且省略了说明施动者、受动者等的麻烦。

4. 该部门先由一个预支账目支取款项缴付该等物品的费用,待用户从该部门提取物品时才向该用户收回费用：GLD pays for the cost of these items from an advance account in the first instance and recovers the costs from the end-users when they draw the goods from GLD. 这里注意顺序及逻辑关系。为了说明逻辑关系,这里"用户"译为 end user 比较清楚。

5. 政府物流服务部门代为采购的货品种类繁多：此句可以译为 The goods purchased by GLD on behalf of user departments are diverse,或者转换主语,变译作 On behalf of user departments, GLD purchases diverse goods。

6. 政府物流服务部门除就公务合约的招标程序及合约管理事宜提供一般指引及技术上的意见外,还备存一套认可的工程承包商名册,以及工程承包商表现评核报告制度,必要时还要协助审核承包商的财政能力：这句较长,先从结构上分清主干部分,使用一些介词短语如 in addition to, in respect of 使句子层次分明,例如：In addition to giving general guidance and technical advice on tendering procedures and contract administration matters in respect of works contracts, GLD maintains a register of approved works contractors and a central works contractor's performance report system and provides financial vetting support where necessary.

## Relevant Words and Expressions

海运 shipping
货轮 cargo boat / steamer / carrier; freighter
货物 goods; freight; cargo
空运 air freight
快递 express
供应链 supply chain

存货控制 inventory control
定制物流 customarized logistics
货物运输 goods traffic; carriage of freights / goods
企业物流 business logistics
社会物流 societal logistics
虚拟物流 virtual logistics
船务代理人 shipping agent
第三方物流 TPL [third-party logistics]
货柜集装箱 container
增值物流服务 value-added logistics service
直复营销服务 direct marketing solution
美国运输与物流协会 ASTL [American Society of Transportation and Logistics]
中国国际贸易促进委员会 CCPIT [China council for the Promotion of International Trade]
复合 / 联合运输；多式联运和铁路运输 intermodel and railway transportation

# 口译技能

# Interpreting Skills

## 语篇理解(2)：逻辑思维

对原文的精确理解是做好口译的关键，那么译员如何确定自己对言语的判断是正确的呢？译员中流传着这样一个故事：有一次在布鲁塞尔机场发生了这样一件事，当时地面情况有点繁杂，一架联合国官员乘坐的飞机在空中盘旋，一直没有降落。一位译员问布鲁塞尔机场官员飞机不降落的原因。那位官员解释说："The pilot cannot land"。译员乍一听觉得非常奇怪，飞行员怎么可能不会降落呢？后来，他略加思索，考虑到当时的情况，推测官员用了一种特殊的表达方法，其意思应该是："The pilot could find no free runway because of the disorderly conditions of the airport"，经核实得到确认。这一事例说明对言语意义的正确理解离不开逻辑思维判断。译员除了具备语音、词汇、句法、内容方面的知识，对演讲语篇的理解还需依赖于对语境、交际对象、言辞的逻辑分析，尤其是当做较长段落讲话的口译时。

要理解、记忆长段的语篇，逻辑分析必不可少。口译中的逻辑分析指对讲话进行纵向和横向的分析。纵向分析是指分清关键信息和辅助信息，即找出逻辑的层次。通常听完一篇讲话应该概括出讲话的主题，这是第一层次；围绕这一主题展开，谈了几方面内容，这是第二层次；每一方面又扩展开去，又是一个新层次。横向分析指明确各信息点之间的逻辑关系，如因果关系、分类组合、比较对照、过程分析、举例说明、时间顺序等。英语里有很多表示这些逻辑关系的线索词汇，这些词语也是交传笔记强调要记的逻辑连接词。

逻辑分析的目的是为了透彻地理解原讲话的内容，对信息的点（具体的信息内容）、线（各点之间的联系）和面（整体印象）进行全面的把握，以便于记忆和表达。信息经过逻辑分析加工,会在记忆中留下更深刻的印象。比如:一篇演讲通过分析得出它的主题是:大学生活是有压力的,而压力来自三方面:学业、经济条件、个人性格,然后又就每一类压力扩展开去,或举例说明或作因果分析等。这样一分析讲话的脉络就非常清晰地呈现出来,再长的段落或篇章也可以应付自如。当然在实际口译中,难免也会遇到有些发言主次不分、层次不清,所以平时需要有意识地做一些训练,比如在规定时间内改写一些逻辑混乱、反复冗长的发言讲稿,或是直接做口头修改,以提高快速逻辑分析与归纳的水平。

另外,讲话内容是由演讲人决定的,所以对演讲的逻辑分析离不开对演讲人的分析和了解。社会地位、政治倾向和职业等都决定着发言者的观点和态度。很明显,生产商和消费者对商业市场的态度会不同,所以了解讲话人的身份背景有助于理解讲话的目的、观点和态度,对讲话进行合理的分析和预测,帮助准确理解语篇内容。

还有一些场合译员不仅需要用耳朵,而且还要用眼睛来"听",帮助分析语篇意义。偶尔会发生这样的情况,说话者的意思无法仅从语言正确判断。意义来自于说话人,而非仅仅在于词语,所以译员需要一边听,一边观察说话者的脸部表情、手势、身体语言,同时接收语言和非语言交际信息,比较它们之间的含义是否完全吻合,只有这样才能理解说话者所表达的表层意思和真正的内在含义。

语篇层次上的意义还受到文化和思维方式的影响,西方"线性"的理性思维方式和东方的"悟性"、"意会"表现在语篇结构和逻辑层次性上就有很大的不同,这也是译员应该注意的地方。

## 口译练习 Enhancement Practice

### 第一项 Project 1
句子精练 Sentences in Focus

**A. Interpret the following sentences from English into Chinese.**

1. The company also provides value-added services like "collection on delivery", "paid by addressee", "agent customs clearance", and so on.
2. The company now opens many high-end products like domestic "next-morning delivery", "next-day delivery", international "time-certain delivery", and so on.
3. With the help of China Postal Airlines, the company has established an "overnight flight" concentration and distribution network with Shanghai as the hub, which helps fulfill next-day delivery in over 200 cities in China.
4. Canada Courier Service Corporation (CCSC) mainly operates domestic and international EMS services and is the largest provider in Canada's express service industry currently.
5. By adopting high technology, the company now has a 4 in 1 around-the-clock real-time track and trace system including its own website, short message, call center and retail counter.

**B. Interpret the following sentences from Chinese into English.**

1. 公司拥有员工2万多人,业务通达全球200多个国家和地区以及国内近2000个城市。

2. 我们的任务是系统地评估您公司的供应链,使您的公司能高效运作。
3. Express特快专递业务自1980年开办以来,业务量逐年增长,业务种类不断丰富,服务质量不断提高。
4. 公司建的信息平台覆盖全国318个城市,全国共有200多个处理中心,其中上海、北京和广州处理中心分别达到2万余平方米、3万平方米和3.7万平方米,并且已经开始运行。
5. 市场的国际化以及对提高效率和降低成本的越来越高的要求迫使企业寻找越来越灵活的解决方案,从而提供企业的核心竞争力。

第二项 Project 2
段落口译 Paragraph Interpreting

**A. Interpret the following paragraph from English into Chinese.**

FedEx Express is part of transportation powerhouse FedEx Corporation. FedEx Corp. provides customers and businesses worldwide with a broad portfolio of transportation, e-commerce and business services. With annual revenues of $32 billion, the company offers integrated business applications through operating companies competing collectively and managed collaboratively, under the respected FedEx brand. Consistently ranked among the world's most admired and trusted employers, FedEx inspires its more than 260,000 employees and contractors to remain "absolutely, positively" focused on safety, the highest ethical and professional standards and the needs of their customers and communities.

**B. Interpret the following paragraph from Chinese into English.**

作为业内领先、国际一流的远洋承运人,我们为您提供首屈一指的门到门运输服务。我们拥有500多艘集装箱船以及140万个集装箱,保证为您提供可靠的全球服务。大规模、现代化的集装箱船队随时听候您的吩咐。我们拥有各种尺寸和类型的集装箱,保证满足您的需求。我们的船队是最现代、最安全、最环保的远洋船队之一。因此我们将保证您的货物顺利、安全地抵达目的地。

第三项 Project 3
篇章口译 Passage Interpreting

**A. Listen to the tape and interpret the following passage from English into Chinese.**

Ladies and Gentlemen,
 Good morning! Here I'd be proud to introduce TNT.
 TNT provides businesses and consumers worldwide with an extensive range of services for their mail and express delivery needs. Headquartered in the Netherlands, TNT offers efficient network infrastructures in Europe and Asia and is expanding operations worldwide to maximize its network performance. TNT serves more than 200 countries and employs around 159,000 people. Last year, TNT reported 10.1 billion in revenues and an operating income of 1,276 million.

TNT Express is the world's leading business to business express delivery company. The company delivers 4.1 million parcels, documents and pieces of freight a week to over 200 countries using its network of nearly 1,200 depots, hubs and sortation centres. TNT Express operates over 23,400 road vehicles and 44 aircraft and has the biggest door-to-door air and road express delivery infrastructure in Europe. TNT's express division employs over 54,000 staff worldwide. It is the first organisation to have achieved global recognition as an investor in people. The division reported revenue of 6.01 billion last year. The operating income was 580 million, up 21.8% compared to last year.

TNT Greater China is a business unit of TNT Express. It provides distribution services through two business areas—Express and Direct Marketing. TNT employs around 15,000 skilled professionals across its Greater China network.

TNT Mainland China delivers value to our customers by providing the most reliable and efficient international distribution solutions. With 26 wholly-owned branches and 3 fully functioning international gateways serving more than 500 cities. We take pride in providing personalized service that aims to delight our customers every step of the way. Our extensive global reach and first-class network infrastructure allow us to deliver what our customers need when and where they need it.

TNT's acquisition of Hoau Group is a significant milestone for TNT. It expands TNT's network coverage to about 1,200 depots throughout China which gives TNT a clear competitive advantage by improving our network coverage and distribution options for our customers.

Hoau has the most densely populated road network of any private company in the country. They provide transportation for freight and parcels to more than 160,000 customers. It has a network of 1,200 depots, 3,000 vehicles and 56 hubs covering all major and second-tier cities in China. Hoau currently has 12,000 employees. Hoau has been granted the rating of 5A, the highest category for the transportation industry in China.

With over 25 years of experience in providing world-class direct marketing solutions in Europe, TNT now offers Direct Marketing Services in Mainland China. This was launched to provide integrated direct marketing solutions including planning and implementation, data analysis and management, telemarketing, response management and analysis.

**B. Listen to the tape and interpret the following passage from Chinese into English.**

各位同仁：

大家好！

如大家所知，"中美物流会议"已于7月18—19日在中国国际贸易促进委员会成功召开，来自中美加三国物流行业相关政府部门、物流企业、研究机构和物流媒体等200余名代表参加会议，共同探讨中美物流行业的热点问题。

此次会议由中国国际贸易促进委员会、中国交通运输协会、美国运输与物流协会和美国国家工业运输联盟联合举办，并得到中国和美国两国商务部的大力支持。

## 第 6 单元　现代物流　Modern Logistics

本届会议是中国物流业全面对外开放后，中美物流界首次大规模高层对话，旨在促进中美在运输与物流领域的全面合作。中国交通运输协会会长钱永昌、中国国际贸易促进委员会会长万季飞、美国国家工业运输联盟总裁 John Ficker、美国运输与物流协会执行董事 Laurie Denham 出席开幕仪式并分别代表主办方致辞，美国商务部副助理部长 Ana Guevara 和中国商务部王洪波商务参赞就中美贸易关系发表了主题演讲。此次会议分为十个议题，讨论中美运输与物流现状和发展趋势、入世后的中美物流合作前景以及有关海运、港口和通关、多式联运和铁路运输、空运和快递、危险品物流、教育和培训等行业热点问题。其中每个议题分别由来自中国和美国的政府、企业和研究机构组成专家组进行对话和讨论。

中国空运市场已成为世界第二大空运市场，且正以每年超过 20% 的速度增长。然而目前能提供优质安全服务的国内物流公司较少。除此之外，经验丰富的物流人才的短缺束缚了国内物流业的发展。这次大会为我们提供了美国企业的管理经验，以及中美在资金、基础设施、技术以及管理方面的合作机会，其中重点之一是中美两国间教育机构和行业协会间的合作机会。

# 参考译文
## Reference Version

**篇章口译 A**

针对各位提出来的这些有关物流方面的问题，我想最好的办法就是通过我们 DHL 来解答。DHL 是全球快递、洲际运输和航空货运的领导者，也是全球第一的海运和合同物流提供商。DHL 为客户提供从文件快递到供应链管理的全套物流解决方案。我们在全球快速、安全和及时的运送货物。这其中的基础是我们广泛的网络，结合空中和地面的运输方式以达到最优化的递送效率。一方面，这使我们的服务可以遍及世界每一角落，另一方面，我们可以树立在当地市场上的品牌形象并能充分理解当地市场和客户的需求。

在物流领域，全球化正在创造出比以往更加复杂的供应链。DHL 全球触角和对本土市场了解的结合再一次显示了这是一个重要的竞争优势。我们既提供种类齐全的标准化服务，同时也提供定制化的行业解决方案。这是达成我们的全球客户要求的高标准的唯一方式。DHL 的服务网络遍及全球 220 多个国家和地区。全球约 28.5 万名尽心尽职的员工向 12 万多个目的地的客户提供快捷、可靠的服务。

完成对 Exel 的并购之后，德国邮政全球网络进一步增强了自身的物流实力。并购后的结果是 DHL 开始使用两个新的物流子品牌运营：DHL Exel Supply Chain 和 DHL Global Forwarding。新的 DHL 将通过旗下的五个业务部门满足您所有服务需要。

DHL 快递由前 DHL 环球速递和德国邮政欧洲包裹快递整合而成，提供快递、包裹和货运服务。DHL 快递是满足您全球快递和包裹需求的最佳合作伙伴。我们在全球拥有 4000 多个办事处，且服务网络覆盖全球超过 12 万个目的地。

DHL 货运为欧洲的散货和整装货物提供国际和国内的运输解决方案。我们通过公路、铁路或联运的方式来运输货物。DHL 货运包括整合前 DHL 文件和包裹运输以外的业务以及丹沙欧洲陆运业务。

DHL Global Forwarding 是海空货运行业的市场领导者,同时也是一家业务遍及全球的项目物流服务提供商。一系列的增值服务使我们的产品和服务组合更加完美,这使我们得以在市场上站稳脚跟并向全球范围内的客户提供独特的服务选择。

中外运—敦豪国际航空快件有限公司在北京正式成立之后,合资公司将敦豪作为国际快递业领导者的丰富经验和中国外运集团总公司在中国外贸运输市场的经营优势成功地结合在一起。目前,中外运敦豪在中国拥有56家分公司,业务覆盖全国318个主要城市。过去10年里,公司业务年平均增长率为40%,跃升了60倍之多。现在,中外运—敦豪已稳居中国航空快递业的领导地位。

不论您所经营的行业是医疗保健、科技、航空、汽车、工业或者零售、消费品、时尚行业,对于您的任何复杂的全球性物流任务,我们皆可完成。DHL Exel Supply Chain 为您提供一整套定制的、基于信息技术的供应链解决方案。

除了核心的采购物流、仓储以及销售物流服务外,我们还提供诸多一流的增值服务,譬如货物整理、合并包装、贴价签、开发账单、订单处理,甚至还包括销售促销和金融服务。

作为一家全球物流服务提供商,我们的任务即是网络联结全世界。我们的目标是以具有吸引力的价格、完全环保的运作方式以及社会责任的切实履行为前提,为我们的客户提供最优秀的服务品质。

日益明显的一个事实是:全球性的公司若要保持长期盈利所必须面对的挑战,已经与其所处社会提高全体公民的生活水平所必须面对的挑战紧密结合在一起。我们相信努力成为一名优秀企业公民的承诺不论对公司还是社会来讲,都是创造可持续性价值的基本条件之一,只有这样才能保障我们所从事事业的可持续发展。

## 篇章口译 B

Next, let's talk about GLD. Government Logistics Department (GLD) provides to the bureaux and departments of the Government with logistics support services in the areas of procurement and supplies, transport operation and management as well as printing services. The GLD is the Government's central procurement agent.

The procurement policy of the Government is to obtain goods and services at the best value for money in support of the Government's programmes and activities. We are committed to providing equal opportunities for domestic and foreign suppliers and service providers, participating or competing in Government procurement. This means that contracts for supplying goods or services to the Government are awarded through open, fair, competitive and transparent procedures. No favours. No discrimination.

Equipped with a modern warehouse and delivery fleet, GLD maintains a number of essential items and controlled forms. GLD pays for the cost of these items from an advance account in the first instance and recovers the costs from the end-users when they draw the goods from GLD. GLD also purchases through allocated bulk contracts a wide range of items commonly used by Government departments and many non-government organizations. These include stationery and cleansing materials. The user departments can draw their requirements directly from the contractors against the allocated bulk contracts and pay for the stores from their own account. GLD remains the contracting party and provides contract administration service throughout the contractual period.

In addition, GLD acts as the purchasing agent for specific stores and equipment required by user departments and a few non-government organizations. The user departments will pay for these stores from their own account but rely on GLD for expertise in sourcing, tendering, negotiations and contract administration. The goods purchased by GLD on behalf of user departments are diverse.

Construction services are procured by the individual works departments concerned, under the general supervision of GLD. In addition to giving general guidance and technical advice on tendering procedures and contract administration matters in respect of works contracts, GLD maintains a register of approved works contractors and a central works contractor's performance report system and provides financial vetting support where necessary.

Services procured by the Government also include consultancy services on financial or management aspects as well as other types of service contracts. Typical examples of service contracts tendered by the Government are cleaning, property management, management of parking meters, and operation of transport and waste management facilities.

**口译练习**

第一项 句子精练

A.
1. 公司还提供代收货款、收件人付费、代客清关等增值服务。
2. EMS 相继推出国内"次晨达"和"次日达"、国际"限时递"等高端服务。
3. 依托中国邮政航空公司,建立了以上海为集散中心的全夜航航空集散网,实现国内 200 多个城市间的次日递送。
4. 加拿大速递服务公司主要经营国际、国内 EMS 特快专递业务,是目前加拿大速递行业的最大运营商。
5. 通过采用高科技,公司还建立了以网站、短信、客服电话和柜台四位一体的实时信息跟踪查询系统。

B.
1. The company now employs over 20,000 professional courier staff, and the network now reaches over 200 countries and regions and up to 2,000 domestic cities.
2. Our mission is to systematically evaluate your supply chain and guide your company toward improved operational efficiencies.
3. Since its beginning in 1980, the Express service has witnessed continuously growing volume and categories as well as improving quality.
4. The company has also established an information platform covering 318 domestic cities,

more than 200 processing centers nationwide, among which the over 20,000 m² Shanghai Processing Center, the 30,000 m² Beijing center and 37,000 m² Guangzhou center have begun to run.
5. Internationalization, efficiency and cost control require more and more solutions and modules to strengthen enterprise core competence.

## 第二项 段落口译

**A.**

联邦快递隶属于美国联邦快递集团(FedEx Corp.)，是集团快递运输业务的中坚力量。联邦快递集团为遍及全球的顾客和企业提供涵盖运输、电子商务和商业运作等一系列的全面服务。作为一个久负盛名的企业品牌，联邦快递集团通过相互竞争和协调管理的运营模式，提供了一套综合的商务应用解决方案，使其年收入高达320亿美元。联邦快递集团激励旗下超过26万名员工和承包商高度关注安全问题，恪守品行道德和职业操守的最高标准，并最大程度地满足客户和社会的需求，使其屡次被评为全球最受尊敬、最可信赖的雇主。

**B.**

As a top world-leading ocean carrier, we offer customers second-to-none door-to-door transportation service. With more than 500 container vessels and 1,400,000 containers, we ensure that you get a reliable worldwide coverage. At your disposal is a vast and modern fleet of containers and vessels. We have the size and type of container to suit your needs. Our vessels are among the most modern, secure and environmentally friendly to sail the oceans. Your cargo is therefore assured a smooth and safe voyage.

## 第三项 篇章口译

**A.**

女士们，先生们：

大家好！这里我非常自豪地向大家介绍TNT公司。

TNT集团是全球领先的快递邮政服务供应商。总部位于荷兰的TNT集团，凭借其在欧洲和亚洲的高效网络设施，正不断扩展全球业务网络。TNT拥有15.9万名员工，分布于200多个国家和地区。去年，集团销售收入为101亿欧元，运营收入为12.76亿欧元。

TNT快递是全球领先的企业级快递公司。通过其在全球200多个国家近1200个快递服务中心、转运中心以及分拣中心，每周在全球递送410万个包裹、文件和货件。TNT快递拥有2.34万辆车和44架飞机，以及欧洲最大的"门到门"空陆递送网络。TNT快递拥有5.4万名员工并为全球第一家获得"投资于人"认证的企业。TNT快递在去年的销售收入为60.1亿欧元，运营收入为5.8亿欧元，年度增长为21.5%。

TNT大中国区是TNT快递在中国的分支机构。它通过旗下快递以及直复营销两大业务部门为客户提供整合的商用递送解决方案。在大中国区，TNT拥有约1.5万名专业员工。

TNT中国国际快递业务为客户提供最可靠高效的递送服务。在中国，TNT拥有26家直属运营机构以及三个全功能国际口岸,服务覆盖中国 500 多个城市。TNT 致力于向客户提供个性化的服务,让客户在递送途中的每个阶段均感到满意。凭借四通八达的全球递送网络以及一流的基础设施,TNT 得以为客户在其需要时帮助其运送所需物品。

TNT 对华宇集团的收购是 TNT 发展历程中的一个里程碑。它使 TNT 在中国的营业网点提高到 1200 个。这个庞大的陆运网络强化了 TNT 在中国市场的竞争优势,使 TNT 可以更好地服务客户,实现增长。

华宇集团是中国著名私有的公路零担货运公司。它为超过 16 万个客户提供货物和包裹运输服务,目前在中国拥有 56 家子公司、1200 个营业网点及 3000 辆运输车。服务覆盖中国所有主要大中城市。华宇目前拥有员工 1.2 万名。它是中国运输产业最高级企业认证类别——"5A"级运输企业。

在欧洲拥有 25 年直复营销服务经验的 TNT 在中国启动直复营销服务,向客户提供综合的直复营销解决方案。我们的解决方案包括策划和执行、数据分析与管理、电话营销、回复管理以及分析等。

B.

Dear Colleagues,
　　Good evening!

As we all know, Sino-American Logistics Conference was successfully held in China Council for Promotion of International Trade on July 18th and 19th. More than 200 representatives from the relevant government departments, logistics companies, research institutions, and logistics media from China, Canada and the United States participated in this conference where experts discussed the hot issues concerning the Sino-American logistics industry.

This conference was organized by China Council for Promotion of International Trade (CCPIT), China Communication and Transportation Association (CCTA), The American Society of Transportation and Logistics (ASTL), and The National Industrial Transportation League (NITL). The conference was strongly supported by US Department of Commerce and China's Ministry of Commerce.

This conference was the first large-scale and high-level dialogue between China and US after Chinese logistics industry's opening up. It was aimed at promoting cooperation in Sino-American logistics and transportation fields. Mr. Qian Yongchang, Chairman of CCTA; Mr. Wan Jifei, Chairman of CCPIT; Mr. John Ficker, President of NITL; Mrs. Laurie Denham, Executive Director of ASTL spoke during the opening ceremony. Mr. Ana Guevara, Deputy Assistant to US Department of Commerce, and Wang Hongbo, Commercial Councilor for Ministry of Commerce of China delivered keynote speeches about Sino-American trade.

The conference was divided into ten sessions to discuss the hot topics, such as Current State and Development of China-US Logistics, Post-WTO Sino-American Logistics Cooperation Trends, Shipping, Ports and Customs, Intermodel and Railway

Transportation, Express & Air Freight, Hazardous Materials, Education & Training, etc. Each of those topics was discussed by the experts from China and American government, enterprises, and research institutions.

China is the second biggest aviation market in the world, and increasing at the rate of 20%. However, currently few local logistics firms are capable of providing high-quality and safe-handling services. In addition, the development of the Chinese logistics industry has been hampered by the shortage of skilled logistics professionals. The conference presented the management experience of US companies and the opportunities for the China and US cooperation such as capital, infrastructure, technology and management. Opportunities for cooperation between educational institutions and industry associations will be highlighted.

# 第 7 单元 市场营销

 **Marketing and Sales**

Unit 7

# 篇章口译

## Passage A (E-C)

### Vocabulary Work

Work on the following words and phrases and write the translated version in the space provided.

| | | | |
|---|---|---|---|
| sweep through | Silicon Valley | buzzed with | stunning |
| radiation-repair | profitability | retention | defection rate |
| transatlantic | top-of-the-line | interruption-free | slip into |
| on board | | | |

### Text Interpreting

**Listen to the tape and interpret the following passage from English into Chinese.**

Good morning, ladies and gentleman. Today, we will take a look at the marketing around the world. As we all know, quality and customer satisfaction have become the key competitive weapons of the 21st century. Few organizations will prosper in today's environment without a focus on quality, continual improvement, and customer satisfaction. Corporations across the globe have implemented quality improvement and satisfaction programs in an effort to reduce costs, retain customers, increase market share, and, last but not least, improve the bottom line.

When total quality management swept through corporate America, the emphasis was strictly on product improvement. But product improvement se wasn't the answer. Consider the case of Varian Associates Incorporated, a manufacturer of scientific equipment. The company put 1,000 of its managers through a four-day course on quality. The company's Silicon Valley headquarter buzzed with quality speak. Talk of work teams and cycle times replaced discussion of elections and X rays. Varian went about virtually reinventing the way it did business—with what seemed to be stunning results. A unit that makes vacuum systems for computer clean rooms boosted on-time delivery from 42 percent to 92 percent. The semiconductor unit cut the time it took to put out new designs by 14 days. However, producing quality products wasn't enough. Obsessed with meeting production schedules, the staff in that vacuum-equipment unit didn't return customer's phone calls, and the operation ended up losing market share. Radiation-repair people were so rushed to meet deadlines that they left before explaining their work to customers.

According to Richard M. Levy, executive vice-president for quality, "All of the quality-based charts went up and to the right, but everything else went down."

The drive for quality was often a production-oriented, mechanistic exercise that proved meaningless to customers. And quality that means little to customers usually doesn't produce a payoff in improved sales, profits, or market share. It's wasted effort and expense. Today the new mantra is "return on quality", which means two things: 1) The quality delivered is the quality desired by the target market; and 2) the added quality must have a positive impact on profitability. For example, banking giant NationsBank Corporation measures every improvement in service, from adding more tellers to offering new mortgage products, in terms of added profitability.

The key to making "return on quality" work is marketing research. It is the mechanism that enables organizations to determine what types and forms of quality are important to the target market.

An inextricable link exists between customer satisfaction and customer loyalty. Long-term relationships don't just happen but are grounded in the delivery of service and value by the firm. Customer retention pays big dividends for organization. Costs fall because firms spend less funds and energy attempting to replace defectors. Steady customers are easy to serve because they understand the modus operand and make fewer demands on employees' time. Increased customer retention also drives job satisfaction and pride, which lead to higher employee retention. In turn, the knowledge employees acquire as they stay longer increases productivity. A Bain & Company study estimates that a decrease in the customer defection rate by 5 percent can boost profits by 25 percent to 95 percent.

The ability to retain customers is based upon an intimate understanding of their needs. This knowledge comes primarily from marketing research. For example, British Airways recast its first-class transatlantic service based upon detailed marketing research. Most airlines stress top-of-the-line service in their transatlantic first-class cabins. British Air research found that most first-class passengers simply wanted to sleep. British Air now gives premium flyers the option of dinner on the ground, before takeoff, in the first-class lounge. Once on board, they can slip into British Air pajamas, put their heads on real pillows, slip under blankets, and then enjoy an interruption-free flight. On arrival, first-class passengers can have breakfast, use comfortable dressing rooms and showers, and even have their clothes pressed before they set off for business. These changes were driven strictly by marketing research.

# 篇章口译

## Passage B (C-E)

 **Vocabulary Work**

Work on the following words and phrases and write the translated version in the space provided.

| | | | |
|---|---|---|---|
| 品牌战略 | 先天不足 | 消费品市场 | 芯片 |
| 非一朝一夕之功 | 品牌优势 | 豪言壮语 | 中国国际集装箱集团 |
| 远洋运输公司 | 讲信誉按时供货 | 微波炉生产基地 | 格兰仕商标 |
| 讨价还价 | | | |

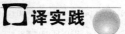 **Text Interpreting**

Listen to the tape and interpret the following passage from Chinese into English.

今天,我们来谈论一下中国企业的品牌战略。在成本、产品与品牌三种优势中,中国企业能尽快获得的最大优势还在于成本优势,尽管成本也在不断提高,但与外国企业相比仍有一定优势。最大的劣势就是品牌劣势,这是先天不足所致。

中国的市场经济刚开始发展,中国的企业刚刚起步,而西方企业的品牌是经过几十年甚至上百年建立起来的。在国际消费品市场上,与外国企业竞争,比在生产资料市场上竞争要困难得多。原因是在生产资料市场上,买东西的人都是专家,所以品牌不如成本重要,只要做出成本低的产品,对方就愿意买。但在消费品市场上,我们面临的都是普通消费者,所以品牌就非常重要,而品牌的建立又非一朝一夕之功。

在中国企业的国际化进程中,如果目前优势只能在成本范围内,就应把我们的成本优势与外国企业的品牌优势结合起来,而不应只凭豪言壮语跟人家竞争。

中国国际集装箱集团公司能成功走向国际,而夏利汽车却不能。道理很简单,全世界的集装箱客户只有100多家,都是大的远洋运输公司,只要质量符合规定,成本低就有市场。当然也需要讲信誉按时供货,但这比创立一个品牌要容易得多。

而生产汽车却不同,即使成本比人家低30%也很难成功,因为汽车卖到国外面对的是有可能成为最大的汽车零部件生产基地,但要在短期内成长出很有名的汽车制造商似乎希望不大。

格兰仕的例子也足以证明这个道理,它也想卖自己的品牌,但是卖不动,虽然它已发展成为世界上最大的微波炉生产基地,产品遍布全世界,但贴的却不是格兰仕的商标。

中国企业要做成世界品牌,有两条路可以走。一条道路是先为人家加工,让人家利用品牌优势赚钱,自己则慢慢积累资金,当企业规模足够大并且有足够的讨价还价能力的时候,再把价格提高,最终把好品牌买过来。

另一条是走类似英特尔公司的道路。英特尔公司是生产芯片的,产品装在计算机里没人看见,于是英特尔公司提出一个战略,所有使用其芯片的计算机必须贴英特尔商标。

# 口译讲评

## Notes on the Text

**Passage A**

1. **in an effort to reduce costs, retain customers, increase market share, and, last but not least, improve the bottom line**:翻译 last but not least 时,要将这个短语的本意讲明:要降低成本、留住顾客、增加市场份额,以及最后具有同等重要性的一点,提高企业盈利程度。
2. **se**:标准误差的意思,即 standard error。
3. **Varian Associates Incorporated**:瓦里安联合公司,建于20世纪30年代后期,是世界一流的科学仪器和真空管制造公司。
4. **The company's Silicon Valley headquarter buzzed with quality speak**:在这里有一个非常好的词组 be buzzed with,意思是"散布着什么样的嗡嗡叫",所以这句话翻译成"公司的硅谷总部充满了议论质量的喧闹"。
5. **return on quality**:是"从质量上求利益"的意思,这有两点含义:1) 提供的质量是目标市场期望的质量;2) 增加的质量必须对盈利能力有正面的影响力。
6. **For example, banking giant NationsBank Corporation measures every improvement in service, from adding more tellers to offering new mortgage products, in terms of added profitability**:在这里 in terms of profitability 可以翻译成"根据赢利能力",因此这句长句可以翻译成"例如,金融业巨头国民银行根据增加的赢利能力来衡量服务中的每项改进,从增加更多出纳到提供新的抵押贷款项目。"
7. **An inextricable link exists between customer satisfaction and customer loyalty**:我们在翻译这句话的时候要改变句式,inextricable 虽然在这里形容 link,但翻译的时候可以放在最后,所以可以翻成"顾客的满意和顾客的忠诚是密不可分的。"
8. **are grounded in the delivery of service and value by the firm**:be grounded in 在这里是"根据"的意思。
9. **Bain & Company**:贝恩咨询公司,建于1973年,主要经营企业咨询业务。

**Passage B**

1. **品牌战略**:通过品牌管理来提高产品竞争力的策略。即通过创立名牌,提高产品和企业的知名度,靠名牌来开拓市场,增大市场份额,提高产品的市场占有率。品牌战略的一个重要原则就是规划差异化、个性化的品牌核心价值与品牌识别,并以此去统率企业的一切营销传播活动,而高度差异化与个性化的信息天然地具有吸引公众的能力,能以较低的成本提升销量和品牌资产。

2. **最大的劣势就是品牌劣势，这是先天不足所致**：这里的"先天不足"宜译成 inherent problem，所以此句可译为 The biggest disadvantage is brand recognition, which is an inherent problem。

3. **而品牌的建立又非一朝一夕之功**：这里的"一朝一夕"可以直接翻成 time，整句话可译成 The same recognition of brand takes time to build。

4. **在中国企业的国际化进程中，如果目前优势只能在成本范围内**：In the process of internationalization, Chinese firms should take into consideration the fact that our advantage is limited to cost.

5. **豪言壮语跟人家竞争**：这里的豪言壮语可直接译成 words，因而整句话可译为 rather than competing solely on words。

6. **先为人家加工，让人家利用品牌优势赚钱**：在翻译这句话的时候，我们在两句短句中加上 by so doing，更加可以达到口译中的良好效果，所以整句译文可为 The first is to begin with assembling parts for foreign manufactures. By doing so, foreign firms take advantage of their brand to make money。

7. **芯片**：chip，其实就是集成电路片，一小片如硅或锗等半导体材料，经过掺杂及其他工序使之具有特定的电子特性，尤指在将其加工成电路元件或集成电路，之前也叫做 microchip。

# 相关词语 *Relevant Words and Expressions*

促销组合 promotional mix
电话营销 telemarketing
独家销售 exclusive distribution
购物抽奖 sweepstake
关系营销 relationship marketing
集中营销 concentrated marketing
减价促销 cents-off promotion
品牌资产 brand equity
特许专卖 franchising
网络营销 network marketing
营销组合 marketing mix
直销策略 direct sales strategy
重新定位 repositioning
差异性营销 differentiated marketing
伏击式营销 ambush marketing
数据库营销 database marketing
推销员奖金 PM [push money]
顾客终身价值 LTCV [lifetime customer value]
营销信息系统 MIS [marketing information system]

战略市场计划 strategic market planning

# 口译技能
# Interpreting Skills

## 衔接（1）

口译中经常遇到一个难题:有时说话人的句子较长,所含信息较多,对听者的心理压力较大。译员常顺着两条思路来改进口译效果:第一,增强句子前后部分的衔接关系,例如使用关联结构,使用语义明显的实词与前文呼应,缩短语义相关词汇之间的距离,等等。第二,使用分流的办法,把一部分信息分流到一个相对独立的结构中去,这就等于扔掉一个包袱,然后译员便可集中精力处理剩余的信息。

汉语大量使用关联结构,如"如果……,那就……","虽然……,但是……"等。英语中也有关联结构,但使用频率很低,例如 If...,句型远比 If...,then...句型常见。但在口译实践中,译员往往高频率地使用英语关联结构,这样可使上下句之间的关系更为清楚,更便于听众听懂。当前面半句特别长时,更需要在后面用 then 等关联词来提醒听众注意上下句之间的关系。

下面简单介绍一下译员常使用的三种关联结构:

1. If...,then...是正确的英语,但不如只用一个连接词 If 的结构常用,不如汉语的"假如……,那就……"使用频率高。译员经常使用这种结构,虽然从文风上看未必十分妥帖,但从语义结构上来看则十分清楚。

例如:如果你要求我把它说得具体一点的话,那我可以概括一下:本届政府现在面临着要干的几件事情可以概括为"一个确保,三个到位,五项改革"。If you expect me to give you some specifics, then I can just make a generalization of the tasks that this government is expected to accomplish... 在口语中或在长句中可使用关联结构 If...,then...,以加强前后的衔接。事实上译员经常使用此关联结构,以便于听者理解。下面一例情况相似,只是关联词略有改变:

但是只要双方从大局出发,从促进国际市场的繁荣和稳定出发,大家都做一点让步,那么达成协议是很有希望的。As long as the two sides can make concessions out of the larger interest and out of the larger interest of promoting prosperity and stability of the world market and trade, then I'm very hopeful that we'll be able to reach an agreement.

2. As (Because)...,so...不是正确的英语结构,在书面中不能接受,但英语本族人在口语中经常使用。我国的译员有时也使用这种结构,在文风上损失较大,但能达到澄清语义结构的效果。笔者认为不宜频繁使用这种结构,但当前半句很长时可考虑使用。毕竟,口译的首要任务是清楚地传递信息。

例如:从根本上来讲,因为它(科索沃)是在南斯拉夫范围之内的一个问题,因此它是一个南斯拉夫的内部事务。Fundamentally speaking, as the Kosovo issue is within

Yugoslavia, so it's an internal matter of Yugoslavia. As (Because)..., so... 这一关联结构虽然不太地道，但很便于听众理解。

3. Although..., yet... 是一个正确的英语结构，但书卷气较重。译员使用这一结构从文风上看有欠妥当，但能清楚无误地传达转折的意义。

例如：我们虽然还没有进入 WTO，但是我们的很多改革比我们原来承诺的还发展得更快。Although China is still not a member of the WTO, as a matter of fact, yet the results of many of our reforms have already gone beyond the commitments made by us.

为了便于听者轻松听懂，可将"虽然……，但是……"口译成英语中不太常用的关联结构：Although..., yet (as a matter of fact)...。

此外，还有 both..., and... 与 not only..., but also... 这两个关联结构也值得我们注意。由于受原汉语的影响，译员常使用这两个结构，但有时会产生一些困难：汉语主要讲究意合，不讲究形合，各种词语很容易合在一起使用。汉语的词性也很灵活，受到的语法限制较少，便于各种词汇搭配使用，在"既……，又……"和"不但……，而且……"这两个结构中很容易填入各种词汇。而英语对词性的要求比较严格，在并列的结构中要求填入相同词性的词汇。但译员在译到后面一半时可能一时想不出相同词性的词汇，也可能已经忘记前面词汇的词性，因而容易出现语法错误，当句子较长时尤其容易出错。如果译员改用断句（也即大分流）的办法，前后词汇的词性就不必保持一致，因此也就不容易出错。此外，在 is not only..., but also... 结构中，中国学生在口译时很难想到在 is 与 not only 之间插入有关词语，从而简化全句结构。可能未简化的结构更符合多数中国学生的心理。

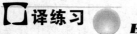

## 译练习 Enhancement Practice

第一项 Project 1
句子精练 Sentences in Focus

**A. Interpret the following sentences from English into Chinese.**

1. The company went about virtually reinventing the way it did business—with what seemed to be stunning results.
2. The drive for quality was often a production-oriented, mechanistic exercise that proved meaningless to customers.
3. Few organizations will prosper in today's environment without a focus on quality, continual improvement, and customer satisfaction.
4. Obsessed with meeting production schedules, the staff in that vacuum-equipment unit didn't return customer's phone calls, and the operation ended up losing market share.
5. Corporations across the globe have implemented quality improvement and satisfaction programs in an effort to reduce costs, retain customers, increase market share, and, last but not least, improve the bottom line.

## 第7单元 市场营销 Marketing and Sales

**B. Interpret the following sentences from Chinese into English.**

1. 保留顾客的能力建立在对他们需要的真切理解上。
2. 在成本、产品与品牌三种优势中,中国企业能尽快获得的最大优势还在于成本优势。
3. 中国的市场经济刚开始发展,中国的企业刚刚起步,而西方企业的品牌是经过几十年甚至上百年建立起来的。
4. 我们应该把成本优势与外国企业的品牌优势结合起来,而不应只凭豪言壮语跟人家竞争。
5. 但在消费品市场上,我们面临的都是普通消费者,注重对于品牌的选择,而品牌的建立又非一朝一夕之功。

第二项 Project 2
段落口译 Paragraph Interpreting

**A. Interpret the following paragraph from English into Chinese.**

Marketing research can be viewed as playing three functional roles: descriptive, diagnostic, and predictive. Its descriptive function includes gathering and presenting statements of fact. For example, what is the historic sales trend in the industry? What are consumers' attitudes toward a product and its advertising? The second role of research is the diagnostic function, wherein data or actions are explained. What was the impact on sales when changed the design on the package? The final role of research is the predictive function. How can the researcher use the descriptive and diagnostic research to predict the results of a planned marketing decision?

**B. Interpret the following paragraph from Chinese into English.**

市场研究在市场营销系统中有两个关键的作用。首先,它是市场营销信息反馈过程中的一部分。它为决策提供了关于现行营销组合有效性的数据,以及对于必要的策略改变的见解。市场研究也是在市场上探求新机遇的主要工具。细分市场研究和新产品研究帮助营销经理识别出最能赢利的机会。

第三项 Project 3
篇章口译 Passage Interpreting

**A. Listen to the tape and interpret the following passage from English into Chinese.**

In today's marketing world, a business is generally doomed to failure if it does not look at the product through the eyes of the consumer. Successful marketing starts with a product that is salable at a price that the right consumer would be willing to pay. Then, the marketer must get it to the marketplace where the consumer can buy it. The marketer must promote it, that is, advertise it to convince the consumer to buy it.

A great deal of work goes into the planning, development and implementation of an overall marketing program before any form of advertising can even be considered. For example, the marketer has to find the answers to many questions concerning the marketing mix:

Product: Is the product what the consumer wants? Does it satisfy his needs? Is it better than competitive products? Does it offer a competitive consumer benefit? Either real or emotional?

Price: Is the product competitively priced where the consumer is willing to pay for it?

Place: Is our product located in a place where it can be conveniently seen and purchased by the consumer?

Promotion: Is the competitive benefit of our product persuasively communicated to the right consumer?

As you can see, the promotion, in the form of the advertising, is only one part of the marketing program. It is important to note at this point that unless the product offers a competitive benefit at a price the consumer is willing to pay—and unless the product is in distribution—the greatest advertising plan ever devised will absolutely fail and fail absolutely. In fact, effective advertising will speed demise of an inadequate product. Effective advertising strategies can only come from effective marketing strategies. Good marketing is always the basis for good advertising.

Nowadays, the Integrated Marketing Communications (IMC) approach is becoming so popular among marketers. But why is the IMC approach welcomed by most marketers? The most fundamental reason is that marketers are recognizing the values of strategically integrating the various communication functions rather than having them operate autonomously.

## B. Listen to the tape and interpret the following passage from Chinese into English.

联想为什么成功呢？与宏基相比，联想的成功就在于利用了一开始中国人买电脑时关注成本与价格的特点。因为那时外国电脑都很贵，国人又都不富裕，所以喜欢买价廉的电脑。于是，联想就利用自身的成本优势和产品差异化优势，逐步占领亚洲市场，成为中国乃至亚洲最大的电脑制造商。当然，它能不能成为国际知名品牌还有待证明。而宏基电脑出口已经20多年了，至今仍在亏损，它是靠OEM来补贴的，可见做成一个品牌有多难。

海尔的国际化战略是走一条"先难后易"的道路，首先从最难进入的市场——美国、德国做起，在美国制造电冰箱，然后再向落后地区发展。美国是最发达的国家，最愿意为品牌付钱，但海尔在美国不具品牌优势，主要是靠经销商的品牌，因为经销商都是经过几十年锻炼出来的，消费者信得过。

如果靠人家的品牌，人家一讨价还价，我们的产品就要大打折扣。比如在美国生产的电冰箱放在沃尔玛卖，一台进价500元，顶多给海尔300元。如果海尔的产品成本足够低，也还能赚钱，逐步创立自己的品牌；但只要在美国生产，成本就不可能低于美国产品，可见它在相当长一段时间内是要亏损的。这就要靠在其他国家赚足够的钱或者通过其他融资渠道来弥补。

海尔能否成功，关键是看它的资金链条。如果融资链条能够支持10年，亏损10年补10

年,海尔就可能变成一个成功的国际品牌;如果无法支持这10年,就可能前功尽弃。

# 参考译文

## Reference Version

**篇章口译 A**

  女士们、先生们,早上好。今天我们要放眼全球的市场营销。众所周知,质量和顾客已经成为21世纪营销关键的竞争武器。在当今形势下,如果不重视质量、连续改进和满意顾客,没有企业能够兴旺发达。全世界的公司都实施了质量改进和顾客满意项目,试图降低成本,留住顾客,增加市场份额,以及最后具有同等重要性的一点,提高企业盈利程度。

  当全面质量管理遍及整个公司式的美国时,重点便严格地集中在产品的改进上。但是产品每个标准误差的改进并不能解决问题。看一下科学仪器生产商瓦里安联合公司的情况吧。该公司对1000名经理人员进行了为期4天的质量方面的培训。公司的硅谷总部充满了议论质量的喧闹。关于工作团队和工作循环次数的谈话取代了有关电子和X射线的讨论。瓦里安实际上在着手重新制定运作企业的方式,并带来了似乎令人惊讶的结果。一个制作真空吸尘器系统的生产单位把准时交货率从42%提高到了92%。半导体生产单位把推出新设计的时间缩短了14天。然而,仅仅制作高质量产品是不够的。在真空吸尘器设备生产班的雇员忙于满足生产期限的要求,所以没有回复顾客的电话,其结果是失去了市场份额。散热器修理部的人急急忙忙地工作,以达到最后期限的要求,他们没有时间向顾客解释他们的工作。负责质量的执行副总裁里查德认为:"所有关于质量的图表都在增加,但是其他的一切都在减少。"

  以前的追求质量的努力经常是一种以生产为导向的机械的活动,对顾客没有什么意义。而且这种对顾客毫无意义的质量在改善销售、利润和市场份额之后没有带来什么好处,它只是浪费了精力和财力。如今新的口头禅是"从质量中求收益"。这有两点含义:1)提供的质量是目标市场期望的质量;2)增加的质量必须对盈利能力有正面的影响力。例如,金融业巨头国民银行根据增加的赢利能力来衡量服务项目的改进,新增项目很多,从增加更多出纳到提供新的抵押贷款项目都有。

  使"从质量中求收益"发挥效用的关键是市场研究。正是这一机制使企业能够认定什么类型和什么形式的质量对目标市场是重要的。

  顾客的满意度和顾客的忠诚度是密不可分的。保持长期的关系不会是一种偶发现象,它以公司提供服务和价值为基础的。回头顾客的保持为企业带来了大效益。由于企业在弥补流失顾客方面(培养新顾客)花费较少的资金和精力,成本便降低了。向稳定的顾客提供服务比较容易,因为他们懂得双方妥协的方式,而且花费雇员较少的时间。顾客的回头率也推进了工作的满意度和自豪感,进而带来了更多雇员的保留。保留的雇员由于工作时间长而获得更多的知识,进而又可以提高生产率。贝恩咨询公司的一项研究评估认为,顾客流失率降低5%可以增加利润25%到95%。

  保留顾客的能力是建立在真切理解顾客所需的基础上。这种认识主要来自对市场的研究。例如,英国航空公司改造跨越大西洋的头等舱的服务便是以详细的市场研究为基础的。大多数航空公司都重视越洋航班头等舱的服务工作。然而英国航空公司的研究发现,大多数头等舱的乘客仅仅是想睡觉。于是英国航空公司为特等舱乘客提供了起飞前在地面贵宾休息室用餐的选择。一旦上了飞机,他们便可以套上英国航空公司的睡衣,躺在真正的枕头上,钻进毯子里,然后享受一次没有打扰的空中旅行。到达目的地时,头等舱乘客可以吃早餐,使用舒适的卫生间和淋浴室,甚至可以在开始工作前就有人把他们的衣服熨好。这些变化完全是由市场研究所推动的。

**篇章口译 B**

　　Today, we'd like to talk about the brand strategies. Among the three advantages, namely, cost, product and brand, the biggest advantage Chinese firms can quickly obtain is the cost advantage. Although our costs are on the rise, we still have some edge over foreign firms. The biggest disadvantage is brand recognition, which is an inherent problem.

　　The market economy in China is still a new phenomenon, so is market-oriented operation of Chinese firms. In contrast, western enterprises have established their brands over a period of several decades, even over a hundred years. It is generally more difficult to compete with foreign business on international consumer goods market than on capital goods market. This is because on capital goods market, buyers are all experts in their respective fields. Therefore, brand is not as important as cost. As long as low cost products are turned out, buyers would be interested. On the contrary, consumer good market faces the general public who are picky about brands, the same recognition of which takes time to build.

　　In the process of internationalization, Chinese firms should take into consideration the fact that our advantage is limited to cost. Therefore, we should combine our cost advantage with brand advantage of foreign counterparts' rather than competing solely on words.

　　As an example, China International Container Group Corp. succeeded in the acquisition of the international market whereas Xiali automobiles did not. The reason is very simple. There are altogether only over one hundred container customers worldwide, most of which are large transnational transportation companies. As long as quality complies with stipulations, low cost will open up the market. Of course timely delivery is needed, but it is much easier than building a new brand. However, producing automobiles is quite another story. It is still hard to succeed even with a cost 30% lower than our counterparts' because to sell cars abroad we have to face millions of ordinary consumers. They cannot have enough knowledge and means to examine if the cars are of decent quality. Therefore it is reasonable to forecast that China may emerge as the biggest auto-parts production base in the world. However, there appears to be little hope that China will be able to turn out a brand name automobile manufacturer in a short period of time.

# 第7单元 市场营销 Marketing and Sales

  This forecast can be borne out by the example of Glanz. Although Glanz has become the largest microwave production base in the world and its products is available all over the world, they still have to carry brands other than Glanz in order to sell.

  To build a world-famous brand, Chinese firms are faced with two choices: The first one is to begin with assembling parts for foreign manufactures. By doing so, foreign firms take advantage of their brand to make money while we accumulate funds. When we become big enough to have enough bargaining power, we may raise price and ultimately buy the brand.

  Another choice is that of Intel Corp. Intel produces computer chips, which can not be seen from outside the computer box. The strategy of Intel therefore is to require that all computers that carry Intel chips be properly labeled.

## 口译练习

### 第一项 句子精练

**A.**

1. 这家公司实际上在着手重新制定运作企业的方式,并带来了令人惊讶的结果。
2. 以前的追求质量的努力经常是一种以生产为导向的机械的活动,对顾客没有什么意义。
3. 在当今形势下,如果不重视产品质量,不重视不断改进,不重视顾客满意度,企业就不可能兴旺发达。
4. 由于只重视生产期限,生产真空吸尘器设备班的雇员没有回复顾客的电话,其结果是失去了市场份额。
5. 世界各地的公司都实施了质量改进工程和顾客满意度工程,以求降低成本,留住顾客,增加市场份额,以及最后具有同等重要性的一点,改善企业盈利。

**B.**

1. The ability to retain customers is based upon an intimate understanding of their needs.
2. Among the three advantages namely cost, product and brand, the biggest advantage Chinese firms can quickly obtain is the cost advantage.
3. The market economy in China is still a new phenomenon, so is market-oriented operation of Chinese firms. In contrast, western enterprises have established their brands over a period of several decades, even over a hundred years.
4. We should combine our cost advantage with brand advantage of foreign counterparts' rather than competing solely on words.
5. But in the consumer goods market, we face the general public who are picky about brands, the same recognition of which takes time to build.

### 第二项 段落口译

**A.**

  市场研究工作可视为三个功能,即描述、诊断和预见功能。描述功能包括收集数据、讲述事实。比如,要了解某个产品的历史销售呈现了何种趋势,了解消费者对于一个产品以及它的广告持何种态度。第二个作用是诊断功能,要对数据和行为进行解释。当我们改变包装设计,要了解对销售产生的影响。最后一个作用是预见功能,即研究者如何能使用描述研究和诊断研究来预见一个设计好的营销策略的结果。

**B.**
　　Marketing research plays two key roles in the marketing system. First, it is part of the marketing intelligence feedback process. It provides decision makers with data on the effectiveness of the current marketing mix and provides insights for necessary changes. Market research also is the primary tool for exploring new opportunities in the marketplace. Segmentation research and new product research help identify the most lucrative opportunities for marketing managers.

## 第三项 篇章口译

**A.**
　　在如今的营销世界中,如果一个企业不注重消费者眼中的产品,将会以失败告终。成功的营销首先应该有在某个价格水平上能够销售出去的、消费者愿意去购买的产品。然后,营销者要把此产品带到市场,让消费者能够购买。而且营销者需要做促销工作,即做广告,说服消费者购买这个产品。

　　在考虑做广告之前,需要有一个完整的营销计划,包括计划制定、展开和实施等步骤。比如,营销者首先要回答以下一系列有关营销组合的问题:

　　产品:此产品是否是消费者所需要的?它是否能够满足消费者的需求?与其他竞争对手相比,它是不是更具竞争力?能否向消费者提供具有竞争力的好处?是真的还是出于情感诉求?

　　价格:此产品的定价是否具有竞争力,从而有顾客愿意购买?

　　市场:我们的产品所在位置是否能够让消费者很容易看见从而进行购买?

　　促销:我们产品的好处是否极具说服力地向消费者进行了说明?

　　你可以清楚地看到,广告作为促销的手段,只是营销计划中的一部分。有一点很重要,那就是除非产品具有竞争力,定价适当,有特色,否则最好的广告也将以失败告终。事实上,有效的广告可以加速普通产品的买卖。只有有了好的营销策略,才会有好的广告策略。好的营销永远是好的广告的基础。

　　如今整合营销传播方式在营销中越来越受到欢迎。那么为什么他们会受到如此大的关注呢?最根本的原因就是营销者已经认识到把各种传播方式进行整合营销的价值所在,而不是任凭那些不同方式自主发挥效用。

**B.**
　　Why did Lenovo Group succeed? Unlike Acer Group, Lenovo took advantage of the consumption pattern of Chinese computer buyers at the beginning, namely, their focused attention on cost and price. Because at that time foreign-made computers were very

expensive while the income level of ordinary Chinese was low. As a result, they preferred to purchase inexpensive computers. Based on its cost advantage and product differentiation, Lenovo gradually took over the Asian market and became the largest computer manufacturer in China and Asia. However, it still needs to be proven whether it can become a world-famous brand. In contrast, Acer Group has been exporting computer for 20 years and is still in the red and being subsidized by OEM. It is apparent how difficult it is to build a brand.

Haier Corp follows an internationalization strategy that tackles the hard part first. It started by entering the markets which are the most difficult to gain access to—the United States and Germany. It manufactures refrigerators in the United States and spread to other less developed areas of the world. The United States is the most developed nation. Americans are willing to pay high prices for brand name products. However, Haier has no brand advantage. Therefore, it has to rely on the brands of distributors which are established over several decades through their hard work and consumer trust.

A negative effect of relying on foreign brand is the huge discount we have to provide in case of strong bargaining power on the part of foreigners. For example, Walmart may offer \$500 to an American-made refrigerator, but only \$300 to Haier. If the cost of production is low enough for Haier's products, it can still make money and gradually establish its own brand. However, the cost of Haier's products can not be lower than that of American-made products if they are produced in the United States. Therefore Haier will have to endure a long period of losses, which are to be financed by profits made elsewhere in the world and through other channels.

The key to Haier's chances of success is its financing chain. If its financing support can last 10 years and subsidize the losses during this period, Haier may become a world brand name. Otherwise, all its previous efforts will become fruitless.

# 第 8 单元 企业文化

## Unit 8 Corporate Culture

# 篇章口译

## Passage A (E-C)

### Vocabulary Work

Work on the following words and phrases and write the translated version in the space provided.

| | | | |
|---|---|---|---|
| corporate culture | EMBA | initiative | organizational chart |
| hierarchy | intangible | motto | value set |
| Hewlett-Packard | align | asset | cultivate |
| vision | elevate | self-esteem | stakeholder |
| embrace | instill in | knowledge-driven economy | marketable |
| gravitate to | | | |

### Text Interpreting

**Listen to the tape and interpret the following passage from English into Chinese.**

Ladies and Gentlemen,

　　Good morning! Today I'm going to talk about corporate culture, which is also an important part of your EMBA program.

　　Well, the concept of corporate culture is not new. We hear a lot about a company's culture, but what determines corporate culture? Corporate culture consists of the beliefs, values, initiatives, attitudes and behavior commonly shared by members of a corporate. Corporate culture is the sum of the formal and informal behaviors that a company adopts as their way of doing business. The formal side includes written statements of value such as respect for individuals, and a written organizational chart. The informal side deals with how work gets done, how employees treat one another, how willing they are to share ideas and information, and how the hierarchy allows employees to cross boundaries to get work done. Corporate culture is not intangible and abstract, but reveals substantially the company's goals, image and mottos.

　　It's true that every organization has its own unique culture or value set. Most organizations don't consciously try to create a certain culture. The culture of the organization is typically created unconsciously, based on the values of the top management or the founders of an organization. Firms with strong cultures achieve higher results because employees sustain focus both on what to do and how to do it. Hewlett-Packard is a company that has, for a long time, been conscious of its culture (The HP Way) and has worked hard to maintain it over the years. Hewlett-Packard's corporate culture is based on respect for others, a sense of community and plain hard work. It has been developed and maintained through extensive training of managers and employees. HP's growth and success over the years has been due in large part to its culture.

Nurturing a sound and healthy culture is the top concern of many companies. But, a healthy culture is the result of several aspects that are aligned toward common goals.

First, companies should focus on people and win people's heart. Staff is the most important asset of the company. The company's management should lay great emphasis on fairness and justness, cultivating a working mood of focusing on people and winning people's heart. You should build up a pleasant, healthy working environment in which people trust and respect each other. You should also make your employees feel the company is just another family in which they can find warmth, care, mutual support and inspiration. In return, employees will be motivated to perform duties diligently and face challenges positively and follow the company's institution and achieve targets.

Second, companies should create a grand and inspiring vision which elevates the energy, enthusiasm and self-esteem of everyone in the company while ensuring that everybody sees a benefit in following the vision. Corporate vision is a short and inspiring statement of what the organization intends to become and to achieve at some point in the future. It may contain commitment to creating an outstanding value for customers and other stakeholders, developing a great new product or service and developing a great company. For example, GE's vision is: We bring good things to life.

Third, companies should demonstrate their effective leadership. By embracing open communication and active listening, outstanding leaders instill in staff members a sense of ownership and pride in the business. Encouraging creativity and allowing employees to make some mistakes are strong contributors to job satisfaction, performance excellence and employee loyalty. Top management should be constantly amazed by how much people will do when they are not told what to do by management. Managing less is managing better. In the new knowledge-driven economy, people should make their own decision. And good leaders also focus on new ideas and innovation to adapt to rapidly changing economy and markets.

In today's strong economy, talented employees have more options, and are looking for opportunities to grow and enjoy their work. They expect to take some risks, and are more open to challenge. They are looking for education and experiences that will keep them marketable. A company is only as good as its employees. It is reasonable to expect good employees to gravitate to and stay with healthy organizations. Healthy cultures attract productive employees, and productive employees help build profitable companies. Therefore, how to build a healthy culture becomes the top priority of many business leaders.

So, I hope my talk has just given you a general picture of what corporate culture is, and you may conduct further discussions based on the current practice of your own company.

Thank you for listening.

# 篇章口译

## Passage B (C-E)

### 词汇预习 Vocabulary Work

Work on the following words and phrases and write the translated version in the space provided.

| 市场经济 | 企业业绩 | 体制陈旧 | 管理层次繁多 |
| 命令重重 | 稚嫩 | 美国通用电气公司 | 日本松下电器公司 |
| 长盛不衰 | 运作习惯 | 官僚 | 一体化 |
| 生产工序创新 | 家用品 | 海尔集团 | 勾画 |
| 全球战略 | 宝洁公司 | 战略问题 | 人文、诚信和服务 |

### 口译实践 Text Interpreting

Listen to the tape and interpret the following passage from Chinese into English.

女士们、先生们：

很高兴在这里谈谈中国的企业文化及其未来的发展。随着社会主义市场经济的不断发展，企业文化在中国企业中的作用越来越突出。确实，企业之间的竞争最终是文化的竞争。实践表明企业文化与企业业绩之间有着直接的联系。

中国的企业文化长期受到中国传统文化的影响。许多企业体制陈旧，管理层次繁多，指令重重。此外，由于中国市场经济运作时间不长，企业管理还处于不成熟阶段。因此，中国目前的企业文化状况还很稚嫩。

纵观世界成功的企业，如美国通用电气公司和日本松下电器公司，我们可以发现它们长盛不衰的原因主要有三个，即优质的产品、强大的销售和先进的企业文化。中国企业如果想在国际市场上与外国企业竞争，急需发展先进的企业文化。

对于大多数中国企业而言，发展健康的企业文化，首先要摆脱旧的观念、运作习惯以及官僚的束缚。随着世界经济的一体化和中国加入世贸组织后，中国企业应树立强大的市场观念，善于在市场变化中抓住机遇，并按国际惯例做事。

其次，中国企业还应该注重建立创新的文化，这是企业文化中很重要的部分，也是企业

# 第 8 单元　企业文化　Corporate Culture

生存和成功的关键。创新包括组织机构创新、战略创新、技术创新、生产工序创新、产品创新和市场创新。创建像中国家用品领军企业的海尔集团那样的优秀企业文化可以帮助中国企业勾画其全球战略。海尔集团视中国最富创新的公司,是企业文化创新的典范。海尔文化的核心是创新。海尔今天的成功很大程度上依赖于其不断发展的先进的企业文化。

还有,中国企业应该重视人才,并最大限度发挥个人的潜力。企业领导要不断鼓励员工的创造力和主动性,提高员工的自信心,并为员工提供一个良好的工作环境。素有"全球第一CEO"之称的杰克·韦尔奇说过:"人才是企业发展的关键因素。人是企业的主体,是企业的活力之源。"微软公司能够长久兴盛,在很大程度上依赖于其长远的人才战略。宝洁公司也把人才视为公司最宝贵的财富。因此,如何吸引、留住优秀人才已成为中国企业发展中必须重视的战略问题。

此外,人文、诚信和服务也是企业文化中重要的因素,应该受到中国企业的重视。

女士们、先生们,企业文化并不是一成不变的,它随着时代的变化而发展。中国企业要在全球经济中更具竞争力,必须抓住机遇,通过不断学习世界上优秀企业的先进文化来调整和发展自己的企业文化。

谢谢各位。

## 口译讲评

# *Notes on the Text*

**Passage A**

1. **corporate culture**:corporate culture 译成中文是"企业文化",很少说"公司文化"。此外,"企业文化"的英语表达还有 organizational culture、entrepreneurial culture 等。
2. **EMBA program**:EMBA 的英语全称是 Executive Master of Business Administration,即"高级管理人员工商管理硕士"。一般在中文里也采用 EMBA 这个说法,因此口译时无须将其译成对应的中文。
3. **The informal side deals with how work gets done, how employees treat one another, how willing they are to share ideas and information, and how the hierarchy allows employees to cross boundaries to get work done**:这个长句含有四个以 how 引导的排比句,口译时要注意四个句子内容的完整性。若四个排比句的次序颠倒,则无妨。此外,这里的 hierarchy 原意是指"等级森严的组织",在这里可根据讲话的背景直接口译成"公司"或"公司管理层"。一般来说,公司都有不同的管理层组成,存在着等级制度。口译时一定要能够快速推理意思。
4. **Hewlett-Packard**:广为人知的著名电脑公司,中文是"惠普公司"。口译时,尤其是商务方面的口译,译员经常会碰到许多公司的名称。有些是译员熟知的,有些则会超出译员的知识范围。英译中时,若不知道中文的名称,则可保留英语的说法。但中译英时,情况则会比较尴尬。因此,译员平时对一些大公司的中、英名称都要熟记。
5. **Second, companies should create a grand and inspiring vision which elevates the energy,**

enthusiasm and self-esteem of everyone in the company while ensuring that everybody sees a benefit in following the vision：这是一个较长的复合句。口译处理时，首先要在 which 前断句，同时还要抓住 while 这个表示状语从句的连接词。这样处理译员比较容易记忆和理解整句的意思。

6. **For example，GE's vision is：We bring good things to life**：这是一句广告词。一般来说，广告词都有现成的译文，而且用词到位，句子优美，但这对口译员来说是个巨大的挑战。当然，在不了解官方译文的情况下，译员可采取直译的方法。就这句广告词而言，如果不知道"我们让生活更美好"，而译成"我们给人们的生活带来好的产品"，这样直译，虽然句子不美，但意思是准确的。

7. **Top management should be constantly amazed by how much people will do when they are not told what to do by management**：这句话中的 when they are not told what to do by management 可采用"反话正译"的口译方法，将其灵活地译成"当员工自己主动完成任务时"。

8. **They are looking for education and experiences that will keep them marketable**：marketable 这里指"人"时应表示"具有竞争力"，而不是指商品"有销路的，畅销的"。口译时译员一定要机智、灵活。

## Passage B

1. **企业文化在中国企业中的作用越来越突出**：中文表达中经常出现"……的作用突出"口译时可灵活将这句译成 corporate culture is becoming increasingly important to Chinese enterprises。

2. **许多企业体制陈旧，管理层次繁多，命令重重**：这句中的"管理层次繁多"和"命令重重"口译成英语时，分别可用 many levels of management 和 chains of command（指挥链）。这样的搭配比较符合英语的说话习惯。如果用 levels of command，这样的搭配则会使英语显得不地道。

3. **因此，中国目前的企业文化状况还很稚嫩**：这里的"稚嫩"根据上下文应理解成"处于初期"，因此可译成 at its infant stage。

4. **我们可以发现其长盛不衰的原因主要有三个**：这里的"长盛不衰"是指"长期的成功"，因此，口译时可以相应地译成 success over the years / for a long time。口译的关键是准确理解原文，并用简洁明了、达意的目的语将其译出。

5. **其次，中国企业还应该注重建立创新的文化**：这里"创新的文化"是指"关于创新的文化"，应译成 a culture of innovation，而非 innovation of culture 或 culture innovation（文化创新）。口译时由于时间紧张，译员一定要辨清这两个概念，尤其是当它们同时出现在一个句子中时。

6. **创新包括组织机构创新、战略创新、技术创新、生产工序创新、产品创新和市场创新**：这句列举的内容较多，但记忆时若根据常识，即按产品从决策至最终投放市场的过程来记忆，则会比较有效。因此，口译时译员的常识可以说是举足轻重的。

7. **企业领导要不断鼓励员工的创造力和主动性，提高员工的自信心，并为员工提供一个良好的工作环境**：中文里对企业的管理者一般笼统地称呼"领导"，而英语中一般用 management。若是高层管理者，则用 top management。当然，这里也可以用 organizational leader。

8. **中国企业要在全球经济中更具竞争力，必须抓住机遇，通过不断学习世界上优秀企业的先进文化来调整和发展自己的企业文化**：这里的"更具竞争力"可相应地译成 gain more competitiveness 或 become more competitive。这里的"优秀企业"可相应口译成 companies with the best performance。

## 相关词语  Relevant Words and Expressions

顾客满意 customer satisfaction
奖励机制 reward system
人事政策 personnel policy
商业行为 business conduct
员工授权 employee empowerment
职位描述 job description
着装标准 dress code
弹性工作制 flexible work schedule
领导层管理 leadership management
授权给下属 to delegate authority to subordinates
团队领导层 team leadership
无边界组织 boundaryless organization
员工的士气 employee morale
带薪休假福利 paid time-off benefits
公司的行为准则 behavioral norms of an organization
充满活力的工作环境 dynamic work environment
高度阶层森严的公司 a highly hierarchical organization
领导、管理层的融合 leadership-management synergy
团队为主、平行结构的公司 team-based, flat lattice organization

## 口译技能

## Interpreting Skills

### 衔接（2）

一、总分关联

汉语中有不少总分关联结构，如"有两件事，一件是……，另一件是……"。笔译成英文时不必啰嗦地译成 There are two things: one is A and the other is B，只需译成 There are two things: A and B，也可译成 Things to do are: First, A; and second B。也就是说英译

文不必把前后两处的关联词都译出。但在口译中,如能采用啰嗦的形式,也即把前后的关联词都译出,可给听众提供更多的线索,使他们更容易跟上译员的思路。

例如:10年以后,有人认为全世界会有三大货币:欧元、美元,但是亚洲不知道会不会有日元还是人民币? Some people believe that there'll emerge three major currencies in the world, that is, one is Euro and another is the American dollar. And do you think there will be one major currency emerging in Asia?

如按笔译要求简练地译成...three major currencies in the world: the Euro and the American dollar...,信息密度增大,译员可能会感到缺少喘息、思考的时间,听众也容易感到疲劳。

## 二、实词衔接

在口译时应尽量避免使用语义不具体的关系代词 which、that 等来指代远处的词语,而应改用实词来与前面的词语衔接呼应,这样有利于听者轻松地听懂。

例如:(他们反对)美国克林顿政府现在奉行的对华全面接触政策.... the China policy pursued by the Clinton Administration of the United States, which is a policy of comprehensive engagement with China.

如仅说 which is comprehensive engagement with China,听者需要费点劲才能发现 which 指代前面的 policy。现此译员添加实词 a policy of,成为 which is a policy of comprehensive engagement with China,前后衔接十分清楚。如删除 which is,仅用同位语 a policy of comprehensive engagement with China 也可,因为实词 a policy 与前面的 the China policy 之间的呼应关系已足够清楚。

## 三、近距离衔接

在书面英语中,即使语义相关的词语被隔开一定距离,读者仍能通过前后寻找辨认出相关词语之间的关系。在口译中,听者不可能退回去重听一遍,所以译员应避免给听者制造额外的麻烦,尽量将语义相关的词汇安排在一起。例如,虽然我们在笔译时不应无故使用被动语态,但在口译中,有时使用被动语态有助于把语义相关的词汇(如动词与宾语)连接在一起,有助于减轻听者的心理负担。

例如:建设有中国特色社会主义的目标就一定能够实现。We are bound to make our objective of building socialism with Chinese characteristics a reality.

译员水平较高,把"实现"译成 make (our objective of building socialism with Chinese characteristics) a reality。但由于 make 与 a reality 之间插入了八个单词,译者必须将这八个单词储存在大脑中,增加了短时记忆的负担。学生可简单译成 we are bound to realize our objective of building socialism with Chinese characteristics。

TMD 是远远超出了有关国家多次表示过的所谓"正当自卫"的需要的。TMD will go far beyond their legitimate defense needs, which the relevant country has repeatedly indicated.

通常不应无故使用英语被动语态,所以 which the relevant country has repeatedly indicated 是正常语序。但在口译中由于 indicated 与前面的宾语 which 之间距离拉得较远,增加了听众的心理负担。这时如改用被动结构 which has been repeatedly indicated by the relevant country,所有语义相关的词汇都紧密相连,听众自然容易听懂。

# 第8单元 企业文化 Corporate Culture

## 翻译练习 Enhancement Practice

### 第一项 Project 1
#### 句子精练 Sentences in Focus

**A. Interpret the following sentences from English into Chinese.**

1. Finding the right corporate culture is very important to your employees' future. Their progress in an organization will depend a great deal on their compatibility with it.
2. Corporate culture has actually gained in importance because employers need to attract talented people and employees want to find increased meaning in their work.
3. The most progressive companies continually evaluate their fundamental styles to keep pace with changing times. Firms and companies must project an appealing corporate culture when competing to attract and keep top employees.
4. We work hard at maximizing individual potential, maintaining an emphasis on product quality, and cultivating an environment where creativity can flourish. A fundamental belief in our people and their abilities continues to be the key to our success.
5. When the staff follow the company's operation mode, values and work requirements, there will be unity, team spirit and consistency of decision and work outcomes. As a matter of fact, a first-class corporate depends on first-class institution, which depends on first-class corporate culture.

**B. Interpret the following sentences from Chinese into English.**

1. 我们公司创立了独特的文化，那就是将传统的中国文化与西方管理理念相结合。
2. 对中国公司而言，学会理解中西方文化的差异及懂得如何将两种不同文化有机地结合是成功的关键。
3. 我们以创新为主的企业文化将使我们公司成为世界顶级金融服务机构之一，并成为金融行业中的领先者。我们相信我们的创新能力将有助于我们在中国保持领先的地位。
4. "建立企业文化"是今天许多中国公司主管最为关心的问题之一。"令顾客满意"也是他们同样需要关注的问题。许多公司在努力实现发展与"令顾客满意"保持一致的企业文化。
5. 作为一个中国公司，我们的业务建立在团结、干劲、好学与创新之上。我们追求将创业精神与独特的职业精神相结合，以获得持久的成功。我们的员工追求正直、信任，并为取得最好的成绩而不断努力。

### 第二项 Project 2
#### 段落口译 Paragraph Interpreting

**A. Interpret the following paragraph from English into Chinese.**

Our company needs people who are creative, energetic and bright, absolutely passionate and committed to our mission of helping others realize their potential. These people share the values such as passion for customers, partners and technology, open and respectful with others and willingness to take on big challenges and committed to personal excellence and self-improvement. We also encourage and nurture lateral thinking. Our workers are given a high level of autonomy to offer innovative solutions. If this is important to you, it is highly likely you will enjoy the environment our company offers. A place where you can get things done and have fun at work.

**B. Interpret the following paragraph from Chinese into English.**

我们公司建立在强大的中国文化和传统的基础上，不断追求获得全方位的优秀业绩。我们的使命是为投资者带来稳定的回报，提高资产价值。我们公司的目标是为我们的客户提供最好的服务。对于公司的员工，我们致力于成为一个负责任的雇主，并为他们提供良好的工作环境和职业发展机会。对于我们的社会，我们致力于回报社会，并为我们国家的持续发展做出贡献。

第三项 Project 3
篇章口译 Passage Interpreting

**A. Listen to the tape and interpret the following passage from English into Chinese.**
Ladies and Gentlemen,

Good afternoon! Microsoft has an innovative corporate culture and a strong product development focus that is designed to keep us on the leading edge of the industry. We believe that our employees are the company's most important asset. They are the source of our creative ingenuity and success so we empower each staff member to take initiative in solving problems, coming up with new ideas and improving the organization.

Microsoft values diversity and respects each person's individuality. When you sell software to 180 million people, in 70 countries, speaking 150 languages, you can't afford to have a singular point of view. Microsoft employs people from many nationalities and backgrounds.

Now, I'd like to share with you more about the culture and values of Microsoft. As for the top management, the following are really the key to our success.

**Who we look for:** Microsoft concentrates on hiring people we believe fit into the company culture: people who are driven to succeed, enthusiastic about how they can contribute to the organization and unafraid of suggesting and implementing new ideas. Microsoft attracts creative people from all types of backgrounds, bringing together passion and new ideas to meet challenges and realize their potential. Our recruits are not always IT professionals; many come from backgrounds such as the banking, law or pharmaceutical industries.

**Diversity:** Microsoft has made a firm corporate commitment to the principle of diversity and respects each person's individuality. We have established a number of initiatives to promote diversity within our own organization, including education and training programs that provide employees with the awareness, skills, knowledge and ability to embrace differences. Microsoft employs a diverse workforce representing a broad range of cultural, linguistic, socio-economic and ethnic backgrounds including disabled employees and people from all corners of the globe.

**Community Spirit**: Amazing things can happen when the right people, tools and resources come together. Since 1983, Microsoft and our employees around the world have donated more than $100 million in cash, $100 million in software and thousands of volunteer hours in our communities around the world. Across our Asia, each Microsoft subsidiary has its own local initiatives for social giving and community outreach.

**Work & Life Balance**: Microsoft is firmly committed to creating a healthy, flexible, and productive work environment that allows employees to engage in a challenging career while balancing their work and life needs. At Microsoft, we aim to make the workplace as flexible as possible to enable our employees to have freedom, balance and autonomy.

**Women in IT**: Microsoft is proudly an equal opportunity employer of women and actively seeks to ensure our workforce embraces excellence in gender diversity. Annually, Microsoft supports and actively participates in the Global Women's Forum and across Asia our subsidiaries have internal networking and support groups for our female employees.

**Parents in Workforce**: Microsoft supports parents in the workforce by having flexible and convenient programs in place to ensure you can have balance between your family and your career. Microsoft enjoys a family friendly environment so it is not uncommon to see spouses and children dropping by for lunch onsite.

I'm sure you must have learned quite a bit from my speech about the philosophy of Microsoft.

Thank you.

**B. Listen to the tape and interpret the following passage from Chinese into English.**

尊敬的来宾们，女士们、先生们：

今天很荣幸有机会和大家交流一下3M中国有限公司的企业价值观。

3M中国有限公司1984年成立于上海。目前3M公司在中国建立了13家分公司、8个生产基地、20个办事处、3个技术中心，和一个研发中心，员工超过4800人。

3M中国长期致力于不断创新、开发新技术和新产品，做到让客户满意。公司尊重每一位员工的价值，并鼓励员工创新，为员工提供具有挑战性的工作环境及平等的发展机会。正如3M有限公司大中华区董事总经理所说，"成为使员工引以为荣的企业"是3M中国有限公司企业四大核心价值之一。因此，强大的企业文化是我们公司获得成功的关键。

3M中国公司能够有今天的业绩主要是因为致力于3M公司具有百年传统的创新文化。我们的企业价值观主要体现在以下方面：

首先，我们尊重客户。作为企业，我们必须聆听及了解顾客的需要，并以革新技术、卓越的品质、价值和服务满足我们顾客的需求。我们的使命是在所服务的市场中成为备受推崇的供应商。

其次,我们尊重员工的个人尊严和价值。我们公司除了给员工提供有市场竞争力的工资,还为员工提供基本技能训练,创造良好的工作环境。我们尊重和发展员工不同的才能、主动性和领导能力。在3M中国的大家庭中,员工获得晋升的机会很多,这对员工很有吸引力。

第三,我们尊重投资者。3M中国坚持持续发展,为股东提供可观的回报。并让投资者看到企业是否更具有发展前景。

第四,我们尊重社会和自然环境。追求最大利润一向都不是3M中国公司的主要动力或首要目标。我们在企业所在的地方,积极担负起公民的责任。我们积极参与向社会捐钱、赠送产品及保护环境的各项活动。

我坚信既然3M中国在努力建设强大的未来,那么我们还将继续保持我们独特的文化和价值观。

谢谢大家。

# 参考译文
## Reference Version

**篇章口译 A**

女士们、先生们:

上午好!今天我要讲讲企业文化,这也是你们EMBA课程中重要的一个部分。

企业文化这个概念很早就有了。关于企业文化我们也听到了许多,但什么是企业文化呢?企业文化是指公司成员共同拥有的信念、价值观、主动性、态度和行为。企业文化是指公司所采纳的指导商业运行的正式与非正式行为的总和。正式部分包括价值观的书面说明,如对个人的尊重以及书面的组织章程。非正式部分指工作如何完成,员工如何相处,如何愿意分享观点和信息,公司如何允许员工跨越界限完成工作。企业文化不是无形和抽象的,而是在很大程度上体现了公司的目标、形象和理念的文化。

诚然,每个公司都有自己独特的文化或价值体系。大部分公司并不是有意识地去创建某种文化。公司的文化通常是在高层管理者或创始人的价值观的基础上不知不觉被创立起来的。有着强大文化的公司能达到更高的目标,这是因为员工们长期思考该做什么以及如何去做。惠普公司是一个长期以来注重自己文化的公司(惠普特色),并一直努力保持自己的文化特色。惠普的企业文化是建立在对别人的尊重,有群体感和平凡、努力的工作之上。这种企业文化通过对管理者和员工的广泛培训得以发展和保持。惠普多年来的发展和成功很大程度上归功于它的文化。

培育合理、健康的企业文化是许多公司最为关心的问题。但是,健康的文化是几个方面朝着共同目标一起发展的结果。

首先,公司应该关注人,并且赢得人心。员工是公司最为宝贵的财富。公司管理层应非常重视合理和公正性,重视养成一种关注人、赢得人心的工作模式。公司应建立一个愉快、

# 第8单元 企业文化 Corporate Culture

健康的工作环境,在这个环境中员工相互信任、相互尊重。公司还应让员工感到公司是另外一个家庭,在这个家庭里员工可以得到温暖、关爱、相互支持和启发。作为回报,员工会努力、勤奋工作,勇敢面对挑战,并且遵守公司的制度,达到目标。

其次,公司应该建立一个宏大而又鼓舞人心的目标。这个目标能提高每位员工的干劲、热情和自尊,同时还要保证让每位员工看到实现目标带来的益处。公司的目标是一个简短而又鼓舞人心的口号,表明公司在未来某阶段将要达到的目标。公司的目标可以是致力于为顾客和其他股东创造杰出的价值,提供高质量的新产品和服务,以及创建一个优秀的公司。比如,GE公司的目标是:我们让生活更美好。

第三,公司应体现有效的领导。杰出的领导者通过公开交流和积极听取的方式,逐步让员工感到自己是公司的主人并为公司感到自豪。鼓励创造力和允许员工犯错大大有助于工作满意度、表现优秀和员工的忠诚。当员工自己主动完成任务时,高层管理应经常表示出惊喜。管理得越少,管理得越好。在新知识经济时代,人们应该自己做出决定。出色的领导还应关注新的想法和创新来适应快速变化的经济和市场。

在今天强大的经济时代,有才能的员工拥有更多的选择,并且他们不停地寻找机会发展、享受工作的乐趣。他们期望冒险,也更能面对挑战。他们希望有更好的教育和更多的经历使自己更具竞争力。有好的员工才会有好的公司。期望员工能被健康的公司吸引,并服务于它是理所当然的。因此,如何创建健康的企业文化是许多商业领袖首先要关注的。健康的文化能吸引高效的员工,同时高效的员工能使公司创利。

希望我的讲话能让大家对何为企业文化有了大概的了解,你们可以根据各自公司的运作情况作进一步的讨论。

谢谢。

## 篇章口译 B

Ladies and Gentlemen,

It's a great pleasure to talk about Chinese corporate culture and its future development. With the continuous development of socialist market economy, corporate culture is becoming increasingly important to Chinese enterprises. It's true that the competition among enterprises is ultimately the competition of culture. It's proved that there are strong links between organizational culture and organizational performance.

Chinese corporate culture has long been influenced by its traditional culture. Many enterprises are operated under the outdated institution, with many levels of management and chains of command. What's more, the operation of market economy in China is something which is only very recent and business management is still unsophisticated. Therefore, corporate culture in China is still at its infant stage.

Looking at the most successful companies in the world, such as American GE and Japanese Panasonic, we may find their success over the years is largely due to three factors, namely, quality products, powerful sales and advanced corporate culture. Chinese enterprises have been urged to develop advanced corporate culture if they want to compete with their foreign counterparts in the international market.

As for most Chinese enterprises, they should first get rid of old ideas, practice and bureaucracy while developing a healthy culture. With the integration of world economy and China's accession into the WTO, Chinese enterprises should cultivate a strong sense of market, seize the opportunities in the changing market and do business according to the international practice.

Second, Chinese enterprises should focus on creating a culture of innovation, which is an important part of corporate culture and the key to the company's survival and success. Innovation includes organizational innovation, technology innovation, strategy innovation, process innovation, product innovation and market innovation. Creating an excellent corporate culture like Haier Group, the leading Chinese home appliances maker, is the guideline for Chinese companies in mapping out their global strategy. Haier Group, the best innovative company in China, is a good example of innovation of organizational culture. The core of Haier corporate culture is innovation. The success of Haier largely depends on its ever-changing, advanced organizational culture.

Third, Chinese enterprises should pay more attention to talented people and maximize individual potential. Organizational leaders should constantly encourage their employee's creativity and initiatives, boost their confidence and create a better work environment for them. Jack Welch, who has been crowned as world No. 1 CEO, once said that talented people are the key to company's growth and they are the leading role in the company and the source of company's vitality. The success of Microsoft for a long time greatly depends on its long-term strategy focusing on talented people. P&G also sees its people as the asset of the company. So, how to attract and keep talented people has become the strategic issue which deserves great attention in the development of Chinese enterprises.

On top of that, humanity, credit and service are also key factors in corporate culture, which should not be overlooked by Chinese enterprises.

Ladies and Gentlemen, corporate culture does not remain unchanged; instead, it develops over time. Chinese enterprises must grab opportunities, readjust and develop their culture by keeping learning advanced culture of companies with the best performance in the world if they want to gain more competitiveness in the global economy.

Thank you.

**口译练习**

**第一项 句子精练**

**A.**

1. 找到合适的企业文化对员工的未来非常重要。员工在公司的发展很大程度上取决于他们是否适应该公司的文化。
2. 企业文化事实上已变得非常重要，因为雇主们需要吸引有才华的人才，并且员工也想使自己的工作不断变得有意义。
3. 最先进的公司不断评估他们公司的基本风格以便与时俱进。公司在竞争吸引和留住最好的员工时，必须制定吸引人的企业文化。
4. 我们努力充分发挥个人的潜力，强调产品的质量，培养一个让创造力能得到发展的环境。对我们员工及其能力的基本信心仍将是我们成功的关键。
5. 当员工遵循公司的运作模式、价值观和工作要求时，会出现团结、团队精神、决策的连贯性和工作成果。事实上，一流的公司依赖于一流的体制，这个体制依赖于一流的企业文化。

B.
1. Our company has created a unique corporate culture, which incorporates traditional Chinese culture with Western management ideals.
2. For Chinese companies, learning to understand the cultural differences between China and foreign countries and getting to know how to integrate two different cultures are the key to their success.
3. Our innovation-oriented corporate culture will make our company one of the world's top ranking financial services and a leader in the financial industry. We believe that our ability to innovate will help us maintain our leading position in China.
4. "Building the corporate culture" is among the top concerns of China executives today. An equally important concern is "meeting the needs of customers". Many companies are doing their best to achieve the goal of developing a corporate culture that is geared toward "meeting the needs of customers".
5. As a Chinese company, our business is based on unity, energy, learning and innovation. We seek to combine a pioneering spirit with distinctive professionalism to achieve lasting success. Our employees focus on integrity and trust and are continually striving for the highest achievements.

第二项 段落口译
A.
　　我们公司需要的员工是富有创意、充满活力、聪明热情的人员，并且能致力于我们旨在帮助他们实现潜力的使命。这些员工能分享我们公司的价值观，如对客户、合作伙伴及技术的热情；他们开朗、尊重别人，愿意接受严峻的挑战，致力于个人的优秀成绩和自我发展。我们也鼓励和培养横向思维的方式。我们的员工享有极高的自主权来提供创新的方案。如果这对于你来说是重要的，那你会在很大程度上喜欢我们公司所提供的工作环境。这里你可以做事成功，并且工作愉快。

B.
　　Our company is built on a strong foundation of Chinese culture and tradition, constantly seeking to achieve excellence in all aspects of its business. Our mission is to produce stable return and boost asset values for our investors. Our company aims to provide the best service for our customers. For employees, we are committed to becoming

a responsible employer and provide them with good working environment and career development opportunities. For society, our commitment centers on the company's pursuit of giving back to society and contributing to the sustainable development of our country.

第三项 篇章口译

**A.**

女士们、先生们：

下午好！微软公司有着创新的企业文化和强大的产品发展目标，这使得我们处于这个行业的前沿。我们深信我们的员工是公司最宝贵的财富。他们是我们创造发明和成功的源泉，所以我们授权每位员工积极主动地去解决问题、提供新的想法和改进我们的公司。

微软尊重多样性，尊重每个人的个性。当你将软件卖给1亿8000万人，他们分布在70个国家，说着150种不同语言，这时你不可能只拥有一种观点。微软雇用来自不同国家和背景的员工。

现在我想和大家谈谈更多有关微软的文化和价值观。对于高层管理而言，以下这些是我们成功的关键。

**寻找什么样的员工**：微软注重雇佣那些我们认为符合我们公司文化的人员：那些有动力去获取成功的人；那些热衷于如何为公司做出贡献的人；那些不怕提出建议并能贯彻新思想的人。微软吸引来自不同背景、富有创造力的人，他们将热情和新的想法结合在一起以迎接挑战，并挖掘自己的潜能。我们招聘的并不总是IT专业人员，许多人有着诸如银行、法律或制药业的背景。

**多样性**：微软坚定地致力于多样性的原则，尊重每个人的个性。我们建立了一系列措施来促进我们公司内部的多样性，包括教育和培训项目，这些项目为员工提供接纳不同文化所需的意识、技巧、知识和能力。微软雇用一支具有多样性的队伍，这支队伍代表着不同的文化、语言、社会、经济和种族背景，包括残疾人员以及来自地球每个角落的人员。

**社区精神**：当合适的人员、工具和资源聚合在一起时，惊奇的事会发生。1983年以来，微软和我们世界各地的员工已捐赠了1亿多美元的现金、价值1亿美元的软件以及在世界各地我们的社区里，作为自愿者服务了几千个小时。在亚洲，每个微软的子公司有自己回馈社会和帮助社区的活动。

**工作与生活之间的平衡**：微软坚定地致力于创建一个健康、灵活和高效的工作环境，这个环境使得员工在从事具有挑战的职业的同时，能保持工作与生活需求之间的平衡。在微软，我们的目标是尽可能将工作场所变得灵活，使员工享有自由，保持平衡，有自主权。

**IT行业中的女性**：微软骄傲地说自己是一个给女性员工提供平等机会的雇主，并且积极确保公司接纳不同性别的员工。每年，微软支持和积极参加《全球妇女论坛》，并且在全亚洲，我们的子公司有服务于女性员工的内部网络和后援团。

**工作场所中的父母**：微软支持在工作场所中的员工扮演父母的角色，向他们提供各种灵活、方便的服务，以保证他们保持工作与家庭之间的平衡。微软享有家庭友好的工作环境，所以在公司看到员工的配偶和孩子用午餐的现象也就不稀奇了。

我相信通过我的讲话，你们对微软的公司理念肯定有所了解了。

谢谢各位。

**B.**

Distinguished Guests, Ladies and Gentlemen,

It's my great honor to share with you the values of 3M China Ltd.

3M China Ltd. was established in Shanghai in 1984 and now it has thirteen subsidiaries, eight productions bases, twenty offices, three technology centers and one research and development center in China, with its employees of over 4,800.

3M China has long been committed to continuous innovation, developing new technology and products, and achieving customer satisfaction. 3M respects every person's value, encourages innovation and offers challenging work environment and equal opportunities for career development. As said by the Managing Director of 3M Ltd. Greater China, "Making 3M a company that its people are proud of is one of the four core values of 3M China". Therefore, a strong corporate culture is the key to our success.

3M China has become what it is today is because the company seeks to engage in 3M's century-old tradition of a culture of innovation. The following are our corporate values:

First, we respect our customers. As an enterprise, we must listen to our customers, get to know their needs and satisfy our customers with innovative technology, superior quality, value and service. Our mission is to become the most admirable supplier in the market where we serve.

Second, we respect the dignity and value of our employees. Our company provides for our people not only competitive salary, but basic skill training and better work environment as well. We also respect and develop every person's diverse talents, initiatives and leadership. In the big family of 3M China, employees have great opportunities for promotion, which is a magnet for our people.

Third, we respect our investors. 3M China seeks sustainable development and provides an attractive return for our shareholders. We also let our investors know if the company has great prospects for future development.

Fourth, we respect our social and physical environment. Working to maximize profits has never been the motive or prime concern of 3M China. In the areas where we have our business operation, we actively take on the responsibility as a citizen there. We are actively engaged in donating either money or products to the society, and environmental protection.

I believe as 3M China is working to build a strong future, we will continue to live our unique culture and values.

Thank you.

# 第 9 单元　保险业务

## Unit 9　Insurance Business

# 篇章口译

## Passage A (E-C)

### Vocabulary Work

Work on the following words and phrases and write the translated version in the space provided.

| | |
|---|---|
| pension | social stabilizer |
| retiree | sustainable retirement solution |
| formidable task | China Insurance Regulatory Commission |
| co-sponsor | insurer |
| municipal authority | annuities |
| expertise | occupational pension |
| backbone | tax incentive |
| pension solution tailored to its specific situation | |

### Text Interpreting

**Listen to the tape and interpret the following passage from English into Chinese.**

Excellencies, ladies and gentlemen,

It is a pleasure and an honor to represent my company ING at the International Pension and Insurance Forum in Dalian. It is a beautiful city, of which I am since yesterday proud to call myself an honorary citizen. Today, local and international experts will share their recommendations with us of pension reforms in China.

Pensions are a hot topic all over the globe. Chairman Wu referred to pension earlier as an essential social stabilizer. But social stabilization comes at a price. In many countries the population is aging very rapidly and as a result, a smaller and smaller group of workers will have to support a larger and larger group of retirees.

China also can't ignore this challenge. According to predictions by the United Nations, the current ratio of nine workers for one retiree will shift to a ratio of less than 3 workers for every retiree over the next forty years.

The Chinese government recognizes this challenge and is determined to seek sustainable retirement solutions for current and future generations. In this country with over 1 billion inhabitants and large regional differences in terms of demographics and economic development, that is a formidable task.

China is consciously seeking to include best practices from other countries in reforming its pension system. Our seminar today is a wonderful example of that approach.

The idea for this seminar was born in February of this year, when the Vice Mayor of Dalian, Mr Dai Yulin, visited ING in Amsterdam. The China Insurance Regulatory Commission greatly supported the idea and suggested that ING co-sponsor the seminar together with Tai Ping Life, a highly reputable Chinese insurer that had also made the suggestion.

I am pleased and proud that, thanks to the good cooperation of the Chinese central government, the government of the Liaoning Province, the Dalian municipal authorities, the China Insurance Regulatory Commission, Tai Ping Life and ING, we now have an excellent program with outstanding speakers from different countries and different organisations. I would like to thank each of our international speakers for their willingness to travel to Dalian and to share their expertise with us today.

Excellencies, ladies and gentlemen, I believe that each country needs pension solutions tailored to its specific situation. But, countries can learn from each other and introduce approaches that have been successful in other markets for the benefit of reforming their own systems. I hope and trust that today's program, which brings together so much expertise, will provide useful directions for China's future in this area.

In my home country, the Netherlands, occupational pensions are the backbone of the pension system. I will review that system in the presentation later today. In many countries, we see a gradual shift from state pensions to occupational and private pensions. I believe that increasing the size and scope of company and personal pensions will also be vital to reinforce the pension system of this country. The government can stimulate this development through tax incentives and the insurance industry can play a crucial role by offering products such corporate annuities and individual pension plans.

The success of pension reforms depends first and foremost on the commitment and cooperation of all stakeholders, all the parties involved. Here in this area, we really need to work together. My company ING is ready to contribute its global expertise and experience, and we are proud to sponsor the seminar. I wish you a fruitful and inspiring conference.

**Thank you!**

# 篇章口译

## Passage B (C-E)

### Vocabulary Work

Work on the following words and phrases and write the translated version in the space provided.

| | | | |
|---|---|---|---|
| 保险业 | 有划时代意义的 | 保险业务 | 品牌建设 |
| 保费 | 投资型保险产品 | 分红 | 股东 |
| 商险、责任险事业部 | 车险管理 | 理赔 | 考核体系 |
| 制度文化 | 责任文化 | 绩效文化 | |

### Text Interpreting

Listen to the tape and interpret the following passage from Chinese into English.

各位同仁，各位嘉宾，大家好：

今年，对于中国保险业来说是极不寻常的一年。国务院颁布了《关于保险业改革发展的若干意见》。这一具有划时代意义的纲领性文件，将在今后很长一个时期对中国保险业的改革与发展产生巨大而深远的影响，标志着中国保险业迎来了新的发展的春天。

今年是华泰的丰收年。公司保险业务实现了健康较快的发展，投资业务创下了历史最好成绩，品牌建设也迈上了一个新台阶。全年公司直接保费收入14.78亿元，同比增长25.58%，投资型保险产品规模达到了66.56亿元。公司实现投资收益3.03亿元，创下历史最好水平。华泰成为了国内唯一一家自成立以来连续10年实现盈利和分红的保险公司。这不仅是华泰人的骄傲，也是对华泰股东的忠诚回报。与此同时，华泰"规范管理、稳健经营、创新发展"的品质已经得到监管部门和社会公众的广泛认可和赞誉。今年，公司相继被评为"中国优秀企业公民"、"世界市场中国（保险）十大年度品牌"、"中国保险市场十强诚信品牌"。

今年是华泰的改革年。销售费用管理改革对于规范经营行为和提高销售能力都具有重大意义；组建商险、责任险事业部，成立车险管理部以及理赔集中管理等，有效地提高了华泰集约化、专业化和精细化管理水平；建立新的薪酬激励机制，也将为华泰加快发展提供强劲的动力。

今年也是华泰的创新年。面对日趋激烈的市场竞争，我们坚定不移地实施"蓝海战略"，在全力推动管理创新的同时，积极推动产品和服务创新。"华泰一号"的成功再一次展示了华泰在投资型产品方面的持续创新能力。一批技术含量高、市场前景广、得到政策鼓励的险种产品相继推出。客服中心的建立、社区门店试点等，是服务创新的新举措，将有力地推动个险业务健康快速发展。

明年是华泰的执行年和开拓年。面对新形势和新任务，公司正式启动和实施长期激励计划，并建立新的经营目标考核体系。公司文化也由以往的"制度文化"和"责任文化"步入"绩效文化"阶段。我们要发扬二次创业的精神，励精图治，奋发有为，用勤劳和智慧开拓华泰的"蓝海"，全力完成今年的预算目标，力争提前实现"三年翻一番、五年翻两番"的发展目标。

明年，让我们再次出发。

# 口译讲评

## Notes on the Text

**Passage A**

1. **Social stabilization comes at a price**：社会稳定是需要付出代价的。这篇讲话的主题是养老金，所以这句译为"社会稳定是需要花钱的"更切合题意。

2. **the population is aging very rapidly**：population aging 为"人口老龄化"之意。人口老龄化给我国的经济发展、人口、资源、环境和社会保障等方面提出了严峻的挑战，保险业是解决这一问题的途径之一。

3. **the current ratio of nine workers for one retiree will shift to a ratio of less than 3 workers for every retiree over the next forty years**：目前劳动人口与退休人口9∶1的比例将在40年后变为3∶1。Nine for one, three for one, 是表示比例的方法。

4. **China is consciously seeking to include best practices from other countries in reforming its pension system**：此句中，consciously 译为"有意识地"不如"积极地"更准确。中国正积极探索如何博采他国之长，推进本国养老体系改革。

5. **China Insurance Regulatory Commission**：中国保险监督管理委员会，简称中国保监会。是国务院直属事业单位。根据国务院授权履行行政管理职能，依照法律、法规统一监督管理全国保险市场，维护保险业的合法、稳健运行。

6. **pension solutions tailored to its specific situation**：tailor 为"度身定做"之意，这里指"依据本国的实际情况建立的养老金体制"。

7. **occupational pensions are the backbone of the pension system**：目前，很多发达国家的养老金都由三部分组成：基础的国家养老金（state pension）、补充的集体养老金（occupational pension）和额外的个人养老金（private pension），我国也正向此方向发展。

8. **stakeholders**：这里指"利益相关者"，这里无需译出，"各方面的承诺和合作"就已含有此意。

**Passage B**

1. **《关于……若干意见》**：有几种译法：Guidelines on... 或 (Guiding) Principles on...

2. **中国保险业迎来了新的发展的春天 / 进入了发展的黄金时期**：都可以表达为 come into /

enter a new prime of development。

3. 今年是华泰的丰收年：丰收可以用 rewarding、fruitful、productive 等表示。
4. ...3.03亿元，创下历史最好水平：with a record investment income of RMB ￥303 million。例如，儿童癌症慈善机构今年的收入创下了历史最高水平：Children's cancer charity enjoys record income this year.
5. 连续10年：ten consecutive years。
6. 规范管理、稳健经营、创新发展：为了追求表达效果，最好采取排比的手法，所以需要适当地进行词性转换，可译为 professional management, steady operation, and innovative development。
7. 得到广泛认可和赞誉：gain extensive awareness and high praise。
8. 中国保险市场十强诚信品牌：Top Ten Reliable Brands in China's Insurance Market。"十大品牌"、"十佳产品"、"十首上榜歌曲"等都可以用 top ten 来表示。
9. 一批技术含量高、市场前景广、得到政策鼓励的险种产品相继推出：Huatai also extended its product portfolio by introducing products with high technological components, large market potentials and strong government support. 这里采用了定语后置的方法，符合英文的表达习惯，也进行了词性转换，使译文更简单，符合口译的表达习惯。product portfolio 是 a range of products 之意。

# 相关词语 Relevant Words and Expressions

保单 policy
保费 premium
续保 renew coverage
保险费 insurance expense; premium
财产险 property insurance
投保人 insurance applicant; insurant; the insured
保险范围 insurance coverage; risks covered
保险索赔 insurance claim
保险佣金 insurance commission
疾病保险 sickness insurance
健康保险 health insurance
人寿保险 life insurance
社会保险 social insurance
有效保单 in-force policy
运输保险 transportation insurance
保险经纪人 insurance broker
保险中介人 insurance intermediary
航空运输保险 insurance against air risk; air transportation insurance

陆上运输保险 overland transportation insurance; land transit insurance
保险商;保险承运人 underwriter

# 口译技能
## Interpreting Skills

### 司仪口译

　　大会司仪口译主要是在各种外交、商务以及政务场合与大会司仪配合进行双语主持或自己独立用双语主持。口译的主要任务是担任领导人出访或外国领导人来访时双方或多方谈判、会谈、交谈时的现场翻译,在各种场合的演讲、讲话或参观访问时的介绍等即席口译。

　　司仪口译的内容决定了它具有别于其他领域口译的特点:首先,在译政治性和政策性较强的内容时,由于内容大多是有关国家的立场和政策等,所以稍有差错就可能影响到一个国家的政治、经济利益、形象、声誉、地位及其国际关系,就可能给国家和人民造成无可挽回的损失。由于口译工作的时效性,工作时间紧,所以译员不但要充分做好准备工作,更要具有相应的素质。

　　要成为一个合格的司仪口译,必须具有一些特别的素质。首先就是听能力。只有听明白了原话,才能进行翻译。因此,译员是否具有敏锐的听觉是极其重要的。译员有好的听力,还需要有良好的收听条件。做司仪口译往往站在领导人或主持人的后边或旁边,这样的位置有利于译员听清楚。但译员有时不得不在各种环境里进行翻译。如在大型记者招待会上,译员需要听明白记者从远距离提出的问题。有时要在人声嘈杂的地方进行翻译,就会影响收听效果。对于这些影响收听的因素,译员在大多数情况下是无能为力的。为了确保较好地完成口译任务,译员应该提前到场,做好准备工作。重要的是平时从主观上采取有针对性的措施,提高自己的听力。例如要多听带各种口音的人讲英语的录音带,总结规律、熟悉口音。扩大知识面、熟悉情况和所谈问题,帮助我们根据所听的大概的声音进行"合理"的猜测(intelligent guess),以求正确理解原话。

　　在司仪口译中,讲话者每讲几句话或一段话就会停下来,让译员进行翻译。现场翻译时间紧,不给翻译斟酌的时间,这就要求翻译反应快、语言水平高、语言转换能力强。在大多数外交场合,特别是中外领导人在讨论双边关系和交换对国际形势、国际问题的看法时,他们的谈话内容往往政策性很强,有时十分敏感。在这种场合,翻译必须准确无误、完整无漏,从政策高度把握分寸。

　　司仪口译的形象也很重要,所谓形象,除了译员的相貌特征,也指综合意义的整体形象,是一个译员在具体场合中的思想感情、言谈举止给大会听众的整体印象,这种大众传播角色,既要代表特定的政治、经济利益,又要满足听众的需要。

　　司仪口译还须注意语气和语调。语气是在具体思想感情支配下语句的声音形式,又都来源于对场合内容的精心分析和具体感受,不同的内容应有不同的语气。用不同的语气表达不同的思想感情。语调表现为要根据具体的内容,将文字转化为语言的艺术再创造。在口译之前，应该对当时的主题内容，有全面深刻的了解，掌握一些最鲜活、最有价值的信息，以便不时之需。

不同的场合要求译员除了具备良好的思想素质、敬业精神、语言能力等共性素质之外，还在知识结构、专业能力、性格特征等方面对译员提出了相应的要求，要求译员具有自己的表达风格。在司仪口译中，译员对现场气氛的变化应保持高度的敏感，以便用适当的方法进行调整，并在口译过程中时刻把握分寸，从而保证最终的成功。

为了应对因受到某种因素干扰而被打断的情况，应该事先对整个大会议程的安排有一个明确的了解。译员要及时调整自己的表达方式，以语言、表情或其他姿势来强化自己的节奏感，做到自然得体。总之，司仪口译是连接大会与听众之间的桥梁。只有注重信息的准确传达和气氛的把握，才会使大会取得最终的成功。

# 译练习 Enhancement Practice

第一项 Project 1
句子精练 Sentences in Focus

**A. Interpret the following sentences from English into Chinese.**

1. The underwriters are responsible for the claim as far as it is within the scope of cover.
2. The extent of insurance is stipulated in the basic policy form and in the various risk clauses.
3. We can serve you with a broad range of coverage against all kinks of risks for sea transport.
4. Health insurance is merely a means by which people pool money to guard against the sudden economic consequences of sickness or injury.
5. Generally speaking, aviation insurance is much cheaper than marine insurance.

**B. Interpret the following sentences from Chinese into English.**

1. 保险费用按照货物类别的具体情况而有所不同。
2. 这个问讯处为顾客提供大量关于货物投保方面的信息。
3. 我们已经将这些货物按发票金额加10％投保综合险。
4. 我想知道基本健康保险所列的项目是否应包括医院门诊、住院、手术及药品等费用的赔偿。
5. 我们所收取的费率是很有限的，当然，保险费用要根据投保范围的大小而有所不同。

第二项 Project 2
段落口译 Paragraph Interpreting

**A. Interpret the following paragraph from English into Chinese.**

　　AIG Global Pensions, with operations in more than 40 countries and jurisdictions, has over 50 years' experience in pension management for multi-national enterprises. AIG

Global Pensions has provided professional consultancy services on pension reforms for countries and jurisdictions such as Mainland China, Hong Kong, India, Thailand, Mexico and Romania, etc., and for international organizations like World Bank, Council of Foreign Relations and USAID etc. AIA, with decades of experience in global pensions management, possesses sophisticated technology and teams of dedicated professionals. In Hong Kong, AIA has been serving the pension market for more than 30 years.

**B. Interpret the following paragraph from Chinese into English.**

目前，公司拥有约18.5万名寿险营销员，约18.4万名从事人寿及财产保险产品销售和市场营销活动的员工，各级分支机构及营销服务部5000余个，拥有比较完善的销售和服务网络，为各地的个人和公司客户提供包括人身险和财产险在内的全方位风险保障解决方案、投资理财和资产管理服务。

第三项 Project 3
篇章口译 Passage Interpreting

**A. Listen to the tape and interpret the following passage from English into Chinese.**
Ladies and Gentlemen,

May I introduce you our Corporation—American International Group, Inc. (AIG). It's a world leader in insurance and financial services, a leading international insurance organization with operations in more than 130 countries and jurisdictions. AIG companies serve commercial, institutional and individual customers through the most extensive worldwide property-casualty and life insurance networks of any insurer. In the United States, AIG companies are the largest underwriters of commercial and industrial insurance and AIG American General is a top-ranked life insurer. In addition, AIG companies are leading providers of retirement services, financial services and asset management around the world. AIG financial service businesses include aircraft leasing, financial products, trading and market making. AIG growing global consumer finance business is led in the United States by American General Finance. AIG also has one of the largest US retirement service businesses through AIG SunAmerica and AIG VALIC, and is a leader in asset management for the individual and institutional markets, with specialized investment management capabilities in equities, fixed income, alternative investments and real estate. AIG's common stock is listed in the US on the New York Stock Exchange and ArcaEx, as well as the stock exchanges in London, Paris, Switzerland and Tokyo.

American International Assurance Company, Limited (AIA) is a wholly-owned subsidiary of American International Group, Inc. As a multinational whose original roots can be traced back over decades to China, AIA has always valued its strong ties with the country. The first foreign-funded insurance company allowed to operate in China after the country was opened up to the outside world, AIA has always focused on making contributions to China and the Chinese in terms of education, medical and health service, etc.

In cooperation with four well-known universities—Fudan University, Zhongshan University, University of Science and Technology of China and Peking University—AIA has established four Actuarial Centers to provide training for students taking professional examinations of the US Society of Actuaries. The Centers have helped produce internationally recognized actuarial professionals, and accelerated the development of the life insurance industry in China.

AIA Shanghai and Shenzhen, active participants in voluntary blood donations, have also contributed RMB ¥1.05 million to equip Shanghai and Shenzhen with bloodmobiles. AIA was granted a "Voluntary Blood Donation Promotion Award" by the Ministry of Health, The Red Cross China and the Health Department of The General Logistics of the People's Liberation Army.

When the country was fighting the SARS epidemic, AIA branches and sub-branches nationwide launched special green passages for SARS claims, and made donations in support of front-line medical workers.

This is the AIG we know with all your dependence and trust in it.

Thank you!

**B. Listen to the tape and interpret the following passage from Chinese into English.**
女士们、先生们：

上午好！

正如大家所知,中国保险品牌精英高峰论坛是由中国保险品牌精英俱乐部(IBEC)发起主办的全国性大型行业会议。IBEC是一个为中国保险业的健康发展助力加油的非赢利性组织,它以"打造保险品牌,倡导诚信行风"为宗旨,以"品质服务,诚信天下"为理念,以健康(Health)、诚信(Honest)、高品质(High Quality)的"3H"为基本原则。

中国保险品牌精英俱乐部高峰论坛的前身是中国保险营销管理精英大会,从去年至今已连续举办了三届。

首届中国保险营销精英大会在南京召开。江苏省保险行业协会的领导以及多家保险公司参加了这次大会。国内著名经济学家茅于轼作了题为《21世纪中国经济发展》的报告,精辟分析了新世纪中国经济的发展趋势,以及中国经济形势对保险行业的影响。

第二届大会在山水甲天下的桂林举行。国内12家保险公司1200多人参加了会议,桂林市副市长潘建民为大会作欢迎词,国务院特派稽查员、中国四大著名演讲家之一的刘吉到会作了精彩演讲。

第三届大会在国内风景名胜区黄山隆重召开。黄山市委书记黄启敏为大会致欢迎词。本次大会特别邀请了环球小姐张萌到会主持。在闭幕式上,大会组委会向黄山市捐赠了3万元资助贫困学生上大学,在当地引起了强烈反响。

为纪念中国保险200周年,第四届大会与中国保险学会合作在广州举办。

宏大的场面,千人参加的大会,实战实用的专业培训,各地保险精英零距离共商保险大计,这就是历届精英大会的真实写照。欢迎您的加入,我们将为您提供机会！

# 参考译文

## Reference Version

**篇章口译 A**

各位嘉宾、女士们、先生们：

非常荣幸能够代表我们 ING 来到大连参加此次国际企业退休金与保险发展论坛。大连是一座美丽的城市，我昨天骄傲地成为了这座市的荣誉市民。今天，中外专家将与我们分享他们对中国养老金改革的一些建议。

目前，养老金是全球热点话题。吴主席曾指出，养老金就是整个社会基础性的稳定器。但这个稳定器是需要花钱的。在很多国家，人口老龄化的速度非常快，造成日趋减少的劳动人口不得不供养越来越多的退休人群的局面。

中国同样无法回避这一挑战。按照联合国的预测，目前劳动人口与退休人口9∶1的比例将在40年后变为3∶1。

中国政府已经意识到这个问题，并开始着手为当代和子孙后代建立坚实稳固的退休和养老机制。对于中国这样拥有 10 多亿人口，且各地人口和经济发展存在巨大差异的国家来说，这是一项艰巨的任务。

中国正积极探索如何博采他国之长，推进本国养老体系改革。我们今天这个研讨会就是这种探索的一个绝佳的例子。

召开这样一个研讨会的设想最初产生于今年2月份大连市副市长戴玉林先生在阿姆斯特丹访问 ING 期间。中国保监会非常支持这一想法，并建议 ING 与另外一家也曾提出类似建议的知名机构"太平养老"共同承办。

我非常高兴和自豪，通过政府的支持，以及中国保监会、辽宁省政府、大连市政府、太平人寿和 ING 的合作，我们今天召开了这样一个有来自不同国家和组织的多位杰出专家出席的、高级别的国际性研讨会。在此，我要特别感谢各位演讲嘉宾专程来到大连，与我们共享他们的专业经验。

各位嘉宾，女士们、先生们，我相信，每个国家都需要依据本国的实际情况建立各自的养老金体制。但各国可以相互学习，通过借鉴他国的成功经验来进一步促进本国养老金的改革。我希望并相信，通过本次论坛，通过汇集这么多专家的智慧，将为中国在这个领域的发展提供有益的帮助。

在我的祖国荷兰，企业年金是养老金体制的支柱。在后面的演讲中我将介绍这一内容。在很多国家，国家养老金正逐步转变为企业年金和私人养老金。我相信企业年金和私人养老金的不断壮大将对增强养老金体系产生积极的意义。政府可以通过税务优惠政策促进年金事业发展，保险业也可以通过提供企业年金和私人养老金计划在年金市场发挥重要作用。

养老金改革的最根本也是最重要基础是各有关方面的承诺和合作。因此，我们要通力协作。ING 愿意提供这方面的专业知识和全球经验。能够有机会赞助此次论坛，我们感到非常自豪。预祝大会圆满成功！

谢谢！

## 篇章口译 B

Dear colleagues and guests,

Good evening!

This year was a very special year for the insurance industry of China. In this year, the State Council issued "Guidelines on Reform and Development of Insurance Industry". This epoch-making programmatic document will exert an enormous influence on the insurance industry of China in a long run. It indicates that China's insurance industry has entered a new prime of development.

This year was a very rewarding year for Huatai. The Company's insurance business achieved a healthy and fast development, its investment income reached the historically high, and the branding construction work also had outstanding achievement. The Company's direct premium income increased by 25.58% compared to the prior year to RMB ¥1.478 billion, and the balance of investment-type insurance products increased to RMB ¥6.656 billion. The Company had a best-ever investment performance since it was founded, with a record investment income of RMB ¥303 million. Huatai became the only insurance company in China which managed to have profit and dividend distribution for ten consecutive years since its establishment. This extraordinary achievement is a pride for Huatai, and also brings exceptional returns to our shareholders. Meanwhile, Huatai's business philosophy of "professional management, steady operation, and innovative development" has gained extensive awareness in the market and high praise from regulators and the public. This year the Company was awarded as the "Excellent Enterprise of China", "Annual Top Ten Brands (Insurance) of China in the World Market" and "Top Ten Reliable Brands in China's Insurance Market".

This year was a reforming year for Huatai. The reform of marketing expense management has historical significance in enhancing the Company's transparency and sales capability. The establishment of Commercial Line Unit, Casualty Unit, Automobile Business Unit, and the centralization of claims service will effectively improve the Company's management to a more intensive, professional and elaborate level. The new performance-based compensation appraisal program also provided momentum to the future development of Huatai.

This year was also an innovative year for Huatai. Facing ever-fierce market competition, the Company has been firmly implementing the "Blue Ocean Strategy" by promoting initiatives in its management, product and service. The success of "Huatai No. 1" once again demonstrated the innovation strength of Huatai in investment-type products. Huatai also extended its product portfolio by introducing products with high technological components, large market potentials and strong government support. As for customer service, there are initiatives to promote the growth of personal lines business, such as setup of customer service centers and service shops inside residential communities.

The next year is an execution and exploration year for Huatai. With our new mission under the new market conditions, the Company officially launched its long-term incentive plan and established its new performance appraisal mechanism. Our corporate culture is turning into a new stage of "performance-oriented culture" from previous "discipline-oriented culture" and "responsibility-oriented culture". We will continue our entrepreneurial spirit, work arduously and collaboratively to implement our "Blue Ocean Strategy". We are dedicated to achieve this year's business plan and try to realize ahead of our plan the goal of "doubling production in three years and quadrupling in five years".

Let us start our new march towards the future next year.

## 口译练习
### 第一项 句子精练
**A.**
1. 只要是在保险责任范围内,保险公司就应负责赔偿。
2. 保险的范围写在基本保险单和各种险别的条款里。
3. 我公司可以承保海洋运输的所有险别。
4. 健康保险就是筹集一些钱以预防疾病或受伤而突然发生的经济困难。
5. 通常空运保险要比海运保险便宜。

**B.**
1. The cover paid for will vary according to the type of goods and the circumstances.
2. This information office provides clients with information on cargo insurance.
3. We've covered insurance on these goods for 10% above the invoice value against all risks.
4. I'd like to know whether basic health insurance coverage should include benefits for outpatient, hospital, surgery and medical expenses.
5. The rates quoted by us are very moderate. Of course, the premium varies with the range of insurance.

### 第二项 段落口译
**A.**
　　美国国际集团的环球退休金服务机构遍布全球40多个国家,拥有50多年为跨国企业服务的丰富经验。其间,曾为多个国家或地区政府提供改革退休金制度的咨询服务,如中国、中国香港、印度、泰国、墨西哥、罗马尼亚等政府,以及世界银行、美国对外关系委员会、美国国际发展署(USAID)等机构。友邦保险在海外已经有几十年管理退休金的经验,拥有先进的管理技术和一流的专业团队。在中国香港,友邦保险已在退休金管理市场服务了30多年。

**B.**
　　We have approximately 185,000 insurance agents for our individual life insurance

products and approximately 18,400 employees engaged in direct sales and marketing activities for life and property insurance products. It has over 5,000 branches and marketing outlets and nationwide sales and service network, providing individual and institutional clients with a wide range of risk prevention solutions, financial advices and asset management.

**第三项 篇章口译**

**A.**

女士们、先生们：

请允许我为您介绍美国国际集团（AIG）。它是世界保险和金融服务的领导者，也是全球首屈一指的国际性保险服务机构，业务遍及全球130多个国家及地区，其成员公司通过世界保险业最为庞大的财产保险及人寿保险服务网络，竭诚为各商业、机构和个人客户提供服务。美国国际集团成员公司是美国最大的工商保险机构，旗下的AIG American General更是全美顶尖的人寿保险机构。美国国际集团在全球各地的退休金管理服务、金融服务及资产管理业务也位居世界前列。其金融服务业务包括飞机租赁、金融产品及促进其市场交易。美国国际集团不断发展的全球消费者信贷业务主要由美国的American General Finance管理。同时，通过旗下的AIG SunAmerica及AIG VALIC，集团现已成为全美首屈一指的退休金管理服务机构之一。美国国际集团亦是个人和大型企业投资管理市场中的翘楚，为客户提供专业的股票、定息证券、地产及其他投资管理服务。美国国际集团的股票在纽约证券交易所、美国ArcaEx电子证券交易市场、伦敦、巴黎、瑞士及东京的股票市场均有上市。

美国友邦保险有限公司（简称"友邦保险"或"AIA"）是美国国际集团的全资附属公司。作为一家起源于中国，与中国有着数十载渊源的跨国公司，以及改革开放后第一家获准在中国开展业务的外资保险公司，友邦保险积极承担社会责任，为当地社会的教育、医疗事业的发展贡献力量。

友邦保险先后与复旦大学、中山大学、中国科技大学及北京大学等四所国内著名高校共同成立了四所精算中心，旨在帮助中国学生参加北美精算协会的专业考试，培养国际上认可的精算人才，促进中国寿险业的发展。

友邦保险上海分公司和深圳分公司积极投入无偿献血事业，曾捐款人民币105万元在上海和深圳两地购置采血车。友邦保险获得由国家卫生部、中国红十字会及总后勤部卫生部共同颁发的"全国无偿献血促进奖"。

在全国上下抗击非典期间，友邦保险各分支公司不仅开通理赔绿色通道，同时向捐款慰问战斗在抗非一线的医护人员。

这就是我们所了解的值得信任和依靠的美国国际集团。

谢谢！

**B.**

Ladies and Gentlemen,

  Good Morning!

  As you know, China Insurance Brand Elite Forum is a national conference sponsored by China Insurance Brand Elite Club (IBEC), which is a non-profit organization to promote the development of Chinese Insurance industry. The organization takes "building the insurance brand and creating a healthy environment" as the objective, "outstanding service and credit standing" as the idea, "Health, Honest, High Quality" as the principle.

China Insurance Brand Elite Forum, formerly known as the Chinese Insurance Outstanding Marketing Elite Congress, was formed last year. Up to now, three sessions were conducted.

The first congress was held in Nanjing, the capital of Jiangsu province where it was attended by the leaders of the Jiangsu Province Insurance Practitioners Association and the various insurance companies of China. Mr. Mao Yushi, Chinese noted economist, had made a report entitled "China's Economic Development in the 21st century", which penetratingly analyzed China's economic development tendency in the new century and its influence to insurance industry.

The second congress was held in the beautiful city—Guilin, and over 1,200 insurance agents and managers from various insurance companies present. Guilin Deputy Mayor Pan Jianmin has made the welcoming speech for the congress. Mr. Liu Ji, the State Department Independent Commission regulators, one of the four most famous speakers in China, came to make a speech.

The third congress was successfully held in Huangshan, the well-known scenic spot of China. Mr. Huang Qimin, the Party Secretary of Huangshan city, sent the salutatory for the congress. The congress specially invited Zhang Meng, Miss Universe, to be the congress presider. In closing, the committee donated RMB ￥30,000 to Huangshan City for helping the poor students go to university, which has made a great influence over the local community.

The fourth congress, in partnership with the Insurance Institute of China, was held in Guangzhou, the capital of Guangdong Province, in conjunction with the 200th Anniversary of China Insurance.

Thousands of people have participated in practical specialized training and discussions with insurance elites from different places about the development of the industry, which is the vivid portrayal of the precious congresses. Welcome to join us, we'll offer you an opportunity!

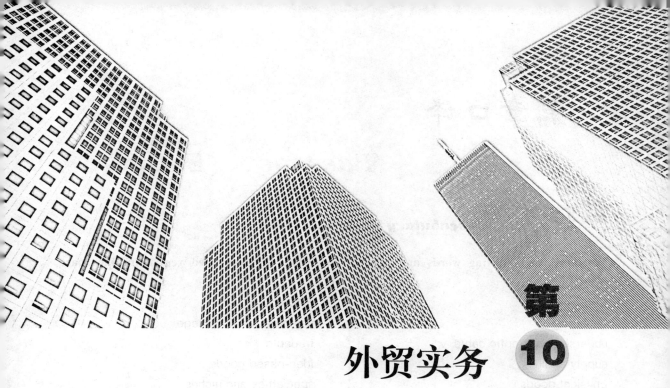

# 第 10 单元 外贸实务

## Unit 10 Foreign Trade

# 篇章口译

## Passage A (E-C)

### 词汇预习 Vocabulary Work

Work on the following words and phrases and write the translated version in the space provided.

- free trade
- offshoring
- undersea fiber-optic cable
- supply-chaining
- physical goods
- idea-driven worker
- knowledge pool
- counterproductive
- outsourcing
- comparative advantage
- tradable
- idea-based goods
- specialties and niches
- churn out
- protectionism

### 口译实践 Text Interpreting

Listen to the tape and interpret the following passage from English into Chinese.

Ladies and Gentlemen,

As an American who has always believed in the merits of free trade, I had an important question to answer after my trips to India and China: Should I still believe in free trade? I know that free trade won't necessary benefit every American, and that our society will have to help those who are harmed by it. But for me the question was: Will free trade benefit America as a whole when the world becomes so closely connected and so many more people can collaborate, and compete, with my kids? It seems that so many more jobs that we think of as "American" are going to be up for grabs. Wouldn't individual Americans be better off if our government erected some walls and banned some outsourcing and offshoring?

David Ricardo developed the free-trade theory of comparative advantage: if each nation specializes in the production of goods in which it has a comparative cost advantage and then trades with other nations for the goods in which they specialize, there will be an overall gain in trade, and overall income levels should rise in each trading country.

When Ricardo was writing, goods were tradable, but for the most part knowledge work and services were not. There was no undersea fiber-optic cable to make knowledge jobs tradable between America and India back then. I don't want to see any American lose his or her job to foreign competition or to technological innovation. I sure wouldn't want to lose mine. So there is some debate among economists about whether Ricardo is still right. Having listened to the arguments on both sides, I come down where the great majority of economists come down—that Ricardo is still right and that more American individuals will be better off if we don't erect barriers to outsourcing, supply-chaining, and offshoring than if we do.

There is a difference between idea-based goods and physical goods. If you are a knowledge worker making and selling some kind of idea-based product—consulting or financial services or music or software or marketing or design or new drugs—the bigger the market is, the more people there are out there to whom you can sell your product. And the bigger the market, the more new specialties and niches it will create. If you come up with the next Windows or Viagra, you can potentially sell one to everyone in the world. So idea-based workers do well in globalization, and fortunately America has more idea-driven workers than any other country in the world. That's why America, as a whole, will do fine in a world with free trade, provided it continues to churn out knowledge workers who are able to produce idea-based goods that can be sold globally and who are able to fill the knowledge jobs that will be created as we not only expand the global economy but connect all the knowledge pools in the world. There may be a limit to the number of good factory jobs in the world, but there is no limit to the number of idea-generated jobs in the world. America as a whole will benefit more by sticking to the general principles of free trade than by trying to erect walls, which will only provoke others to do the same and impoverish us all. While protectionism would be counterproductive, a policy of free trade, while necessary, is not enough by itself. It must be accompanied by a focused domestic strategy aimed at upgrading the education of every American, so that he or she will be able to compete for the new job in the modern world. And it must be accompanied by a foreign strategy of opening restricted markets all over the world, thereby bringing more countries into the global free-trade system—which will increase demand for goods and services, spur innovation, and reduce both unemployment and job migration across the globe.

# 篇章口译

## Passage B (C-E)

 **Vocabulary Work**

Work on the following words and phrases and write the translated version in the space provided.

产业经济论坛    纺织工业    物质和文化消费    产业结构
转移    生产要素    产业链    自由贸易体制
配额    例外条款    积压已久    贸易摩擦
互利共赢    贸易保护主义    公平贸易

 **Text Interpreting**

Listen to the tape and interpret the following passage from Chinese into English.

女士们、先生们：

"全球纺织经济论坛"作为中国纺织工业协会主办的高规格、国际性产业经济论坛，得到了国际经济组织、有关国家非政府组织和驻华外交机构、主要国家和地区的行业协会、跨国商业机构和知名企业的广泛关注和积极参与，也得到了中国政府的高度重视。我代表中国工业经济联合会对参加论坛的各国嘉宾、代表和朋友们表示热烈的欢迎。

纺织工业作为为人类提供物质和文化消费的一个传统产业，曾为世界文明、工业化以及经济发展做出了巨大的贡献，并在世界贸易中占有十分重要的地位。随着经济全球化的进程，各国产业结构发生相应的调整，纺织工业的重心出现了变迁，英国、美国、日本、亚洲四小龙地区、中国内地和东南亚都先后承接了纺织业的转移。这种转移并非是简单的一部分国家进入、另一部分国家退出的替代，而是通过全球范围的投资、贸易和生产要素配制，使全球日益形成相互依存、彼此互补的完整产业链，从而构造出利益互补和生产者与消费者共赢的世界纺织业大格局。

长期以来，全球纺织品贸易体制一直游离于自由贸易体制之外。去年，随着《纺织品与服装协定》的废除，纺织品配额这一关贸总协定规则最重要的例外条款之一因此被埋葬了。配额的取消使中国积压已久的纺织品出口能力得到了一定的释放，行业竞争力得到极大的展现。然而，中国部分纺织品对原配额市场的出口增长，引起了一些世贸成员的关注，引发了一连串的贸易摩擦以及欧盟和美国的设限。随着纺织品和服装配额的取消，国际纺织产业结构和产业区域布局有所调整，种种矛盾和冲突的出现是完全正常的现象。中国作为WTO成员是一个负责任的国家，中国一直致力于维护世界纺织行业的稳定和有序发展，一方面坚决反对贸易保护主义行为，维护中国纺织企业的合法权益，另一方面也在兼顾其他国家和地区的利益,努力在互利、共赢的基础上寻求合作发展。

此次中国纺织工业协会以"合作、发展与公平贸易"作为论坛的主题,邀请了许多国家和地区的高层,相互沟通,共同探讨建立公平贸易体系,共商合作发展大计,对于全球纺织服装业的发展具有十分深远的意义。我希望这次论坛取得圆满成功,让我们携手并进,坚持公平贸易的原则,共创全球纺织工业合作发展的新篇章!

# 口译讲评

## Notes on the Text

**Passage A**

1. **Will free trade benefit America as a whole**:美国作为一个整体能在自由贸易中获益吗? as a whole 指作为一个整体,整个来看,比如:I disliked the acting but enjoyed the play as a whole.(我不喜欢某些表演,但总的来说还是挺喜欢这个剧的。)

2. **be up for grabs**:可得的,供争夺的,人人都可以争取,比如:We've got ＄1000 up for grabs in our quiz. All you have to do is call this number.(只要拨打这个号码,就有可能得到智力竞赛提供的1000美元奖金。)

3. **outsourcing and offshoring**:外包和离岸外包。outsourcing 指公司把部分服务或生产工作交给另一方去完成,这一方可以是另一家公司,也可以是在公司内部。外包是一种降低企业成本的战略。例如美国戴尔公司把部分电脑组件的生产外包给另一家企业。随着全球化的发展,许多公司把外包的目光投向海外,于是就出现了离岸外包(offshoring 或 offshore outsourcing)。离岸外包逐渐地以业务流程外包(business process outsourcing, BPO)的形式出现,公司将某个业务流程整个地外包给海外的某个服务提供企业或者公司在海外的子公司。从某种意义上,外包,尤其是离岸外包造成了本国工作岗位外流。

4. **David Ricardo**:大卫·李嘉图(1772—1823),英国经济学家,是英国古典政治经济学的杰出代表和完成者。李嘉图最著名的著作是《政治经济学及赋税原理》,这本书引入了比较优势理论。根据李嘉图的理论,即使一个国家在所有制造业中比其他国家更加高效,它也能够通过专注于其最擅长领域、与其他国家进行贸易交往而获取利益。比较优势学说构成了现代贸易理论的基石。

5. **I come down where the great majority of economists come down**:我同意大多数经济学家的观点。

6. **idea-based goods**:知识密集型产品,也可以译为"创意产品"或"点子产品"。

7. **the bigger the market, the more new specialties and niches it will create**:市场越大,细分程度就越高。niches 指(特定产品或服务的)用户群。

8. **Viagra**:万艾可,俗称"伟哥"。

**Passage B**

1. **全球纺织经济论坛、中国纺织工业协会、中国工业经济联合会**：这三个组织的英文名分别为 The Global Textile Economic Forum、China National Textile and Apparel Council 和 China Federation of Industrial Economics。

2. **亚洲四小龙**：指亚洲四个面积不大但工业发达的新兴经济体，即韩国、新加坡以及我国的台湾和香港地区。英文中有用 East Asian Tigers、Four Asian Tigers、Asia's Four Little Dragons 指代亚洲四小龙的说法。在学术类期刊书籍中一般都译为 Newly Industrialized Economies，简称 NIEs，较少用直译。此外，在亚洲地区特别是中文地区，亚洲四小虎另有所指，指的是泰国、马来西亚、菲律宾和印度尼西亚四个国家，其经济在20世纪90年代都像20世纪80年代的亚洲四小龙一样突飞猛进，因而得名。

3. **《纺织品与服装协定》**：Agreement on Textiles and Clothing（ATC），自1995年起WTO的《纺织品与服装协定》取代了《多种纤维协定》(Multi-Fibre Arrangement，简称MFA)，该协定包括10个条款和1个附件，至2005年1月1日，全球纺织品贸易实现一体化，该领域完全纳入GATT规则中，纺织品配额制终止，进口国不能再对出口国实施歧视，《纺织品与服装协定》本身也不再存在。它是《WTO协议》中唯一规定了自行废止内容的协议。

4. **关贸总协定**：General Agreement on Tariffs and Trade（GATT）是关于关税和贸易准则的多边国际协定和组织。1995年12月12日，关贸总协定128个缔约方在日内瓦举行最后一次会议，宣告关贸总协定的历史使命完成。根据乌拉圭回合多边贸易谈判达成的协议，从1996年1月1日起，由世界贸易组织（World Trade Organization，简称WTO）取代关贸总协定。

5. **配额的取消使中国积压已久的纺织品出口能力得到了一定的释放，行业竞争力得到极大的展现**：The elimination of quota system has given a chance to the Chinese textile and apparel industry to release its long-pressed textile export capability and give full play to its competitiveness.

6. **欧盟**：European Union，简称 EU，是由欧洲共同体（European Communities）发展而来的，是一个集政治实体和经济实体于一身，在世界上具有重要影响的区域一体化组织。1991年12月，欧洲共同体马斯特里赫特首脑会议通过《欧洲联盟条约》，通称《马斯特里赫特条约》(简称《马约》)。1993年11月1日，《马约》正式生效，欧盟正式诞生。总部设在比利时首都布鲁塞尔。

## 相关词语  Relevant Words and Expressions

配额 quota
反倾销 anti-dumping
普惠制 Generalized System of Preferences
国民待遇 national treatment
经贸摩擦 economic and trade frictions

贸易逆差 trade deficit
贸易平衡 balance of trade
贸易顺差 trade surplus
外汇收入 exchange earnings
非关税壁垒 non-tariff barrier
自由贸易区 free trade area
多边贸易协定 Multilateral Trade Agreements
进／出口许可证 import／export license
扩大市场准入 increase market access
缩小南北差距 narrow the North-South gap
互利共赢的开放战略 win-win strategy of opening-up
通行的国际经贸规则 internationally recognized economic and trade rules
贸易和投资自由化便利化 the liberalization and facilitation of trade and financial systems
通过磋商协作妥善处理经贸摩擦 properly resolve economic and trade frictions through consultation and collaboration
推进贸易和投资自由化便利化 advance the liberalization and facilitation of trade and financial system

# 口译技能

# Interpreting Skills

## 记者招待会

1. 记者招待会的性质与特点

记者招待会（press conference），有时也叫新闻发布会（news briefing），是指有关部门，包括政府、商业公司及其他机构，召集新闻媒体公布有关国家的政治、经济、外交等的最新动态；商业公司的业务发展、变化及新产品的投放市场；其他机构的一些重大决策及活动情况。它是集时事、信息于一体的重大场合。

记者招待会的特点是形式正规，气氛隆重，现场感强。记者招待会的参加者多为相关部门的领导人、发言人以及各大新闻媒体的中外记者。

2. 记者招待会的过程

记者招待会主要由三个部分组成。首先，司仪简要概括本次活动的主题内容及安排，并介绍出席招待会的领导、嘉宾及主要的媒体单位。其次，相关部门的领导人就主题内容作发言。最后，主谈人回答记者的提问。就口译形式而言，记者招待会一般采用即席口译或同传与即席口译并用。

3. 译员的准备及口译技巧

(1) 作为译员,在接受口译任务后应及时向主办方索取相关资料,尽可能了解活动的主题背景、相关内容及程序安排。译员应对参加本次活动的主要人员及新闻媒体单位做一份中英对照的表格并加以熟记,以免口译时出现忙乱及差错。此外,译员还应充分了解主谈人的身份并寻找机会了解其讲话的风格,包括发音及语速。

(2) 由于记者招待会采用现场回答问题,译员事先无问与答的相关稿件作参考,并需做即席口译。这要求译员须有效地做好笔记,因为有时问题会很长。例如:I'm with *Wall Street Journal*. International investors are now very interested in the China's stock market. Do you think the rise of the stock market over the past two years went too far, too fast and the average Chinese investors might be risking too much? What further measures is your government considering to cool down or regulate the market? And yet another related topic to investment. The government has announced new plans for agency to manage diversification of China's foreign exchange reserves. Can you tell us what kind of assets does this agency invest in? 这位记者一共提了两个问题,并且每个问题的前面都先作一番评论。这也是记者提问的一贯方式。由于机会难得,每位记者只能提一个问题,但他们往往将几个问题合并成一个。因此,译员一定要做好充分的准备,做笔记时应将问题分行记录,以免混淆。

(3) 译员必须学会如何预测可能遇到的问题及相应的回答。一般记者招待会的主题都比较明确,这无疑限定了"问"与"答"的范围。因此,译员在主题背景知识的基础上,应努力领会问与答的内容;口译时尽量做到达意、完整,以免漏译、错译,以至于最终直接影响双方的交流并导致误会。

(4) 译员还须听懂不同英语讲话者的提问。毕竟,在这种场合中译员会碰到不同国别的记者。如果实在无法听清提问的内容,译员可以让讲话者重复刚才的问题。当然,一般来说,驻外记者的英语还是应该达到一定的水准。还有一种情形译员也要有所准备,即在中英互译时,有些外国记者会用中文提问。此时,译员除了将问题译成目的语外,还应了解中文的听众是否听懂了他/她的中文。必要时再重复一下中文的问题。

(5) 在记者招待会的场合,由于译员完全暴露于观众,因此他/她还须克服怯场的心理。此外,译员还须学会如何排除来自会场上的各种干扰,包括记者的镁光灯、观众的讲话及工作人员的来回走动等等。因此,记者招待会的译员需比其他口译场合的译员具备更高的注意力和排除干扰的能力。

4. 常用句型

1) Ladies and Gentlemen, today we are holding the press conference of..., we have invited here....

2) We would like to express our thanks to... for sparing time from his/their very busy schedule to meet with our correspondents and answer questions.

3) The floor is now open.

4) Now Ladies and Gentlemen, Mr./Ms..../the panel would like to take your questions.

5) My name is... I am with (from)... (work unit)

6) I would like to ask... about...
7) What's your comment on.../How do you comment on.../Can I have your comment on.../Would you comment on...
8) How do you react to...
9) Do you think...
10) Could you be more specific about...
11) My question is,...
12) Would you please give us some of your views on...
13) Mr./Ms.... will take the last question.
14) Ladies and Gentlemen, thank you for coming. This concludes the press conference.

# 译练习 Enhancement Practice

第一项 Project 1
句子精练 Sentences in Focus

**A. Interpret the following sentences from English into Chinese.**

1. Infrastructure bottlenecks, congested ports and freak weather have held back the coal exports of Australia, the world's largest exporter of coal.
2. The export trade is subject to many risks. Ships may sink or consignments be damaged in transit, exchange rate may alter or buyers default.
3. Free on Board (FOB) means that the seller fulfils his obligation to deliver when the goods have passed over the ship's rail at the named port of shipment.
4. International organizations such as the WTO and European Free Trade Association (EFTA) regulate tariffs and reduce trade restrictions between member countries.
5. The terms of payment are an important part of business contract. A letter of credit is a banker's guarantee that payment will be made on presentation of all the required shipping documents.

**B. Interpret the following sentences from Chinese into English.**

1. 普惠制是国际贸易的一种优惠政策,是发达国家给予发展中国家商品的一种减免关税的政策。
2. 纺织品是中国的出口产品之一,其盛名可以追溯到几百年前。我们的纺织品在欧洲市场很畅销。
3. 透明的包装使顾客可以清楚地看到包装在里面的瓷器的优美形状和漂亮色彩,方便超市销售。
4. 我们将建立更加开放的市场体系,在更大范围、更广领域、更高层次上参与国际经济技术合作和竞争。
5. 海洋运输保险保护进出口商免遭本来需要承受的经济损失,如果他们的货物在从装运港至目的港的途中损坏或丢失。

第二项 Project 2
段落口译 Paragraph Interpreting

**A. Interpret the following paragraph from English into Chinese.**

　　In today's world a country can and will lose its comparative advantage in one field much more quickly than before. Countries like India and China can now compete in many more fields, fields that were once seen as the exclusive preserve of developed Western nations. These developed Western countries will need to adapt, and move into still newer fields, much more quickly, if they want to maintain their standards of living. At the same time, as India and China develop, they will lose their comparative advantage in certain lower-rung fields, like basic manufacturing or textiles, to places like Vietnam or Madagascar. No country is immune to these economic laws of gravity.

**B. Interpret the following paragraph from Chinese into English.**

　　进口和出口是对外贸易的两个方面。国家花钱进口货物，通过出口赚取外汇。虽然对外贸易非常重要，进口货物造成的竞争有助于降低国内市场的价格，而出口可以为国内产品提供广大的国外市场，但是政府有时候也不得不对此加以限制。为保护国内的工业，进口可能受到控制或需要交纳关税；或者因为发展中的国内工业所需而限制某种原料出口。

第三项 Project 3
篇章口译 Passage Interpreting

**A. Listen to the tape and interpret the following passage from English into Chinese.**

　　South-East Asia looks set to undergo an invigorating new round of opening up its trade with the rest of the world. Negotiators from the Association of South-East Asian Nations are expected to meet their Indian counterparts next week to discuss a free-trade pact that could be signed early next year. The EU is starting its free-trade talks with ASEAN this year. South Korea agreed a trade pact with ASEAN last month. The United States, having already opened free-trade talks with Thailand, will start negotiating with Malaysia shortly. America has also struck a tariff-cutting deal with Vietnam.

　　All good news, but things could be better. The apparent enthusiasm of regional governments for talking free trade to all and sundry is largely due to diminished hopes for the worldwide Doha round of trade talks, which could do more for the flow of goods and services than any bilateral or regional deal.

　　And there is plenty that could still go wrong. The trade pacts South-East Asia is preparing to enter may, like those already signed, be riddled with exceptions, sometimes affecting precisely those goods and services in which trade liberalization would be most beneficial. Thailand is refusing to sign the ASEAN-South Korea deal because the Koreans insisted on excluding rice, of which Thailand is the world's biggest exporter. India originally had a list of more than 1,400 "sensitive" items that it wanted excluded from tariff cuts in the proposed ASEAN deal. It has narrowed these down to a mere 850.

Just as bad are the bureaucratic procedures laid down in regional and bilateral trade deals, which may be so onerous that the pacts end up doing little to free trade. Tariff cuts agreed under such pacts are not automatically granted; exporters have to apply for them. They must show that their wares comply with complex rules designed to stop goods being smuggled in from outside the free-trade zone. Firms often find it less bother simply to pay the original tariffs.

Worse still, the bureaucratic requirements vary considerably from one trade pact to another. So an exporting firm based in a country that has lots of free-trade deals with its neighbours does not, in practice, feel as though it is operating in a giant single market. All that the proliferation of deals may do is thicken the hotchpotch of incoherent agreements.

America is pressing for bilateral deals in South-East Asia as bilateral deals are easier to wrap up quickly than trying to deal jointly with a shambling bunch like ASEAN. But the Asian Development Bank is worried that such deals will divert trade away from the region's poorest states, such as Cambodia and Laos.

In America and Europe, firms play a big part in shaping trade deals. But consultation with businesses has been lacking in many of South-East Asia's recent negotiations. Agreements are often drawn up by lawyers with little understanding of business or basic economics. And the result is upsetting.

**B. Listen to the tape and interpret the following passage from Chinese into English.**

女士们、先生们：

值此金秋十月，亚太经合组织工商领导人峰会今天在上海隆重开幕了。我谨代表中国政府，对各位莅临中国上海，表示热烈的欢迎；对峰会的召开，表示热烈的祝贺！

峰会汇聚了亚太地区众多工商领导人，共商亚太地区乃至世界经济面临的现实问题，探讨企业的发展策略，增进相互的理解，共同构建合作的框架，受到APEC各经济体高层领导人和政府的重视。

APEC不同经济体的企业完全可以发挥各自的比较优势，加强区域间的经济技术合作，进行更大范围、更大规模的资源优化配置，在追求企业利润最大化的过程中，达到共赢的结果。

中国非常注重与APEC其他经济体的友好合作，它们是中国重要的经贸合作伙伴。去年中国与APEC各经济体的贸易额以及从APEC各经济体引进的外资金额，都超过了中国对外贸易、引进外资总量的70%。中国同样鼓励有条件的国内企业到境外投资和经营，积极参与国际竞争与合作，中国的对外投资也主要集中在APEC各地区。

中国加入世贸组织后，中国市场与世界市场更加紧密地融为一体，中国的经济发展也更加依赖于与世界其他国家和地区特别是亚太地区的经济往来与合作，开放的中国离不开世界。中国以积极的姿态推进全方位、多层次、宽领域的对外开放。正处在新的历史起点上的中国孕育着前所未有的贸易和投资机会。在此，我们真诚欢迎各经济体的企业到中国来，把握商机，谋求更大的发展。

我相信，通过APEC各成员体持续不断的努力，亚太地区的经济一定会生机勃勃；亚太地区人民的生活一定会得到进一步改善。

我预祝本届APEC CEO峰会取得圆满成功！

# 参考译文
## Reference Version

**篇章口译 A**

女士们、先生们：

作为一个一直以来都确信自由贸易会带来好处的美国人，我在结束印度和中国之行后产生了一个很大的疑问：我应该继续相信自由贸易吗？我知道，自由贸易当然不会使每个美国人都受益，而且社会必须要帮助那些在自由贸易中受损的人们。我的问题是：当世界的联系如此紧密，如此多的人可以和我的孩子合作或竞争时，美国作为一个整体能在自由贸易中获益吗？似乎有众多我们认为应该是美国人的工作将被世界各地的竞争者瓜分，要是我们的政府采取保护措施，禁止外包和离岸外包业务，那么每位美国人的生活不是会更好吗？

大卫·李嘉图创立了基于比较优势的自由贸易理论：如果每个国家专门生产本国具有比较优势的产品，然后用各自的产品进行交换，贸易各方都会从这种交易中获益，各自的整体国民收入都会提高。当李嘉图提出他的理论时，只有商品是可以做贸易的，而大部分的知识产品和服务是不可以交易的。当时美国和印度之间没有海底光缆，因而无法支持服务贸易。我不愿意看到任何美国人由于国外的竞争或因技术改造而失业。我自己当然更不想丢饭碗。因此经济学家之间开始争论李嘉图的比较优势理论是否依然准确。我听了双方的论战，我同意大多数经济学家的观点，李嘉图依然是正确的：只要我们不阻止外包，不切断国际供应链，不禁止离岸外包，更多的美国人的生活会更好。

知识密集型产品和一般的实物产品是不同的。如果你掌握有较高的知识水平，从事生产和销售一些知识密集型产品，比如提供咨询服务或金融服务，提供音乐产品或电脑软件，或市场营销、工程设计、研制新药等，那么市场越大，你产品的销量就越大；而市场越大，细分程度就越高。要是你能设计出新一代视窗操作系统或万艾可药品，你的销售对象将是全世界。所以，掌握较高知识水平的人可以从容应对全球化。幸运的是美国拥有全世界最多的知识工人。这就是为什么美国作为一个整体能在自由贸易体系中运作自如，只要它能持续不断地培养出大量掌握先进知识技术的工人，他们能创造出供全球销售的知识产品，而且能胜任因全球经济扩张和知识汇集所创造出来的新的工作岗位。世界上好工厂的工作岗位也许是有限的，而知识创意引发的工作岗位却是无限的。

作为一个整体，美国坚持自由贸易所得到的好处将超过实行贸易保护主义。保护主义只会激起其他国家的报复，从而损害大家的利益。当然，虽然保护主义是有害的，自由贸易政策是必需的，但仅仅有自由贸易政策还是不够的，还必须着手提高美国公民的受教育程度，以帮助每一个美国人有能力竞争现代世界的工作岗位。同时，自由贸易政策还需结合世界范围内的市场开放，使更多的国家纳入全球自由贸易体系，从而在全球范围内增加对商品和服务的需求,激励创新,降低失业率和工作流动。

**篇章口译 B**

Ladies and Gentlemen,

  The Global Textile Economic Forum, hosted by China National Textile and Apparel Council, is a high level international economic forum on industrial economic issues. It has got hold of wide attentions from international economic organizations and non-governmental organizations overseas, foreign diplomatic missions in China, leading industrial organizations from many countries and regions, and global trade organizations and companies. Representatives from those organizations have actively participated in the forum. The Chinese government has also attached great importance to this annual event. On behalf of the China Federation of Industrial Economics, I would like to extend my sincere greetings and warm welcome to all the distinguished guests, delegates and friends who have participated in the forum.

  Textile industry, as a traditional industry that meets people's material and cultural needs, has made great contributions to the world civilization, industrialization and economic development and it has played the important role in the international trade. With the development of global economic integration, industries have undergone the restructuring: the geographical center of textile production has successively shifted to the UK, the United States, Japan, "Four Little Dragons" in Asia, the Chinese mainland and Southeast Asia. Such shift is not a simple substitution process where some economies have entered while some others have withdrawn. Instead, it has turned the world into an interdependent and complementary complete industry chain via investment, trade and reallocation of production elements on a global basis, thus forming a globally integrated textile industry structure, a mutually beneficial and win-win solution for both producers and consumers.

  For many years, the world textile trading system had dissociated from trade liberalization. With the phasing-out of the ATC, the textile quotas, one of the most significant exceptions to the GATT rules, were buried last year. The elimination of quota system has given a chance to the Chinese textile and apparel industry to release its long-pressed textile export capability and give full play to its competitiveness. However, the sharp growth of textile exports to the formerly quota-restricted markets had aroused concern by some WTO members and led to a series trade disputes and limitations set by EU and the United States. With the abolishment of textile quotas, both the structure and regional distribution of the world textile industry have changed, so it is quite normal that there are various contradictions and conflicts. As a responsible member of the WTO, China has been dedicating its efforts to keeping the world textile industry to develop in a stable and orderly way, on the one hand, China strongly opposes trade protectionism and safeguards the legal interests of Chinese textile enterprises; and on the other hand, it pays attention to the interests of other economies and regions and seeks the way of cooperation and development on the mutual-benefit and win-win result.

This time, China National Textile and Apparel Council has chosen "Cooperation, Development and Fair Trade" as the theme of the forum and invited the high-rank representatives from many countries and regions to exchange ideas, exploit the possibility of setting up a fair-play system and discuss future development program. I think this will be of great significance to the development of global textile and apparel industry. I wish the forum a great success. Let's make joint efforts, stick to the fair-play principle, to write a new chapter for the cooperation and development of global textile industry.

口译练习
第一项 句子精练
A.
1. 基础设施瓶颈、港口拥堵和反常的气候,制约了全球最大的煤炭出口国澳大利亚的煤炭出口。
2. 出口贸易常常遇到很多风险。船舶可能沉没,或货物在运输途中受损,汇率发生变动,或买主违约。
3. 装运港船上交货指的是当货物在指定装运港越过船舷时,卖方即履行了交货义务。
4. 像世界贸易组织和欧洲自由贸易联盟这样的国际组织调控关税并减少成员国之间的贸易限制。
5. 支付条款是商业合同的重要部分。信用证是银行出具的保证,保证在提交全套必要的装运单据后即付货款。

B.
1. The Generalized System of Preferences is a system of preference in international trade. It is a policy for reducing or relieving the tariffs on the commodities of the developing countries implemented by the developed countries.
2. Textile is one of China's export products and its popularity dates back hundred of years. Our textile products are selling quickly in European markets.
3. The transparent packaging gives the customer a clear view of the graceful shape and beautiful colors of the porcelain packed therein and facilitate its marketing in supermarkets.
4. We will build a more open market place and participate more broadly in international economic and technological cooperation and competition with still wider and higher dimensions.
5. Marine insurance exists to protect importers and exporters against the financial loss which they would otherwise suffer if their cargoes were damaged or lost while en route from the loading port to the destination.

## 第10单元 外贸实务 Foreign Trade

第二项 段落口译
A.
　　在今天这个世界，一个国家会比以前更快地失去在某一领域的比较优势。像印度、中国这样的国家在很多领域都有竞争能力，而这些领域曾被认为专属于发达的西方国家。要维持生活水准，这些发达国家必须很快适应并迅速进入更新的领域。而同时，随着印度和中国的发展，它们会失去某些较低级领域的比较优势，像在制造业和纺织业方面会不如越南、马达加斯加这样的国家。没有任何一个国家可以免于这一经济领域的万有引力定律。

B.
　　Importing and exporting are the two aspects of foreign trade: a country spends money on goods it imports and gains money through its exports. Though foreign trade is valuable for keeping domestic prices down by creating competition at home and providing large markets abroad, governments may have to put restrictions on it. Imports may be controlled or subjected to a customs duty to protect a home industry, and exports may be restricted to conserve a particular raw material required by a developing home industry.

第三项 篇章口译
A.
　　东南亚似乎正进入一轮新的贸易开放期。东盟的谈判代表下周将和印度代表见面，双方有可能在明年初签订自由贸易协议。欧盟也会于今年开始与东盟的自由贸易谈判。韩国已于上月和东盟签订了一项贸易协议。美国正在同泰国进行自由贸易谈判，与马来西亚的谈判也将很快开始，美国已与越南达成削减关税的协议。
　　听上去不错，但情况原本应该更好。地区政府对自由贸易谈判对象来者不拒、热情有加的原因很大程度上是出于对多哈贸易会谈的信心不足，多哈回合有关货物和服务的自由流通的协定应该好过任何双边或多边的地区协议。
　　而且还会出现很多问题。东南亚国家准备签署的协议，很可能像以前所签的许多协议一样，带有很多例外条款，而这些除外的货物和服务如果能自由流通的话恰恰应该是最为有利的部分。泰国拒绝跟韩国签订协议，因为韩国坚持将大米排除在协定外，而泰国是全球最大的大米出口国。印度向东盟提出的关于削减关税的贸易协定列出了1400多项要求除外的"敏感"商品，现在已经减少到"仅仅"只有850种了。
　　同样糟糕的是地区间和双边贸易协定所规定的种种官僚程序，程序如此繁琐以至协定可能最后对自由贸易没有任何实质性的好处。协定所规定的减税并不是自动进行的，出口商必须提出申请，他们必须证明他们的货物符合旨在阻止区外的货物走私进入自由贸易区的种种复杂规定。出口公司往往觉得还不如干脆付税更省事。
　　更糟的是，每个协议的复杂程序和要求各不相同，所以同周边邻国拥有许多自由贸易协议的出口公司实际上并没有觉得是在与一个很大的单一市场打交道。新协议的大量增加其实可能只是使各种协定之间的混乱状况更为严重。
　　美国在寻求跟东南亚国家的双边协定，因为这比同作为一个整体而行动缓慢的东盟谈判要容易。但是亚洲发展银行担心这样的双边协定会使该地区最贫穷的像柬埔寨和老挝这样国家失去贸易机会。

在美国和欧洲，企业在贸易谈判中起重要作用，但在东南亚国家最近的许多贸易谈判中，没有进行必要的企业咨询。协议往往由不懂业务或基本经济学知识的律师起草。其结果令人沮丧。

**B.**

Ladies and Gentlemen,

In this golden autumn season of October, the APEC CEO Summit solemnly opens in Shanghai today. On behalf of the Chinese Government, I wish to warmly welcome all of you to Shanghai, China and also to offer cordial congratulations on the opening of APEC CEO Summit.

At the APEC CEO Summit, many business leaders across the Asia-Pacific gather together to discuss the immediate economic issues facing the Asia-Pacific region and the world, explore development strategies for enterprises, seek better mutual understanding and make joint efforts to build the framework of cooperation. The Summit has caught the attention of senior leaders and governments of APEC economies.

For enterprises from different APEC economies, it is entirely possible for them to bring into play their respective comparative advantages, boost inter-regional economic and technological cooperation, optimize the allocation of resources in a wider scope and on a greater scale and achieve an all-win outcome while seeking to maximize their profits.

China values its friendly cooperation with other APEC economies. They are China's important partners in economic cooperation and trade. Last year, the trade volume between China and other APEC economies and newly-approved introduction of foreign capital from them both account for more than 70% of China's total foreign trade and absorbed foreign capital. China also encourages viable Chinese enterprises to invest and do business abroad and to take an active part in international competition and cooperation. Moreover, China's overseas investment has been concentrated mainly in APEC regions.

After China's accession to the WTO, the Chinese market and the world market are more closely integrated. China's economic development also depends more on its economic exchanges and cooperation with other countries and regions in the world, especially the Asia-Pacific region. An open China cannot do without the world. China vigorously advances its all-directional, multi-tiered and wide-ranging opening-up. China, at a new historic starting point, faces unprecedented opportunities for trade and investment. Here, we sincerely welcome enterprises from various economies to China to grasp business opportunity and seek even greater progress.

I am sure, through persistent efforts of all APEC members, the economy of the Asia-Pacific region will continue its vitality and the life of people in the region will further improve.

I wish the APEC CEO Summit a complete success.

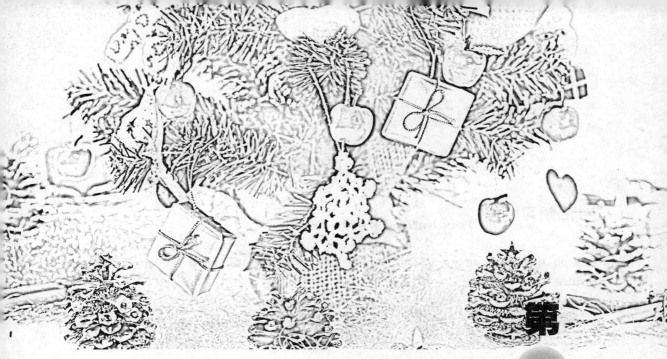

资本市场 第11单元

 Unit 11 **The Capital Market**

# 篇章口译

## Passage A (E-C)

### Vocabulary Work

Work on the following words and phrases and write the translated version in the space provided.

| | |
|---|---|
| Wharton | Merrill Lynch |
| recruiting trip | Theory of the New Economy |
| underlying force | gulf |
| leverage | preeminence |
| financial service | analyst |
| progressive business model | relic |
| the Cro-Magnon era | miraculously |
| wrestle over | brokerage and investment banking |
| in client assets | revenue |
| seminal event | IPO |
| blend | paradox |

### Text Interpreting

**Listen to the tape and interpret the following passage from English into Chinese.**

I'm happy to be here at Wharton, traditionally a wonderful source of Merrill Lynch talent. But I'm not here on a recruiting trip. My purpose today is much broader. I'm here to talk about what I call the Theory of the New Economy.

First, I'll talk about the underlying forces behind the new economy—how they're shaping my industry in general and my company in particular. Next, I'll try to convince you that the gulf said to exist between the Old Economy and the New Economy has been greatly exaggerated. Finally, I'll talk briefly about how Merrill Lynch is leveraging these forces to achieve preeminence in financial services.

Some of you may be wondering whether a CEO of a major financial services firm is the best person to be lecturing about "The New Economy." You are not alone. Here, for example, is what one analyst tried to tell us last spring. He wrote: "With a more progressive business model, we suspect consumers decreasingly view Merrill Lynch as a relic from the Cro-Magnon era of financial services." Thirty years in this business and this is the respect I get!

But that was last year, and now, suddenly, many of the virtues of the so-called "Old Economy" firms are being miraculously rediscovered. It's amazing what 12 months and a 1,600-point loss on the Nasdaq will do! Yes, a bad year for the tech sector has made a lot of experts wrestle over whose prediction was most accurate. But where they all agree is that the underlying trends of the New Economy are no fad. Globalization and technology have introduced fundamental and permanent changes to the way every company does business.

National borders have become almost irrelevant when it comes to asset management, investing, or mergers. Executing a strategy in different markets, with different languages, laws, and cultures is now a fundamental part of the financial services industry. Take Merrill Lynch: Ten years ago, we were basically a two-sector business—brokerage and investment banking—with about \$350 billion in client assets, and 13% of our revenues coming from outside the US Today, we enjoy dominant market positions around the globe in three complementary businesses: Private Client, Investment Management and Investment Banking, supported by 850 research professionals in 26 countries. We hold \$1.8 trillion in client assets, and 35% of our revenues come from outside the US.

In the meantime, technology has transformed every industry, but probably ours more than any other. After all, the biggest-selling consumer item on the Internet is not music, not toys, not books or flowers. It's stock. Three years ago, we launched Merrill Lynch OnLine from a standing start. Today, many experts say our site is the best on the web. We're also using the power of the Internet to reshape how the institutional markets operate.

Globalization and technology are the trends that will be seen as the seminal events of the new economy. They will have far more lasting effects than the bubble in tech stocks or the flood of IPOs. They have taught us many lessons. The most important is that being successful in the new economy requires the proper blend of old and new economy virtues. That's just one of the great paradoxes of our time. In fact, today I want to offer what I call the Five Great Paradoxes of the New Economy.

# 篇章口译

## Passage B (C-E)

### Vocabulary Work

Work on the following words and phrases and write the translated version in the space provided.

| | | | |
|---|---|---|---|
| 股市 | 资本市场 | 股权分置 | 上市公司 |
| 防范风险 | 外汇 | 国际货币基金组织 | 外汇储备多元化 |
| 保值增值 | 超脱 | 微乎其微 | 美元资产 |
| 评功摆好 | 忧患 | 结构性问题 | |

### Text Interpreting

Listen to the tape and interpret the following passage from Chinese into English.

我关注股市的发展，但更关注股票市场的健康发展。去年以来，我们加强了资本市场的基础性制度建设，特别是成功地推进了股权分置改革，解决了历史上的遗留问题。

我们的目标是建立一个成熟的资本市场。这就需要：第一，提高上市公司的质量；第二，建立一个公开、公正、透明的市场体系；第三，加强资本市场的监管，特别是完善法制。最后，要加强股市信息的及时披露，使股民增强防范风险的意识。

你谈到中国的外汇储备如何使用，这确实是我们面临的一个大问题。从我国的经历来看，外汇少的时候，有少的难处。上世纪90年代的时候，我们因缺少外汇，曾经向国际货币基金组织借外汇，他们只借给我们8亿美元。现在外汇多了，超过1万亿美元了，怎么把它使用好？这又成为我们一个新的难题。

中国实行外汇储备的多元化，这是基于外汇安全的考虑。我们是要组建一个外汇投资机构，这个机构是超脱于任何部门的，依照国家的法律来经营外汇，有偿使用，接受监管，保值增值。

中国对外投资时间还短，我们十分缺乏经验。我最近查了一下资料，现在非金融类的对外投资，截至2006年底，只有733亿美元，去年一年新增160亿美元。这同发达国家比起来，简直是微乎其微。

我知道你提出的问题，是关注我们成立这个公司开展对外投资会不会影响美元资产。在中国的外汇储备当中，美元资产占多数，这是个事实。中国购买美元资产是互利的，中国组建外汇投资公司，不会影响美元资产。

近些年来，中国金融体系保持了平稳较快的发展，但无论是过去、现在还是将来，都不必评功摆好。我的脑子里充满了忧患，"名为治平无事，而其实有不测之忧"。中国金融存在着不稳定、不平衡的结构性问题。所谓不稳定,就是投资增长率过高,信贷投放过多,货币流动性过大,外贸和国际收支顺差过高。所谓不平衡,就是城乡之间、地区之间、经济与社会发展之间不平衡。这些都是摆在我们面前需要解决的紧迫问题,而且是需要长期努力才能解决的问题。

# 口译讲评

## Notes on the Text

**Passage A**

1. **I'm happy to be here at Wharton, traditionally a wonderful source of Merrill Lynch talent**:很高兴来到沃顿,这里向来是美林公司理想的人才库。此句中的 Wharton 指的是宾夕法尼亚大学沃顿商学院,是全美最好的商学院之一。

2. **But I'm not here on a recruiting trip. My purpose today is much broader**:然而,我此行并非是招募新人,今天我有更大的目的。此句的翻译采用了结构重组法,若译为"我不是在这里来参加一个招聘的旅行"则显得极为死板,而且不符合汉语的语言习惯,翻译时经常要对原句进行拆分和重组。

3. **I'll talk about the underlying forces behind the new economy—how they're shaping my industry in general and my company in particular**:我想谈一下新经济所蕴涵的力量,以及这些力量如何影响整个行业以及我的公司。此句中的 behind 根据上下文表达了"蕴涵"之意,因而不是机械地译为"新经济背后的力量"。

4. **I'll try to convince you that the gulf said to exist between the Old Economy and New Economy has been greatly exaggerated**:我希望你们确信新经济和旧经济之间存在的鸿沟其实是被过分夸大了。此句中 gulf 一词翻译为"鸿沟",而非本义"海湾",含义抽象化了,英文中很多词语都有引申含义,例如 develop the film 译为"冲洗胶卷"。

5. **You are not alone**:心怀疑问的并非只有你们。此句不可直接翻译为"你们并不是孤独的"。而要根据上下文的含义进行意译。

6. **He wrote**:"**With a more progressive business model, we suspect consumers decreasingly view Merrill Lynch as a relic from the Cro-Magnon era of financial services.**":一位分析师曾试图告诉我们说:"由于采取了更进取的商业模式,我们猜测消费者会逐渐不再将美林视作金融业克罗马农时代的遗物。"克罗马农时代指大约 15—20 万年前,现代智人开始在撒哈拉以南的非洲崛起,然后走出非洲,陆续向欧亚大陆扩散。他们很可能首先到达在冰期中干涸成为盆地或沼泽的地中海地区或中东,与当地的尼安德特人竞争并共存了至少 6 万年之久。大约在 5 万年前,终于适应了冰期严寒气候的现代智人逐渐占了上风,开始陆续进入东欧,自东而西地横扫尼安德特人。其中的一支大约在 3.5 万年前到达欧洲西端的大西洋边,并导致尼安德特人的最终灭绝。人类学家将这个时代称之为克罗马农时代。

7. **They have taught us many lessons**:我们从中获得许多经验和教训。此句中翻译的语态进行了转化,将译句的主语转化为"我们",使得上下文更加连贯。

**Passage B**

1. **我关注股市的发展,但更关注股票市场的健康发展**:I follow closely the development of the stock market, and I particularly hope to see its healthy growth. 此句的第一个"关注"译为 follow,第二个关注的翻译为 see,都采用了意译,符合上下文的短语搭配。

2. **去年以来,我们加强了资本市场的基础性制度建设,特别是成功地推进了股权分置改革,解决了历史上的遗留问题**:Since last year, we have strengthened the development of institutional infrastructure for the capital market. In particular, we have successfully introduced the reform of listing non-tradable shares of listed companies, thus resolving a left-over issue. 此句的翻译采用了断句法,将"特别是"后面的句子拆成了另外一句话,这样不仅符合英文的表达习惯,也给译员留下了喘息的时间。

3. **加强资本市场的监管,特别是完善法制**:We need to enhance oversight and regulation of the capital market and especially improve the relevant legal framework. 注意此句中"监管"的翻译,没有简单地直译为 supervision,而是译为 oversight and regulation,更为精当。

4. **你谈到中国的外汇储备如何使用,这确实是我们面临的一个大问题**:As to the issue of how to use China's foreign exchange reserves you have mentioned, this is indeed a big issue we face. 此句中将"你谈到"转译为一个带 as to 短语的结构,这样处理比起直译为 you mentioned just now...更为生动。

5. **从我国的经历来看,外汇少的时候,有少的难处**:From our own experience, we know how difficult it could be when we lacked foreign exchange. "外汇少的时候,有少的难处"不可直译为 when foreign exchange is insufficient, we have a lot of difficulties,要尽量使用地道的英文进行翻译,不仅传达含义,而且传神。

6. **中国实行外汇储备的多元化,这是基于外汇安全的考虑**:China practices diversification of its foreign exchange reserves to ensure their security. 此句采用了省译法,省略了"这是",将两个分句并成一句话。翻译时经常要对原有句型进行重组。

7. **"名为治平无事,而其实有不测之忧"**:A country that appears peaceful and stable may encounter unexpected crises. 注意此句名言警句的翻译,首先要理解中文原句的含义,然后要翻译成相应的英文,同时还要注意语体的一致。

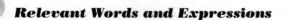

## 相关词语 Relevant Words and Expressions

重组 restructuring
投机 speculation
利率 interest rate
反洗钱 fight against money laundering
制假活动 counterfeiting activities

# 第11单元 资本市场 The Capital Market

公司管理 corporate governance
新股发行 IPO
营业利润 pre-provisioning revenue
外汇储备 foreign exchange reserve
不良贷款 non-performing loan
经营机制 operational mechanism
工商企业 corporate sector
国民待遇 national treatment
金融产品 financial product
通货紧缩 deflation
通货膨胀 inflation
抵御外部冲击 cushion impact of external shocks
早期预警系统 early warning system
支付清算系统 payment and settlement system
防范和化解金融风险 prevent and mitigate financial risks

# 口译技能

# Interpreting Skills

## 商务口译

商务口译是一门专业要求很高的职业。要成为一名优秀的商务口译译员,除了要具备胜任一般口译任务的素质之外,还必须全面熟悉商务知识,掌握商务场合的特点。

1. 直译、意译和音译并举

就商务口译方式而言,可分为直译和意译。在商务活动中,当涉及数量、质量、产品性质、要求、功能、价格等方面的情况时,译员务必使用直译的方式。这种译法,强调原语的形式结构及表层意义,而不需顾及原语表面形式以外的任何意思;"意译"注重语言深层而非表层含义,更不拘泥于原话的语法结构、词的前后位置的对应、字的多少、句的长短等。在商务口译中"直译"并不是"生搬硬套,字应字的翻译",而"意译"也不等于不顾演讲者本意随便翻译,"信口开河,不着边际的翻译"。其实直译和意译的目的是一样的,商务口译是直译与意译二者的有机结合;在商务口译中当涉及商标、地名、人名和国名等的翻译时,需要用音译。例如:Coca-Cola 可口可乐, Intel 英特尔, Pentium 奔腾。

2. 熟悉商务英语专业知识、掌握国际贸易术语

要成为一名优秀的商务口译译员,不仅必须有扎实的两种语言功底,了解两种语言背后的文化,更需要有商务领域的专业知识。译员对商务知识的了解是比较宽泛的。针对每一次会议谈判或专题讨论,译员在接到一项新的翻译任务时,还应该认真准备,在较短的时间内,找到有关的书籍、报刊文章、前期会议文件等资料,了解要讨论的专题和词汇以及

谈话双方的立场，并向有关专家和对这一课题熟悉的人请教，力求尽快抓住本课题的基本概念，本会谈的热点问题，双方的立场态度等等。商务口译的技能很大程度上依赖背景知识的熟悉程度。随着大商务、大经贸格局的形成，商务不再局限于以往的进出口、业务谈判、函电等，而是涵盖贸易金融、经济、商法、营销等。译员有必要在传译任务开始前穷尽性地收集和整理口译活动将涉及的专业术语和专有名词，并且找到它们在另一种工作语言中的语义等值加以强记，做到使用时脱口而出。商务口译人员也许不必成为某一领域的专家，但所有这些商务知识的基本内容却不可不知。比如与 WTO 专题相关的农业政策、反倾销、与贸易相关的知识产权、保障措施、技术壁垒；与宏观经济环境相关的全球化、美国贸易政策、最惠国待遇；与企业管理相关的领导艺术、企业组织框架、项目管理等等。

3. 笔记信息的科学利用

笔记不是听写，也不是速记，更不是诉状记录。笔记是听、理解、抓住信息意义后进行表达的辅助工具。口译一旦完成，笔记就失去其作用。那么商务口译中笔记应该记什么？怎么记？首先，要立足意义理解和意义记忆。译员要关注说话者表述的内容信息，捕捉谈话的实质内容，而不是精确辨认说话者使用的每一个字。抓关键词是关键。关键词指的就是那些意义单一、准确，不产生联想，在句子中承载主要信息的词汇，如数量、质量定值、时间、地点等等。这里值得提醒的是，关键词要抓，但笔记的东西并不一定完全等同说话者所用的词，译者可根据自己的习惯，把关键意义用文字、符号或划线等一目了然的形式在笔记上记录，以辅助口译表达。笔记中使用原语还是译入语，取决于译者本人的习惯。笔记中使用符号或缩写词应该是在译员群中得到共识的。英语单词拼写冗长，可以只记头几个字母。形象符号代替文字可以包含意义，同时又直观明了。商务口译人员对本专业的某些常用术语可以自己发明一些常用记号，常用常新。

4. 灵活处理现场

口译过程时一个复杂而又是创造性的劳动，加之涉及的知识面非常广泛，卡壳也是一种正常的现象。在口译过程中有些词没有听懂或没有听到，翻译中就卡在那里，或绞尽脑汁想又把后面的信息耽误了，常常因小失大。在处理这个问题上，通常采用以下三种方法。

猜测法：碰到生词或没听到的词，可利用背景知识、上下文和整个讲话的主题，将其大概意思猜测出来。这时译员通过解释或用一个泛泛的词来代替这个具体词的意思，让听众明白讲话者要传递的信息。

漏译法：有时由于临场紧张、时间紧迫，或根据背景知识、上下文无法猜测出来，如果再仔细琢磨意味着对后面信息传递的耽误。这时候，译员应果断放弃该信息的翻译，跳过继续往后翻，不用去反复想着漏译的句子。

轻声询问法：这种方法在非常重要的政治、外交场合不可使用。由于口译员的知识经历有限，有时会遇到不懂的专业词汇，如果离发言者较近，这时可以小声快速询问，问明白后，说声"对不起"，继续翻译。

总之，商务口译与其他翻译一样，是一项跨语言、跨国界、跨文化的交际活动，它不仅是个语言转化的过程，还是个大商务形势下推进商务各方理解与沟通的过程，也是发展国际交流与合作的过程，只有不断学习、不断钻研，才能成为一名出色的商务口语翻译。

# 第11单元 资本市场 The Capital Market

## 口译练习 Enhancement Practice

### 第一项 Project 1
#### 句子精练 Sentences in Focus

**A. Interpret the following sentences from English into Chinese.**

1. Effective credit risk management must lie at the very center of the risk management process more generally.
2. Before turning to the subject of the culture of credit, allow me to make a few brief observations about the issues discussed over the course of today's workshop.
3. That emphasis on credit risk is entirely appropriate since I am hard pressed to think of any major banking sector disturbances or crises anywhere in the world.
4. Indeed, the credit decision-making process ultimately entails informed judgments that meticulously balance potential risks against potential returns.
5. Creditors should not lend other people's money unless the lender is highly certain that the resulting debt can be serviced and repaid in a timely fashion.

**B. Interpret the following sentences from Chinese into English.**

1. 这些成就的取得，归功于党中央、国务院的正确领导，得益于大家的鼎力支持。
2. 中国金融业改革发展中也存在不少急需要解决的问题，我们必须妥善处理好这些问题。
3. 我们在银行资产质量上取得了显著提高，按五级标准，不良率下降了5个百分点以上。
4. 近三年来我们取得的进步，犹如一部交响曲的序幕，接下的几年将会是悠扬的主旋律。
5. 亚洲金融危机的教训告诉我们，亚洲经济应该更加有效地建立区域货币合作机制。

### 第二项 Project 2
#### 段落口译 Paragraph Interpreting

**A. Interpret the following paragraph from English into Chinese.**

In every part of the world, financial markets are being remade. The EMU in Europe, and the Big Bang in Japan. In the US, we saw the repeal of the Glass-Steagall Act—a watershed event for this industry. Today we have not one but two banks, and can offer clients the full range of financial services—just as our European competitors have been doing for years.

**B. Interpret the following paragraph from Chinese into English.**

经过多年的改革，中国已初步建立了与社会主义市场经济相适应的金融体制。中国金融业在改革中稳步发展。人民币币值对内对外保持稳定。外债水平较低。到今年3月底，外汇储备已达到2276亿美元，比年初增加154亿美元。国有独资商业银行不良贷款数额和不良贷款占全部贷款的比例都同时下降。

第三项 Project 3
篇章口译 Passage Interpreting

**A. Listen to the tape and interpret the following passage from English into Chinese.**

The weather may be cold and wet, but in the rich world's financial markets it is beginning to feel like August all over again. Credit spreads have widened and shares are pitching from gloom to elation as investors look to the Federal Reserve for solace. The anxiety is unmistakable. But this time the scare is about more than bad mortgage loans and their baleful effect on the credit markets. America may be falling into recession. And a new fear now stalks the markets: that the dollar's slide could spin out of control.

A full-blown dollar crisis on top of a credit crunch and a weakening economy would be frightening. It would send financial markets reeling and tie the hands of the Fed, perhaps forcing it to raise interest rates even as recession looms. The sky-high euro would soar further, choking off Europe's growth. Political tensions would also rise. Already Airbus has called the dollar's decline "life-threatening" and France's president, Nicolas Sarkozy, has given warning of "economic war".

At worst, the shadows could darken further. For half a century the dollar has been the hegemonic currency. A large slice of global trade is counted in dollars. Central banks hold most of their foreign-exchange reserves in dollars, a boon for America that has allowed it to issue debt more cheaply. That dominance has survived dollar slides before, as in the late 1970s and mid-1980s. But now, with the euro as an alternative, the fear is of a sudden shift in the global monetary system, with investors switching quickly from one currency to the other.

So far, this remains only a fear. Although the dollar has been falling at quite a lick, it has seen no chaotic slump, but a slide interspersed, as this week, with brief rallies. Americans' expectations of future inflation have not yet risen much. Yields on government bonds have fallen; clearly, investors do not yet expect higher premiums for safe American assets. Whether disaster strikes depends on what exactly is driving the dollar down and on how policymakers react.

The United States now has a remarkably large current account deficit, both in absolute terms and as a share of GDP. At the moment we don't seem to have any difficulty attracting capital inflows sufficient to finance this deficit, but many observers—me included—nonetheless find the deficit worrisome. The worriers see an ominous resemblance between the current US situation and that of developing countries which also went through periods during which capital flows easily financed large current deficits, then experienced "sudden stops" in which capital inflows abruptly ceased, the currency plunged, and the economy experienced a major setback.

# 第 11 单元　资本市场　The Capital Market

**B. Listen to the tape and interpret the following passage from Chinese into English.**

女士们、先生们：

　　亚洲金融危机表明，亚洲国家和地区要以更加积极的姿态去建立区域货币合作机制，否则就难避免国际金融投机的冲击。据世贸组织统计，前年亚洲商品出口总额为 1.65 万亿美元，其中区域内出口 8000 多亿美元，占 49%。去年年底亚洲 12 个国家和地区的外汇储备超过 1.12 万亿美元，约占全球外汇储备的近 60%。亚洲地区经济与贸易联系的不断加深为区域金融合作奠定了坚实的基础；巨额的外汇储备加强了亚洲资金自我循环和抵御外部冲击的实力。当前，亚洲地区中央银行应进一步加强金融合作。

　　一是进一步开放金融业，支持区内贸易的发展。

　　二是发展亚洲金融市场。东京、香港和新加坡是远东地区重要的国际金融中心，在金融产品的交易方面各有一定优势，应该在竞争中相互协调，共同发展。在继续发展货币市场的同时，要共同研究开发资本市场特别是债券市场。要发挥东亚及太平洋中央银行行长会议（EMEAP）的作用，推动债券交易市场联网，建立本地区支付清算系统。

　　三是加强亚洲各国和各地区中央银行的合作。同时，我们也建议亚洲国家的中央银行在制定和执行利率、汇率政策方面进行必要的协调，维护亚洲国家和地区的汇率稳定。

　　四是加强亚洲各个国家和地区金融监管当局之间的合作，防范和化解金融风险，共同抵御来自各种形式的金融冲击。及时交流各国和各地区金融法规的制定、降低不良贷款和处置高风险金融机构的经验，共同建立亚洲地区金融风险早期预警系统，在反洗钱、打击制假活动方面加强合作。

　　谢谢大家！

# 参考译文　Reference Version

**篇章口译 A**

　　很高兴来到沃顿，这里向来是美林公司理想的人才库。然而，我此行并非是招募新人，今天我有更大的目的。我在此要谈一下我所谓的"新经济理论"。

　　首先，我想谈一下新经济所蕴涵的力量，以及这些力量如何影响整个行业以及我的公司。其次，我希望你们确信新经济和旧经济之间存在的鸿沟其实是被过分夸大了。最后，我简要谈一下美林将如何充分运用这些力量在金融服务业中追求卓越。

　　也许有人正在怀疑，一个大金融公司的首席执行官是不是"新经济"问题的最佳演讲人。心怀疑问的并非只有你们。例如，一位分析师曾试图告诉我们说："由于采取了更进取的商业模式，我们猜测消费者会逐渐不再将美林视作金融业克罗马农时代的遗物。"在此行业干了 30 年，这就是我得到的敬重！

　　然而，这是去年的事情了。如今，所谓"旧经济"企业的优势突然奇迹般地被人重新发现了。纳斯达克 12 个月居然狂跌 1600 点，真叫人不可思议！没错，科技概念股一年来的糟糕表现使许多专家在其最确信的预测上大跌眼镜。但是，他们也都认同新经济潜在的趋势并非一时狂热。全球化和科技正为每一家公司的经营方式带来根本、永久的变化。

国界在资产管理、投资或兼并业务上已经成为无关紧要的概念。在不同市场,以不同的语言、法律、文化来实施经营策略已是目前金融行业的基本部分。以美林为例,十年前,我们有两方面的基本业务:经纪和投资银行,拥有3500亿美元的客户资产,13%的收入来自美国以外的地区。如今,在遍布26个国家850位专业研究人员的支持下,我们在三大互补的业务上拥有全球市场的支配地位:私人客户、投资管理和投资银行。我们拥有1.8万亿的客户资产,35%的收入来自美国以外的地区。

同时,科技改变了每一个行业,而对我们行业的影响比其他行业更大。总之,互联网上销售量最大的商品并非音乐,并非玩具,并非图书和鲜花,而是股票。三年前,我们推出了美林在线。如今不少专家称之为最好的互联网网站。我们同时正运用互联网技术重塑机构市场的运作方式。

全球化和科技,这些趋势将被视为新经济形成和发展的基本因素。他们会比科技股泡沫和IPO(新股发行)热潮更具深远影响。我们从中获得许多经验和教训。最主要的经验是,要在新经济中得到成功,需要将新旧经济中的优势有机结合起来。这仅仅是我们时代的一个大的悖论。

## 篇章口译 B

I follow closely the development of the stock market, and I particularly hope to see its healthy growth. Since last year, we have strengthened the development of institutional infrastructure for the capital market. In particular, we have successfully introduced the reform of listing non-tradable shares of listed companies, thus resolving a left-over issue.

Our goal is to build a mature capital market. To meet this goal, first, we need to improve the performance of listed companies. Second, we need to develop an open, fair and transparent market system. Third, we need to enhance oversight and regulation of the capital market and especially improve the relevant legal framework. Finally, we should see to it that stock market related information is released on a timely basis and make individual stock investors more aware of investment risks.

As to the issue of how to use China's foreign exchange reserves you have mentioned, this is indeed a big issue we face. From our own experience, we know how difficult it could be when we lacked foreign exchange. In the 1990s, China did not have enough foreign exchange, so we borrowed foreign exchange from the IMF. The IMF only lent us 800 million US dollars. Now our foreign exchange reserves have exceeded one trillion US dollars, and how to make good use of them has become a new issue for us.

China practices diversification of its foreign exchange reserves to ensure their security. Yes, we do plan to set up a foreign exchange investment company, and it will not be under any government department. The company will manage the foreign exchange according to law on a paid-use basis. It will be under government oversight and regulation and should preserve and increase the value of the assets.

# 第11单元 资本市场 The Capital Market

As it has not been long since China began to make investment overseas, we have little experience in this area. I recently looked at the statistics, which show that as of the end of year 2006, China's overseas investment in the non-financial category was only 73.3 billion US dollars. It increased by 16 billion US dollars last year. Still, it is insignificant in comparison with that of developed countries.

I know by raising this question, you may wonder whether the overseas investment to be made by this newly established company will affect US dollar denominated assets. China's foreign exchange reserves mainly consist of US dollar denominated assets. This is the fact. China's holding of US dollar denominated assets is mutually beneficial in nature. The setting up of a Chinese foreign exchange investment company will not affect the US dollar denominated assets.

China's financial system has maintained fast yet steady growth in recent years. However, this gives no cause for complacency, neither in the past, nor now, or in the future. My mind is focused on the pressing challenges. "A country that appears peaceful and stable may encounter unexpected crises." There are structural problems in China's finance which cause unsteady and unbalanced development. Unsteady development means overheated investment as well as excessive credit supply and liquidity and surplus in foreign trade and international payments. Unbalanced development means uneven development between urban and rural areas, between different regions and between economic and social development. All these are pressing problems facing us, which require long-term efforts to resolve.

**口译练习**
第一项 句子精练
**A.**
1. 有效的诚信风险管理应该处于整个风险管理的中心位置。
2. 切入正题之前,请允许我简单谈谈对今天的研讨会的想法。
3. 对诚信风险的重视是恰到好处的,因为20年来世界上没有一场大的金融业危机不是由信用问题引起的。
4. 确实信贷决策过程需要睿智的判断审慎地平衡潜在的风险和可能的回报。
5. 贷方不该贷出别人的钱,除非他确信借方能支付贷款利息和及时还贷。

**B.**
1. All these progress would not be possible had it not been for the guidance of our leaders and supervisors and the cooperation of our domestic and overseas clients.
2. However, many problems need to be addressed urgently if the financial sector is to grow further. Therefore, we need to solve these problems in a proper manner.
3. We achieved a remarkable improvement in the bank's asset quality as indicated by the 5 percentage point's decrease in NPL ratio on the 5-tier system.

4. If we compare our achievements and progress of the past three years to the prelude of symphony, the coming years will then be the major movement with more melodious tones.
5. Asian financial crisis has taught us the lesson that Asian economies should work more effectively to set up a mechanism for regional monetary cooperation。

## 第二项 段落口译

**A.**

在世界各地,金融市场正在重塑。欧洲的欧洲货币联盟(EMU),日本的金融大爆炸。在美国我们看到了《格拉斯—斯第戈尔法》的废除,此事可以看做是整个行业转折点的事件。如今,我们拥有两家银行,可以像我们欧洲的竞争者多年来一贯所做的那样,为客户提供全方位的金融服务。

**B.**

Through reform over the years, China has by and large put in place a financial system in line with the socialist market economy with the financial sector growing steadily in the process of reform. The value of RMB has remained stable both at home and abroad and China's external debt is kept within a comfortable range. Foreign exchange reserves reached US\$ 227.6 billion in the end of March, US\$ 15.4 billion more than the beginning of this year. The non-performing loans (NPLs) in the wholly state-owned commercial banks are in decline both in terms of its ratio and in the total lending portfolio absolute number.

## 第三项 篇章口译

**A.**

天气可能变得阴冷而潮湿了,但是富国的金融市场正又一次感受到了8月般的火热。因投资者看好美联储,信贷规模进一步扩展,股市走出阴影迎来光明。然而担忧也是明摆着的。这次恐慌不只是有关不良抵押贷款和它们对信贷市场的不良影响,而是美国可能会进入经济衰退。现在一种新的恐惧正在市场蔓延,那就是美元贬值可能失控。

在信贷紧缩和经济疲软之上爆发一场全面的美元危机将是令人胆战心惊的。它将使金融市场动荡并束缚美联储的手脚,也许会迫使它在经济衰退迫近时提高利率。欧元将进一步升值,这将制约欧洲的经济增长。政治上的紧张关系将加剧。空客公司已经把美元贬值称为是"生死攸关"的。法国总统尼古拉·萨科齐已经发出"经济战"爆发的警告。

最糟糕的是阴影将进一步扩大。半个世纪以来,美元在货币中一直处于霸主地位。全球很大一部分贸易是以美元计价的。各国央行的大部分外汇储备也是美元,这对美国来说是个恩惠,使得它能够以更低的代价来发行债券。这种统治地位过去曾经使美元摆脱了下滑,如20世纪70年代后期和20世纪80年代中期。但是,现在有了欧元的选择,人们担心会出现全球货币体系的突然变动,投资者会从一种货币迅速转向另一种货币。

到目前为止，这还仅仅是一种恐惧。尽管美元已经贬值很多，但还没有出现无序的暴跌，本周在下跌中还有短暂的反弹。美国人对进一步通货膨胀的预期没有增加。政府债券的数量在下降，这清楚地表明，投资者还不寄希望从安全的美国财产中得到更高的收益。灾难是否会袭来取决于是什么原因促使美元继续贬值和政策制定者们做出怎样的反应。

同时，美国还出现了严重的财政赤字，既包括绝对数值，也包括 GDP 产值。目前，我们似乎能够吸引足够的资本流入金融领域，填补财政赤字，但许多观察者，包括我在内，感觉赤字是令人忧心的。担忧者们发现，目前美国经济局势与许多发展中国家极为相似，都经历了资本流入弥补财政赤字的时期，也经历了资本流入突然停止和货币贬值的时期，经济发展遇到很大挫折。

## B.

Ladies and Gentlemen,

Asian financial crisis has taught us the lesson that if Asian economies could not work more vigorously to set up a mechanism for regional monetary cooperation, it would be difficult to avoid speculative attacks. According to WTO statistics, the commodity export of Asia amounted to US＄1.65 trillion the year before last year, out which more than US＄800 billion, or 49％, were intra-exports among Asian countries. The end of last year witnessed the foreign exchange reserves of 12 Asian economies exceeding US＄1.12 trillion, accounting for almost 60％ of the world total. Growing economic and trade links among the Asian countries provide a solid basis for regional financial cooperation while the abundant foreign exchange reserves will serve as a reliable funding source for the region itself, and increase its capacity to cushion impact of external shocks. At the current stage, central banks in Asia should further build up regional financial cooperation among each other.

First, financial sector opening up should intensify to support regional trade expansion. Second, Asian financial market needs to be further developed. As important international financial centers in the Far East, Tokyo, Hong Kong and Singapore, each boasting of unique advantages in trading certain financial products, should increase coordination and grow together in competition. While efforts should be continuously made to promote money market development, joint research should also be conducted on developing capital market, in particular the bond market. EMEAP (Executive Meeting of East Asian and Pacific Central Banks) should play a stronger role in promoting regional bond market development and in establishing regional payment and settlement system.

Thirdly, central bank cooperation within Asia should be strengthened. At the same time, we think it is necessary for central banks of the Asian countries to coordinate in interest rate and exchange rate policies to maintain exchange rate stability in Asia.

Fourthly, financial regulatory authorities in Asia should have more cooperation to prevent and mitigate financial risks and resist external shocks together. It is desirable for them to exchange experiences in the areas of financial legislation, NPLs reduction and disposing of high-risk financial institutions, work together to set up an early warning system for monitoring financial risks in Asia, and strengthen cooperation in fighting against money laundering and counterfeiting activities.

Thank you.

# 第 12 单元 生命科学

## Unit 12 The Biological Science

# 篇章口译

## Passage A (E-C)

 **Vocabulary Work**

Work on the following words and phrases and write the translated version in the space provided.

| | | | |
|---|---|---|---|
| pneumonia | SARS | biomedical researcher | mechanism |
| viral attack | replicate | host | genetic replication |
| immune | infected virus | chemical substance | mutated strain |
| antibiotics | detrimental effects | infection | |

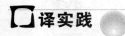 **Text Interpreting**

**Listen to the tape and interpret the following passage from English into Chinese.**
My friends,

The fact of the mysterious pneumonia has been widely spread in in this part of the world drives me to do a literature review on the suspected cause, i. e. coronavirus, of the SARS, or Severe Acute Respiratory Syndrome. As a biomedical researcher, let me show you my concern and make the following suggestions.

The basic mechanism of viral attack is that the viruses replicate themselves using the host's—in this case is "our"—DNA genetic replication system. By doing this, our body couldn't function well due to the massive viral replication. Supposingly, the immune cells in our body will fight off the infected viruses quickly. However, the viruses are so smart that they could be able to produce some chemical substances to cause our immune cells to die. Besides, this coronavirus is a new kind of virus, which belongs to a mutated strain, and our body cannot recognize it. No antibiotics have been proved to be 100% effective in treating viral infection so far. The only effective way to get rid of it is by us. It is like a prolonged battle between the viruses and our immune response. In fact, viruses couldn't kill all the immune cells in a health individual. The stronger the immune function you have, the less the viral injury you get. Therefore, the degree of sickness after infection and the rate of recovery mainly depend on how strong your immune function is.

You cannot avoid the infection unless you avoid from those infected individuals or area. But, you can try your best to boost up your immune function by several regimes. Make sure you are "extremely healthy" at least during this critical period. Stronger immune function could keep the viral damage minimal even you were so unluckily being infected. Also, stronger immune function delays the onset of any detrimental effects from the viral infection. Scientists are now working on tracking the treatment and so make sure you are still surviving until an effective treatment occurs. The following suggestions aim to strengthen your immune function within a short period of time.

1. Antioxidant nutraceuticals: Antioxidants are chemicals found in foods which exert a great value in strengthening our immune system. Boost up your immune function by taking a cocktail of antioxidant supplements.

2. Let green tea to be your daily beverage because it contains tremendous amount of antioxidant flavonoid, catechins. Eat more tomatoes, broccoli or fruits and vegetables in red and dark green color.

3. No intense physical activities during this critical period! It has been shown that intense exercise will suppress your immune function, which is related to the upper respiratory infection, even several days following your workout. Instead of intense exercise, light-to-moderate workout helps if you have been training regularly.

4. Make sure you get enough carbohydrate foods, for example, rice, food concentrated in starch, etc., because carbohydrate is the primary food for immune cells. Do some Gatorade or Pocari if needed since they are both good sources of carbohydrate.

5. Make sure you get enough sleep and don't make yourself so stressful! Anxiety, depression, and tried will influence your body's stress hormones, such as catecholamine and glucocorticoids, and so suppress your? immune status.

6. Mouth-mask helps despite it is not 100% effective. But it can still decrease the chance from infection.

All the above information is supported by peer-reviewed biomedical literatures. That means they are credible and reliable! God bless you, and I really hope that none of you will get infected and I will pray for all of you in every moment!

# 篇章口译

## Passage B (C-E)

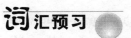

**Work on the following words and phrases and write the translated version in the space provided.**

| 心血管疾病 | 衰老 | 果糖 | 天然糖 |
| 皱纹 | 营养学 | 蛋白质 | 皮肤松弛 |
| 硬化 | 加工食品 | 碳酸饮料 | 葡萄糖 |
| 糖尿病 | 抵抗力 | | |

## 译实践 Text Interpreting

**Listen to the tape and interpret the following passage from Chinese into English.**

女士们、先生们：

我向大家报告一项我们的新发现。我们的研究人员经过两年的研究发现，大量摄取一种叫做果糖的天然糖的老鼠，似乎比其他老鼠衰老得更快。对甜食吃得太多的人来说，情况也可能会如此。

自然存在于蜂蜜和水果中的果糖，被广泛用于从饮料到酸奶的各种食品中。尽管它的甜味很受欢迎，这种糖却能使皮肤起皱纹并影响身体健康。研究员喂给实验鼠大量果糖，他们发现那些吃了果糖的老鼠的皮肤和骨质中的胶原蛋白发生了变化。

胶原蛋白是存在于结缔组织、骨质和软骨中的纤维蛋白质，它的基本作用是将人体各组织结合在一起。胶原蛋白的丧失是导致老年人皮肤松弛和深度皱纹的原因。

胶原蛋白的丧失引起的生理变化通常叫做"交叉相联"。太多的"交叉相联"就会使皮肤降低弹性，发生硬化，这是导致皮肤起皱纹的原因。人也可能是如此，尽管还没有证据证明这一点。我们摄取的加工食品越来越多，例如碳酸饮料、烘烤食品、罐装水果、果酱和乳制品，而这些食品都含有果糖。其他研究也表明，大量摄取果糖会影响人体对葡萄糖的代谢和增强对胰岛素的抵抗力，而这两者是判断患糖尿病可能性的重要指标。

我们的研究人员喂养的老鼠摄取的果糖比普通成人每天可能摄取的果糖多得多，这在此类实验中是符合标准的。在一年的时间里，这些老鼠每天按每千克(2.2磅)体重12.5克的标准摄取果糖。与此相比，一个体重154磅(70千克)的人，喝一夸脱(升)的可乐，大约摄取了60克的果糖，或者说每千克体重摄取0.8克的果糖。

这只是一项初步发现，下最后的定论还有待大量进一步的研究结果给予支持。

## 口译讲评

## Notes on the Text

**Passage A**

1. **The fact of the mysterious pneumonia has been widely spread in this part of the world drives me to do a literature review on the suspected cause, i. e., coronavirus, of the SARS or Severe Acute Respiratory Syndrome**：神秘的非典型性肺炎正在这个地区广泛传播，于是我对引起SARS，即严重呼吸综合征的病因，例如冠状病毒，做了一下研究。本句中增译了"于是"，将一个英文同位语从句拆成汉语中的两个分句。同时，此句还出现了医学上的专有名词coronavirus，注意其对应的汉语。

2. **As a biomedical researcher, let me show you my concern and make the following suggestions**：现在让我从生物医学研究者的角度给您一些建议。此句采用了省译法，省去

了 show you my concern，因为根据上下文的含义，这句的意思已经被包括了，若再译出来，则显得很啰嗦。

3. **The basic mechanism of viral attack is that the viruses replicate themselves using the host's, in this case is "our", DNA genetic replication system**：滤过性病毒能够引起疾病的主要原因是，病毒能够通过使用病人身体中的 DNA 基因复制系统来复制自己。此句根据上下文的含义，采用了"意译法"，将 the basic mechanism 译为"主要原因"，而非"基本机制"，使得上下文更为连贯，读起来朗朗上口。

4. **By doing this, our body couldn't function well due to the massive viral replication**：如果病毒大量复制自己，则我们的身体就不能正常工作了。此句将 due to 的句型译为"如果"，而非"因为"，更符合中文关联词可一词多用的习惯，使得上下文更加流畅。

5. **Supposingly, the immune cells in our body will fight off the infected viruses quickly**：于是，我们身体当中的免疫细胞就会很快的杀掉这些感染病毒。此句将 supposingly 译为"于是"，起到承上启下的作用，同时，将 fight off 译为"杀死"，更加传神。

6. **But, you can try your best to boost up your immune function by several regimes. Make sure you are "extremely healthy" at least during this critical period**：但是，你可以尽你所能调动你的免疫系统，确保你处于"非常健康"的状态，至少在这段非常时期。此句的翻译采用了"联句法"，将英文两句话通过增加一个过渡词连成一句话。翻译时，经常要根据中英文语言的不同语法规则和语言习惯，对原文进行拆分和重组。

7. **Stronger immune function could keep the viral damage minimal even you were so unluckily being infected**：如果你的免疫系统够强，就算你非常不幸地被感染上病毒，也会将病毒的侵害降到最低限度。此句的翻译采用了"增词法"，增加了几个关联词："如果"、"就算"、"也会"。

8. **Scientists are now working on tracking the treatment and so make sure you are still surviving until an effective treatment occurs**：科学家们现在正在研究如何治疗此种肺炎，所以一定要保证你能够活到有效治疗方法研究出来之前。此句中的几个词 track、occur 都不是通常的含义，因而都要根据上下文的连贯采用意译法。

**Passage B**

1. **大量摄取一种叫做果糖的天然糖的老鼠，似乎比其他老鼠衰老的更快。对甜食吃得太多的人来说，情况也可能会是如此**：Rats that eat high levels of a natural sugar known as fructose seem to age faster than other rats—and the same could be true for people who eat too much sweet junk food. 此句翻译采用了并句法，将英文原句的两句话组合成破折号连接的一句话。

2. **自然存在于蜂蜜和水果中的果糖，被广泛用于从饮料到酸奶的各种食品中**：Fructose, found naturally in honey and fruit, is used widely in foods ranging from soft drinks to yogurt. 此句中的"自然存在于"这个分句被移为后置定语，修饰中心词"果糖"，翻译时应注意这种句式的变换。

3. **胶原蛋白的丧失引起的生理变化通常叫做"交叉相联"**：The process affected is known as "cross linking"：本句采用了省译法，省略了"胶原蛋白的丧失"，因为这个概念在前句中已经包括了,只要用 transitional words "the progress" 代替即可。翻译时应注意句与句之间的衔接。

4. 太多的交叉相联就会使皮肤降低弹性,发生硬化,这是导致皮肤起皱纹的原因:Too much cross-linking reduces elasticity and makes the skin stiff and rigid, and these are the conditions that encourage wrinkled skin. 本句采用了增译法,将"发生硬化"译为 make the skin stiff and rigid,其中,增加了"皮肤"这个词,这样翻译使得上下文含义更加明确。

5. 人也可能是如此,尽管还没有证据证明这一点:The same could be true of people, although this has not been shown. 注意这个句型:The same could be true of... 。

6. 我们的研究人员喂养的老鼠摄取的果糖比普通成人每天可能摄取的果糖多得多,这在此类实验中是符合标准的:The rats our researchers worked with were fed much more than the average adult person might eat in a day, which is standard in such experiments. 此句将"摄取"这个主动式转化为被动式 were fed,从而达到上下文的连贯。主被动之间的转化是翻译时常常采用的一种方法。

# 相关词语  Relevant Words and Expressions

繁殖 reproduce
克隆 clone
衰老 aging
寿命 life expectancy
灭绝 die out; extinction
胚胎 fetus
氨基酸 amino acid
染色体 chromosome
恶性肿瘤 malignancy
防癌疫苗 cancer vaccine
化学疗法 chemotherapy
机会因素 chance element
基因工程 gene engineering
基因疗法 gene therapy
基因歧视 genetic discrimination
基因重组 gene recombination / alternation
免疫系统 immune system
老年痴呆症 Alzheimer's disease
DNA 数据库 DNA database
激素/荷尔蒙 hormone

# 口译技能

## *Interpreting Skills*

### 法庭口译

随着中国入世,中国的法庭、仲裁庭将会面临着日益增加的涉外案件。同时,跨国流动犯罪以及涉案人员的权利保证使得合格的庭译人员成为必要。

1. 法庭翻译的类型

法庭翻译,又称司法翻译,泛指在法庭上提供的翻译和任何类型案例中的法律翻译。狭义上的法庭翻译仅指在法庭上提供的翻译。从翻译的类型来讲,除了个别情况的书面互译或手语翻译外,法庭翻译基本上属于口译范畴。结合国外法庭翻译人员资格考试的有关立法与司法实践,法庭翻译主要包括视译(sight translation)、交替传译(consecutive interpretation)和同声传译(simultaneous interpretation)三种模式。在实际中,法庭翻译人员可能需要在这三种模式之间来回切换,这也就自然增加了法庭翻译的难度。

2. 法庭翻译的标准——准确性与完整性

法庭翻译不是从源语到目的语的简单转换,而应该包括三个层面的要求:意愿层面、现实层面以及道德层面,即要怎么译,能怎么译与应怎么译。道德层面对法庭翻译的要求应该是最高层次的,道德层面应该是口译的一个重要方面。作为翻译人员,一旦从事法庭翻译,就必须承担一定的义务与责任,应该受限于法律与翻译的双重道德要求。

法庭口译人员应准确地(不解释、不遗漏、不编辑)进行翻译。法庭口译人员实际上担负着双重责任:确保法庭记录能如实反映非中文(non-Chinese-speaking)诉讼参与人的陈述;确保非中文当事人与中文(Chinese-speaking)当事人在法律程序中处于平等地位。这就意味着法庭口译人员在信息转换成目的语(target language)的过程中有义务保存源语(source language)中的每一个信息因素,即应该忠实地保存所有法庭陈述的原意,包括其风格与语体。若是一味直译有可能会歪曲源语信息,但法庭口译应直接表达源语信息,即使其中包括错误表述等。法庭翻译人员不应掺入任何自己的表述意见。若确需解释口译中的问题(比如出现目的语术语缺项或只有翻译人员才能解释的误解),法庭翻译人员应征得法庭同意后方可提供有关解释。

在某种意义上而言,法庭翻译人员的翻译决定着陪审员或法官(包括人民陪审员)是否信任证人及是否采信证据。因此法庭翻译人员应再现源语信息中所包含的所有信息要素。具体来讲,法庭翻译的准确性与完整性主要体现如下:

1) 法庭翻译人员应该忠实、准确地再现源语发言人的语言水平而不进行任何的润色、编辑或删减。

2) 法庭翻译人员应该准确地保持源语的言语形式,以口语、俚语、淫秽言语、粗俗言语或复杂精深的言语形式如实地再现源语发言人的语言运用情况。

3) 若非中文发言者在其证言中使用了个别中文表述,法庭翻译人员应该用中文重复这些表述。若非中文发言者在其答复或发言中完全使用中文,除非有法庭相反指示,法庭翻译人员不必对此提供翻译。

4) 当在法庭上出现反对意见或疑义时,法庭翻译人员应翻译所提供的引起反对意见或疑义的所有信息,并以手势示意非中文发言者不得发言,直至法庭对此作出裁决。

5) 法庭翻译人员不能因非中文发言者的语言水平所致的可能不能理解而为其简化原有表述;非中文发言者在必要时可以要求法官指示法庭翻译人员作解释或简化原有表述。

6) 法庭翻译人员应尽可能地提供直译。所有的法庭翻译人员都应配备合适的法律双语词典。若出现一词多义或不熟悉的术语或短语,法庭翻译人员应向法庭如实相告。征求法庭许可之后,法庭翻译人员可询问发言人以确定准确含义。

7) 法庭翻译人员不能更正问题中所涉错误事实,不能更正非中文发言者的证人证言,即使该证人证言中存在着明显的语言错误。

8) 除非根据法庭指示,法庭翻译人员不能以概括方式提示法庭程序。

## 口译练习 Enhancement Practice

**第一项 Project 1**
**句子精练 Sentences in Focus**

A. Interpret the following sentences from English into Chinese.
1. The time left to meet the deadline should be measured in hours rather than days.
2. Human genetic engineering is bound to emerge sooner or later, whether we want it or not.
3. How life started we don't know; what we do know is that DNA appeared about three and a half billion years ago.
4. Death rate trend indicates that 85 years is the upper limit on life expectancy, barring biomedical breakthrough to slow aging.
5. It is very likely that developing improved humans will create great social and political problems with respect to unimproved humans.

B. Interpret the following sentences from Chinese into English.
1. 在基因的各种可能性范围内,生物进化基本上是一种随机游动,因而其进展十分缓慢。
2. 在大约第一个20亿年间,DNA复杂性的增长速率应该是每隔几百万年出现一则信息。
3. 我们已经开始了一个新纪元,我们可以增加DNA的复杂性而用不着坐等缓慢的生物进化过程。
4. 在过去的一万年里,人类的DNA没有什么重大的变化。但在下一个千年里,我们很可能会完全重新设计它。
5. 基因的复杂性,或被编入DNA中的信息量,大致来自分子中核酸的数量。每一则信息都可看成是对一个正反问题的解答。

# 第12单元 生命科学 The Biological Science

第二项 Project 2
段落口译 Paragraph Interpreting

**A. Interpret the following paragraph from English into Chinese.**

Today we will talk about life expectancy of our human beings. In last quarter of the 20th century, life expectancy rose sharply in industrialized nations. More people lived 100 years, and average life expectancy in these countries was about 76 years. How long will this trend continue? Will a life expectancy of 100 years or more become routine in richer countries? With these questions in mind, we have invited three experts to air their views upon this issue for which everybody shows much concern.

**B. Interpret the following paragraph from Chinese into English.**

我们将破译遗传密码并征服癌症。19世纪的歌剧中,如果女主角在第一幕中咳嗽的话,观众便会知道她将在第三幕中因肺结核而死。但是由于20世纪抗生素的出现,曾经是那样可怕的不治之症现在成了服点儿药片就万事大吉的事情。由于科学家对基因密码更加了解,而且已将研究深入到了分子水平,许多严重的疾病(比如癌症)对人类的威胁将会变得越来越小。

第三项 Project 3
篇章口译 Passage Interpreting

**A. Listen to the tape and interpret the following passage from English into Chinese.**

Good morning, everyone!

My lecture today will focus on the origin of life and the future of humans.

By far the most complex systems that we have are our own bodies. Life seems to have originated in the primordial oceans that covered the Earth four billion years ago. How this happened we don't know. It may be that random collisions between atoms built up macromolecules that could reproduce themselves and assemble themselves into more complicated structures.

What we do know is that three and a half billion years ago the highly complicated molecule DNA had emerged. DNA is the basis for all life on Earth. It has a double helix structure, like a spiral staircase, which was discovered by Francis Crick and James Watson in the Cavendish lab at Cambridge in 1953.

There are four kinds of nucleic acids. I won't try to pronounce their names because my speech synthesizer will make a mess of them. Obviously it was not designed for molecular biologists. But I can refer to them by their initials, C, G, A and T. The order in which the different nucleic acids occur along the spiral staircase carries the genetic information that enables the DNA molecule to assemble an organism around it and reproduce itself.

As the DNA made copies of itself there would have been occasional errors in the order of nucleic acids along the spiral. In most cases the mistakes in copying would have made the DNA unable to reproduce itself. Such genetic errors, or mutations as they are called, would die out. But in a few cases the error of mutation would increase the chances of the DNA surviving and reproducing. This natural selection of mutations was first proposed by another Cambridge man, Charles Darwin, in 1857, though he didn't know the mechanism for it. Thus the information content in the sequence of nucleic acids would gradually evolve and increase in complexity.

Because biological evolution is basically a random walk in the space of all genetic possibilities it has been very slow. The complexity or number of bits of information that are coded in DNA is given roughly by the number of nucleic acids in the molecule. Each bit of information can be thought of as the answer to a yes-or-no question. For the first two billion years or so the rate of increasing complexity must have been of the order of one bit of information every million years. The rate of increase of DNA complexity rose to about one bit a year over the last few million years.

But now we are at the beginning of a new era in which we will be able to increase the complexity of our DNA without having to wait for the slow process of biological evolution.

**B. Listen to the tape and interpret the following passage from Chinese into English.**

我们的研究人员认为,秋天出生的人比生在春天的人活得长,上了年纪的时候也不容易得慢性病。

我人口研究学院的研究员通过分析奥地利、丹麦和澳大利亚3国超过100万的人口普查数据得出结论,人们50岁以后的平均寿命与出生月份之间存在关联。

母亲在怀孕期间所吃的东西因季节而有不同,一年里不同时间流行的传染病也不一样,两者都会对新生儿的健康发生影响,并进而影响他们到老年时的平均寿命。

我们认为,春天分娩的母亲孕期的最后阶段适逢冬季,因此她摄入的维生素要比夏季时少。她停止哺乳开始让婴儿正常进食的时候又正好赶上夏天最热的那几个星期,这时候婴儿容易发生消化系统感染。

在奥地利,秋天(10至11月)出生的成人大约要比春天(4至6月)出生的多活7个月,而在丹麦这一差异大约是4个月。

南半球的情况也差不多。生于澳洲秋天——欧洲的春天——的成人寿命比春天出生的长大约4个月。

我们的研究人员使用死亡证明和人口普查数据作为参考资料,主要对象是20世纪初出生的人。尽管人们在一年中各个时期的营养状况与那时相比都已经有所改善,这样的季节性差异却依然存在。

# 参考译文

## Reference Version

**篇章口译 A**

朋友们：

神秘的非典型性肺炎正在这一地区广泛传播，这引起我对致发 SARS，即严重呼吸综合征的病因，例如冠状病毒的关注，我因而对此做了一番研究。现在让我从生物医学研究者的角度给您一些建议。

滤过性病毒能够引起疾病的主要原因是，病毒能够通过使用病人身体中的 DNA 基因复制系统来复制自己。如果病毒大量复制自己，则我们的身体就不能正常工作了。于是，我们身体当中的免疫细胞就会很快的杀掉这些感染病毒。然而，这些病毒非常聪明，他们能够产生某种化学物质而导致我们的免疫细胞死亡。除此以外，冠状病毒是一种新型的变异病毒，它不能被我们的身体识别。这样，在我们的免疫系统和病毒之间就会展开一场长时间的斗争。实际上，病毒并不能杀死一个健康人身体中的所有免疫细胞。人身体的免疫功能越强，受病毒侵害的几率就越小。所以，在感染病毒后的病情严重情况和康复的几率基本上看此人的免疫功能有多强。

你无法避免被感染，除非你不去接触被感染者和被感染地区。但是，你可以尽你所能调动你的免疫系统，确保你处于"非常健康"的状态，至少在这段非常时期。如果你的免疫系统够强，就算你非常不幸地被感染上病毒，也会将病毒的侵害降到最低限度。科学家们现在正在研究如何治疗此种肺炎，所以一定要保证你能够活到有效治疗方法研究出来之前。下面是一些在短时期内能够增强你的免疫功能的方法：

1. 抗氧化剂：抗氧化剂是一种存在于食品中的能够很好增强我们免疫系统的化学物质。你可以靠服用一些抗氧化剂保健品来增强你的免疫功能。

2. 每天喝绿茶，因为绿茶中含有大量抗氧化剂类黄酮和茶酸。多吃西红柿、椰菜和其他红色和深色的水果。

3. 在这段非常时期不要做剧烈运动！因为剧烈运动会压抑你的免疫系统功能（与你的上呼吸感染有关的免疫系统功能），并且此压抑情况会持续好几天。如果你以养成定期锻炼的习惯，那么在这段时间你可以做一些轻度或中度运动。

4. 确保你食用足够的碳水化合物食物，例如大米及其他富含淀粉的食物，因为碳水化合物是免疫细胞最重要的食物。喝一些 Gatorade 饮料或 Pocari 饮料，因为这些饮料含有丰富的碳水化合物。

5. 每天保证充足睡眠，不要使自己处于紧张和压力之下。焦虑、紧张都会影响身体的压力荷尔蒙，例如儿茶酚安和糖皮质激素，从而压抑身体免疫功能。

6. 口罩虽然不能 100% 预防感染，但是能够起到一定的作用，仍然可以减少被感染几率。

以上所有信息均有生物医学理论支持，这些建议都是可信和可靠的。愿上帝保佑。我真心希望你们中没有一个人会被感染。我会时刻为你们大家祈祷平安！

**篇章口译 B**

Ladies and Gentlemen,

  I would like to report to you on our recent discovery. In the wake of two-year studies, our researchers have discovered that rats which eat high levels of a natural sugar known as fructose seem to age faster than other rats which do not—and the same could be true for people who eat too much sweet junk food.

  Fructose, found naturally in honey and fruit, is used widely in foods ranging from soft drinks to yogurt. But while its sweet taste is popular, the sugar could cause wrinkles and heal the problems. The researchers fed large amounts of fructose to laboratory rats and found that the fructose-fed rats showed changes n the collagen of their skin and bones.

  Collagen, a fibrous protein found in connective tissue, bone and cartilage, basically holds the body together. The loss of collagen is what causes sagging and deep wrinkles in older people.

  The process affected is known as "cross linking". Too much cross-linking reduces elasticity and makes the skin stiff and rigid, and these are the conditions that encourage wrinkled skin. The same could be true of people, although this has not been shown. We are eating more and more processed foods such as carbonated drinks, baked goods, canned fruits, jams and dairy products that contain fructose. Other studies have shown that high fructose intake can affect how the body handles glucose and increases insulin resistance—which can both be important measures of the tendency toward diabetes.

  The rats our researchers worked with were fed much more than the average adult person might eat in a day, which is standard in such experiments. The rats were fed 12.5 grams of fructose per kg (2.2 pounds) of weight every day for a year. To compare, a person weighing 154 pounds (70kg) who drinks a quart (liter) of cola consumes about 60 grams of fructose, or 0.8 grams per kg of body weight.

  This is just a preliminary finding and much need be done before final conclusions are reached.

**口译练习**

**第一项 句子精练**

**A.**

1. 到最后期限的时间应该用小时而不是用天来计算了。
2. 不管我们喜欢与否,人类基因工程迟早会出现的。
3. 生命是怎么开始的,我们不知道。但我们确实知道的是,35亿年前,DNA就出现了。
4. 死亡率的趋势表明如果不考虑生物医学上延缓衰老的新突破,85岁是预期寿命的上限。
5. 培育改进了的人种对未改进的人类而言会产生社会和政治问题,这是很有可能的。

**B.**

1. Because biological evolution is basically a random walk in the space of all genetic

possibilities it has been very slow.
2. For the first two billion years or so the rate of increasing complexity must have been of the order of one bit of information every million years.
3. We are at the beginning of a new era in which we will be able to increase the complexity of our DNA without having to wait for the slow process of biological evolution.
4. There has been no significant change in human DNA in the last ten thousand years. But it is likely that we will be able to completely redesign it in the next thousand.
5. The complexity of genes, or number of bits of information that are coded in DNA is given roughly by the number of nucleic acids in the molecule. Each bit of information can be thought of as the answer to a yes no question.

## 第二项 段落口译

**A.**

我们今天的话题是有关人的寿命。在20世纪的最后25年,工业化国家的人口预期寿命大幅度增长。百岁老人增多,在这些国家里,平均预期寿命是76岁左右。那么,这种趋势会持续多久?超过100岁的长寿在较富裕的国家里会变得很普通吗?带着这些问题,我们特别请来了几位专家,请他们谈谈这个人人关心的问题。

**B.**

We'll crack the genetic code and conquer cancer. In 19th-century, during the performance of an opera, when the heroine coughed in the first act, the audience knew she would die of tuberculosis in Act 3. But thanks to 20th-century antibiotics, the once-dreaded, once-incurable disease now can mean nothing more serious than taking some pills. As scientists learn more about the genetic code and the way cells work at the molecular level, many serious diseases—cancer, for one—will become less threatening.

## 第三项 篇章口译

**A.**

同学们,大家早上好!

今天我的讲座题目是生命起源及人的未来。

迄今为止,我们所拥有的最复杂的系统是我们的身体。生命看来似乎起源于40亿年前覆盖着地球的原始海洋。这是怎么发生的,我们不知道。可能是原子之间的无序碰撞产生了大分子,这些大分子能复制自己并聚集成更为复杂的结构。

我们确实知道的是,35亿年前,高度复杂的分子DNA就出现了。DNA是地球上所有生命的基础。它有着像螺旋式楼梯一样的双螺旋结构,这一点是由弗朗西斯·克里克和詹姆斯·沃森于1953年在剑桥的卡文迪什实验室里发现的。

有四种核酸,我就不说它们的名字了,因为我的语音合成器会把他们弄乱的。显然它不是为分子生物学家设计的。但我可以用它们的首字母来指代,即C、G、A和T。这些不同的核酸沿着螺旋式楼梯排列成的序列携带着基因信息,使DNA分子能围绕着它聚集成一个有机体并自我复制。

　　DNA自我复制时,偶尔会在核酸的螺旋序列上出错。大多数情况下,复制中的错误会使DNA自我复制终止。这些基因错误(通常叫做突变)会自行消失。但在少数情况下,错误或突变会增加DNA存活和自我复制的机会。突变的自然选择是由另一个剑桥人查尔斯·达尔文于1857年首先提出的。尽管他并不知道其机制。核酸系列中的信息含量就这样逐渐进化并越来越复杂。

　　在基因的各种可能性范围内,生物进化基本上是一种随机游动,因而其进展十分缓慢。其复杂性,或被编入DNA中的信息量,大致来自分子中核酸的数量。每一则信息都可看成是对一个正反问题的解答。在大约第一个20亿年间,DNA复杂性的增长速率应该是每隔几百万年出现一则信息。最近的几百万年间,这个速率逐渐增加到大约每年一则信息。

　　现在我们已经开始了一个新纪元,我们可以增加DNA的复杂性而用不着坐等缓慢的生物进化过程。

**B.**

　　Our researcher have found that people born in the autumn live longer than those born in the spring and are less likely to fall chronically ill when they are older.

　　By using census data for more than one million people in Austria, Denmark and Australia, the researchers at the Institute for Demographic Research found the month of birth was related to life expectancy over the age of 50.

　　Seasonal differences in what mothers ate during pregnancy, and infections occurring at different times of the year could both have an impact on the health of a new-born baby and could influence its life expectancy in older age.

　　We believe that a mother giving birth in spring spends the last phase of her pregnancy in winter, when she will eat less vitamins than in summer. When she stops breast-feeding and starts giving her baby normal food, it's in the hot weeks of summer when babies are prone to infections of the digestive system.

　　In Austria, adults born in autumn (October-December) lived about seven months longer than those born in spring (April-June), and in Denmark adults with birthdays in autumn outlived those born in spring by about four months.

　　In the southern hemisphere, the picture was similar. Adults born in the Australian autumn—the European spring—lived about four months longer than those born in the Australian spring.

　　Our researchers focused on people born at the beginning of the 20th century, using death certificates and census data. Although nutrition at all times of the year has improved since then, the seasonal pattern persists.

# 信息技术

## 第 13 单元

 **Information Technology**

Unit 13

# Passage A (E-C)

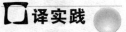 **Vocabulary Work**

Work on the following words and phrases and write the translated version in the space provided.

| | | | |
|---|---|---|---|
| end user | cyber attack | phishing | bogus |
| adware | spy-ware | malicious shareware | vulnerability loophole |
| firewall | anti-virus software | intrusion detection system | program patch |
| spam | intrusive nuisance | congest | fraud |

**Text Interpreting**

Listen to the tape and interpret the following passage from English into Chinese.

Distinguished Guests, Ladies and Gentlemen,

Good morning! I am delighted to deliver the opening speech for the Information Security Forum. This is an important event for IT professionals and industry players to exchange expert views and share knowledge and experience on best practices in information security.

According to research results, the volume of Internet traffic generated by end users worldwide is predicted to nearly double annually over the next few years. More and more offering of electronic services has transformed business operation and take over traditional delivery channels. While the online route serves to please customers and enable businesses to stay competitive, computer users are also exposed to greater risk of cyber attacks such as computer services disruption, data corruption, or leakage of confidential information in the computer. information security is indeed everyone's concern.

Internet surfing, emails and online operation are common sources of cyber risks. For the audience here, you know what phishing and bogus websites are and how they exploit the careless Internet users to disclose their credential information and illegally transfer money from their bank accounts. However, even the vigilant Internet users can become victims of adware, spy-ware or malicious shareware if their information systems contain vulnerability loopholes. To protect our computer networks and systems against the attackers, it is necessary to implement security measures to monitor, detect and block various cyber attacks with the use of applicable technologies such as firewalls, anti-virus software, intrusion detection systems and other defensive mechanisms. Most importantly, users should ensure that program patches are applied properly.

Email has become an integral part of the Internet for users to communicate with others. However, among the emails received in our city, around 60% are spam, and the cost of spam to Internet service providers here was nearly $6 million a month. Spamming is an intrusive nuisance that invades people's personal privacy and breaches IT security. Spam emails can be used maliciously to spread viruses, congest network traffic, transmit illicit contents and facilitate cyber crimes.

Recognizing the damaging effects of spam on our community, our Government has launched a campaign in fighting the spam epidemic. The campaign is setting the scene for a partnership of Government, the IT industry, the e-marketing industry and the community in a united front. Besides, various promotion and publicity activities are being progressively initiated to enhance public awareness of the spam problems, and provide them with accurate and useful information to deal with such problems.

In an interconnected world, information often moves across boundaries within a company or between companies. It is important that data moving across the value chain is protected in a consistent manner. It was shocking news that a data security breach, possibly the largest to date, had recently happened in the US and exposed more than 40 million credit card accounts to fraud.

Increasingly, companies and enterprises have begun to set and polish up their security policies, guidelines and good practices. The government has led by example in strengthening the IT security for government information systems. Back to 2005, a security management framework has been put in place to ensure and enhance internal IT security.

We have to be up-to-date and on the alert constantly on information security as well as discipline ourselves to follow the best practices and be a good citizen of the cyber world. The Government has set up various information resources to facilitate the access of information security related information and current updates by the public and companies. The development of a secure and reliable e-community requires every citizen's concerted effort.

It is most encouraging to see a large number of reputable industry players gathering here for the promotion of IT security to the community. I wish the forum a great success.

# 篇章口译

## Passage B (C-E)

 **Vocabulary Work**

Work on the following words and phrases and write the translated version in the space provided.

| | | | |
|---|---|---|---|
| 数字鸿沟 | 电讯基础设施 | 手机渗透率 | 主力军 |
| 领头羊 | 蓝图 | 中国无线发展中心 | 运营商 |
| 多销售商 | 平台 | 开发周期 | 意识推广 |
| 调控政策 | 企业精神 | 商业头脑 | |

 **Text Interpreting**

Listen to the tape and interpret the following passage from Chinese into English.

尊敬的来宾,女士们、先生们:

很荣幸参加中国国际无线会议。我特别感谢组办方把本领域内许多本地和国际专家请来参加此次会议。

在过去十年里,无线和移动技术一直以令人惊叹的速度在增长。很显然,不仅信息和通讯技术高度发达的国家如此,发展中国家更是如此。有人甚至预计无线和移动设备将成为一种更为高效有用的工具,跨越最不发达国家的数字鸿沟。

中国有着优越的电讯基础设施,是世界上手机渗透率最高的地方之一,目前业已推出3G网络服务,热衷使用各种移动产品的用户在中国占很高比率,因此中国拥有许多制胜元素,能成为各种创新型无线产品、技术和服务发展的主力军,甚至领头羊。

正因为此,政府已将无线技术和服务作为"21战略"中国信息通讯业蓝图中技术发展的一个重要区域。已有一些措施推出,支持该产业的进一步发展。

早在2003年12月,政府资助成立并启动了中国无线发展中心。该中心提供了一个独一无二的与不同标准无线网络相连接的多运营商和多销售商平台,所有商业考虑均面面俱到。无线开发商可以通过不同的运营商和设备,来开发并检验自己的产品,从而大大降低了成本,缩短了开发周期。

去年,政府成立了一个工作组,和该产业一起实施一个包括意识推广、产品开发和专业培训在内的行动项目。为了推进此项目,今年年初成立了一个由产业界、学术界和政府代表构成的新工作组,促进对创新型产品的使用和开发。新工作组旨在发现不同领域共同关注的问题,并解决与无线技术和服务相关问题。

政府会一如既往地建立适当的基础设施、调控政策和商业环境,资助有价值的倡议,在

# 第13单元 信息技术 Information Technology

中国无线科技和产品开发方面起到协助和推动的作用。不过,尽管中国拥有很多优势,发展前景令人振奋,但无线产业的成败与否,和其他产业一样,很大程度上仍取决于创新能力、企业精神和行业人士的商业头脑。

我很高兴地看到今天的会议为参与者提供了一个极好的机会,就无线产业的未来发展以及所面临的挑战交流看法。我相信,有效的交流一定能使与会者得到颇丰的收获。

# 口译讲评

## Notes on the Text

**Passage A**

1. **information security**:即信息安全,主要涉及信息传输的安全、信息存储的安全以及对网络传输信息内容的审计三方面。其中完整性、可用性、保密性和可靠性是信息安全的特征,密码技术和管理是信息安全的核心,安全标准和系统评估构成信息安全的基础。信息安全作为信息时代的安全重点和根本保障,已经越来越成为国家安全、社会安全乃至世界安全的基础,成为经济安全的命脉、国防安全的核心。

2. **phishing**:即网络钓鱼。phishing一词是fishing和phone的综合体,由于黑客始祖起初是以电话作案,所以用ph来取代f,创造了phishing。phishing发音与fishing相同。"网络钓鱼"攻击者利用欺骗性的电子邮件和伪造的web站点来进行诈骗活动,受骗者往往会泄露自己的财务数据,如信用卡号、账户和口令、社保编号等内容。诈骗者通常会将自己伪装成知名银行、在线零售商和信用卡公司等可信的品牌,在所有接触诈骗信息的用户中,有高达5%的人都会对这些骗局做出响应。

3. **adware**:即广告软件,是指未经用户允许,下载并安装或与其他软件捆绑通过弹出式广告或以其他形式进行商业广告宣传的程序。安装广告软件之后,往往造成系统运行缓慢或系统异常。

4. **spy-ware**:即间谍软件,是一种能够在电脑使用者不知不觉的情况下,或者在给电脑使用者造成安全假象的情况下,在用户的电脑上安装"后门程序"的软件。这些"后门程序"可能是一个IE工具条,一个快捷方式或是其他用户无法察觉的程序。虽然那些被安装了"后门程序"的电脑使用起来和正常电脑并没有什么太大区别,但用户的隐私数据和重要信息会被那些"后门程序"所捕获,这些信息将被发送给互联网另一端的操纵者,甚至这些"后门程序"还能使黑客操纵用户的电脑,或者说这些有"后门"的电脑都将成为黑客和病毒攻击的重要目标和潜在目标。总之,间谍软件是目前网络安全的重要隐患之一。

5. **Spamming is an intrusive nuisance that invades people's personal privacy and breaches the IT security**:这个典型的定语从句在翻译时要将原句进行切分,转为几个独立的小分句,"垃圾邮件是个讨厌的不速之客,侵占个人隐私,破坏因特网安全。"

6. **The campaign is setting the scene for a partnership of Government, the IT industry, the e-marketing industry and the community in a united front**:set the scene for... 是一固定词组,意思是"为……创造条件,提供背景",全句可译为"这一系列行动为政府、信息技术产

业、电子市场产业和社会在统一战线上的合作提供了背景。"

7. **It is important that data moving across the value chain is protected in a consistent manner**：in a consistent manner 的意思就是 consistently，此句可以译为"价值链上的数据流动始终处于保护之下，这点非常重要。"

8. **Recently, a special task force on information security has been formed comprising stakeholders in the industry to address specific information security issues and produce a checklist of focus activities for enhancing the information security in our city**：这是一个典型的英语长句，翻译时首先要注意把被动语态转换为主动语态，因为汉语中多用主动语态来组句达意，其次，要注意句中若干关键词的处理，如 stakeholder 这里指的是利益相关方，翻译时可处理为"业内人士"；整句话可处理为："最近，政府就信息安全问题成立了一支由业内人士构成的特别任务组，解决具体的信息安全问题，运作一系列的重点活动，以此提高我市的信息安全。"

9. **We have to be up-to-date and on the alert constantly on information security as well as discipline ourselves to follow the best practices and be a good citizen of the cyber world**：这句话中并列成分很多，翻译时要注意断句与切分，转成多个独立小句，以符合汉语的表达习惯，可译为："我们必须在信息安全方面紧跟时代，时刻不放松，同时规范自己，遵循成功经验，成为网络世界的良好公民。"

**Passage B**

1. **很显然，不仅信息和通讯技术高度发达的国家如此，发展中国家更是如此**：这句话如若处理不好，很容易变成中国式英语的拗口表达，可参考译为 This is evident not only in countries where information and communications technology development has reached an advanced stage, but more so in the developing world。

2. **中国有着优越的电讯基础设施，是世界上手机渗透率最高的地方之一，目前业已推出 3G 网络服务，热衷使用各种移动产品的用户占中国很高比率，因此中国拥有许多制胜元素能成为各种创新型无线产品、技术和服务发展的主力军，甚至领头羊**：这句话中包括的信息太多，在翻译之前，一定要理清逻辑，确定主次，选用具体的结构和语法进行构建，可译为 With an excellent telecommunications infrastructure, one of the highest mobile penetration rates in the world, the roll-out of 3G network services and a high proportion of avid users of mobile applications, China possesses many of the success factors to be a key or even leading player in the development of innovative wireless applications, content and services。

3. **已有一些措施推出，支持该产业的进一步发展**：这句话宜用被动语态翻译，即译成 A number of initiatives have been launched to support the further development of the industry。

4. **该中心提供了一个独一无二的与不同标准无线网络相连接的多运营商和多销售商平台，所有商业考虑均面面俱到**：这句话中，"独一无二的与不同标准无线网络相连接的多运营商和多销售商平台"这个短语中定语成分较长，翻译时要注意短语表达时的对称与平衡，可处理为 a unique multi-operator and multi-vendor platform with connectivity to the

wireless network of different standards。

5. 去年，政府成立了一个工作组，和该产业一起，实施一个包括意识推广、产品开发、和专业培训在内的行动项目："一个包括意识推广、产品开发、和专业培训在内的行动项目"这个短语可以译为 a program of activities covering awareness promotion, applications development and professional training。

6. 政府会一如既往，建立适当的基础设施、调控政策和商业环境，资助有价值的倡议，在中国无线科技和产品开发方面起到协助、推动的作用：这句话在翻译时要理顺关系，找准中心结构，可以把"起到协助、推动的作用"作为句子主干部分，之后顺次粘连其他成分。可译成：The Government will continue to play a facilitating and enabling role in the development of wireless technology and applications in China, by putting in place the right infrastructure, regulatory regime and business environment and funding worthwhile initiatives。

7. 不过，尽管中国拥有很多优势，发展前景令人振奋，但无线产业的成败与否，和其他产业一样，很大程度上仍取决于创新能力、企业精神和行业人士的商业头脑：这个长句的翻译较为挑战，主语"无线产业的成败与否"宜用名词结构，使句子显得较为精简，不致太过冗长，全句可译为 Notwithstanding the strengths of and exciting prospects for China, the success or otherwise of the wireless industry, as with other industries, depends to a large extent on the innovative capability, entrepreneurial spirit and business acumen of our industry players。

# 相关词语 Relevant Words and Expressions

网虫 nerd; nethead
网域 network domain
分时网络 time-shared network
共享网络 shared network
联网产品 networking products
同步网络 synchronizing / synchronous network
网络布局 network topology
网络故障 network out-of-order
网络模拟 network analog
远程登录 remote login
远程主机 remote host
智能终端 intelligent / smart terminal
办公用网络 office network
不安全网络 insecure network; unsafe net
超文本链接 hypertext link
多媒体终端 multimedia terminal

多协议网络 multi-protocol network
因特网协议 IP [Internet protocol]
终端信息包 terminal packet
终端转换器 terminal converter

# 口译技能

## Interpreting Skills

### 视译

  视译即视稿翻译，是会议翻译的一种。在正式场合，发言人为谨慎起见通常会念稿发言，而事先准备的讲稿语言华美，逻辑严谨，不像即席发言那么容易理解和记忆，再加上速度较快，这就要求译员在几乎无所准备的情况下，跟着发言人的速度，将原文稿件用另一种语言译出。视译不允许译员有足够的斟酌余地，稿件又逼译员尽量使译出语正确。做视译时，需要译员灵活运用顺译技巧，注意发言人的速度，最好做到发言人话音刚落，翻译的声音也随即停止，翻译时还要留神发言人是否临时插入讲解或例子，那时就要做无稿翻译。做好视译的关键有三点：译入语的语序、视译单位和连接语。

  译入语有两种可能的语序：1）打破了原句语序，句子结构紧凑。2）基本保持了原句语序，句子结构较松散，把原文的几大部分分为若干小部分，词类转换频繁，连接语较多。前者在同传箱里做视译，基本上行不通。首先，在语序上动这样大的手术，无法跟上发言者的速度。其次，听众也会由于句子太长而无法一听即懂。后者的结构比较适应视译要求，语序大致不变，每个短句部分短而上口，意思表达清楚。这不仅为口译人员赢得了宝贵的时间，也使听众感到舒服得多。

  视译的翻译单位：若要基本保持原文语序，就应该有一种可以依赖的视译单位。可采用"信息基素"作为视译单位，即构成一个较完整的内容信息的基本单位。信息基素应具备以下要素：1）相对独立的概念；2）一目可及的范围；3）前后信息基素的灵活结合。视译单位的三要素是缺一不可的。"具有相对独立的概念"可以从大处保持原文语序，给短距带来极大的方便，使译文口语化，易译易懂。每个视译单位均在"一目可及范围之内"，有助于译员在一个单位内进行词序调整，不致使译文支离破碎。"前后信息基素的灵活结合"通过有机地使用衔接词可以保证一个较完整的内容信息能够流畅地得以转达，给增译留有充分的余地。

  由于视译和同传在译语产出方面有许多共同点，视译练习一直是同声传译训练的重要组成部分。在练习时，第一步可以找一些有译文的发言稿，边听发言录音，边做"同声传读"，逐渐过渡到脱离译稿只看原文进行口译。视译前建议快速通读一下原文，以便对发言的主要内容做到胸中有数，并对语言难点和专业难点做一些"译前准备"。

# 第13单元 信息技术 Information Technology

## 翻译练习 Enhancement Practice

### 第一项 Project 1
### 句子精练 Sentences in Focus

**A. Interpret the following sentences from English into Chinese.**

1. IT development is an evolutionary process that can only be sustained by continuous input in terms of innovation, investment, policy support, and most important of all, commitment of all stakeholders.
2. I would like to take this opportunity to thank the authors of these pieces of advice, and many of them are here today, for all their help in sharing with us their expert input on combating spamming.
3. In view of the community's concerns about information security and economic loss caused by spamming, we shall step up our efforts to maintain a secure environment for the conduct of e-business.
4. To telecommunications operators, particularly Internet service providers, spam adds to your operating costs, with additional server capacity to manage anti-spam systems and additional resources to handle customer complaints.
5. Recently, a special task force on information security has been formed comprising stakeholders in the industry to address specific information security issues and produce a checklist of focus activities for enhancing the information security in our city.

**B. Interpret the following sentences from Chinese into English.**

1. 亚洲不仅扩大了手机的使用人数,而且也增加了更先进的无线服务类型,比如数据服务。
2. 在信息时代,我们要与全球范围内所有的伙伴建立积极有效的联系,利用信息技术增强竞争力。
3. 中国要保持竞争优势,就必须不断提高实力,开发创新型产品、服务和内容,应用信息技术成果。
4. 充足的从事多媒体内容创建的本地人才,以及他们对中国乃至全世界市场十分了解,进一步强化了中国成为无线内容提供商的优势。
5. 世界各国已经制定了适合各自发展的具体策略,充分发挥信息技术的潜力,努力提高生产力,促进经济发展,提高人民生活水平。

### 第二项 Project 2
### 段落口译 Paragraph Interpreting

**A. Interpret the following paragraph from English into Chinese.**

You will agree that as technologies develop, techniques used by spammers will only become more sophisticated. The recent development of spamware illustrates the evolving nature of this problem. Fortunately, we have not all gone over to the dark side.

To help combat spam emails, computer users may install effective email filters, discipline the usage of emails as well as take proactive steps to track down potential intruders or criminals as soon as the suspects appear on their websites. Various anti-spam measures are adopted to curb email spamming worldwide including both the establishment of relevant legislations and non-legislative measures.

**B. Interpret the following paragraph from Chinese into English.**
移动服务的需求风行一时,现在全世界手机用户比固话人数要多。2003年,手机用户从2亿3千万左右增长到13亿多。换言之,每秒钟有超过430个用户登记!预计到2009年,这个数字将超过20亿。期盼已久的第三代手机服务,即3G,也已开始在世界各地站稳脚跟。同时,世界经济不断发展,我们预计无线通讯的需求将进一步增加。

第三项 Project 3
篇章口译 Passage Interpreting

**A. Listen to the tape and interpret the following passage from English into Chinese.**
Ladies and Gentlemen,

Like what they say, "Spring is the best time to make action plans for the rest of the year." I am, therefore, hugely delighted to be able to share with you in the early days of the new spring our action plan in tackling spamming.

Spamming, as you all know well, is a problem that is affecting almost everyone in the information age. It takes many forms, from junk fax to junk e-mail to junk voice or video messages on your fixed line or even your mobile telephone. And it will take on other forms as technology develops.

To individual consumers, spam is an intrusive nuisance that invades your personal privacy, breaches your IT security with virus and spyware, and transmits illicit contents, from pornography to illegal gambling services and even deceptive business practices.

To businesses, spam costs you money in the form of worker productivity reduction and in the need for network capacity upgrade and information security investment.

Without any doubt, spam has become the major 21st century problem that affects all of us without any prejudice, and the only difference in treatment between spam victims lies merely in the degree of damage. Recognizing the damaging effects of spam on our community, we launched a consultation exercise in June last year, with a view to ascertaining the size of the problem and soliciting views from all stakeholders on how the problem should be tackled. We received in total 42 useful submissions.

Ladies and gentlemen, there is no doubt in my mind that we need to step up our fight against spamming. Drawing on the views expressed in the submissions and the trend on recent developments, we can protect ourselves from spam to a large extent by adopting products with suitable technologies. For service providers, the adoption of such products will improve their services to subscribers and ease the load on their network equipment.

While we believe that we should not dictate or recommend individual products or solutions, we can help in the process by facilitating the industry, businesses and consumers to learn more about the latest developments and offerings. We will, therefore, collaborate with the industry in organizing seminars and exhibitions to promote anti-spam technical solutions to all users.

The measures that I have described mark the beginning of our battle against spam, and the measures will no doubt need to evolve over time. Like computer virus, we may never be able to eradicate the problem. But we aim to contain it as far as possible. In this battle, we need the efforts from all quarters of our community. Our plan sets the scene for a partnership of Government, the IT industry, the e-marketing industry and the community in a united front. In this, I see no difference in perspective. You are our allies, and I look forward to working closely with you all in controlling this 21st century problem.

**B. Listen to the tape and interpret the following passage from Chinese into English.**

尊敬的来宾，女士们、先生们：

我很高兴得知今天的会议将无线开发中心在澳大利亚、加拿大和英国的同行一起请来中国，进一步探讨合作的可能性。

今天，无线行业的销售商、服务供应商和开发商共聚一堂，交流技术，探讨产品联手开发、投资和营销，实在是恰逢其时。

亚洲是无线行业非凡发展的引领者，这并不让人惊讶。目前，单是亚洲就占了全世界1亿1000万无线数据用户的75%强。许多人预计，只要无线市场活跃下去，亚洲将继续推动无线数据服务的增长。

中国为促进亚洲无线服务的进一步发展做出了很大的贡献。我们的优势尤其在于我们有能力领导无线产品的开发，这是无线技术应用和财政增长的推动力。

我之所以对我国在无线产品开发上的优势充满信心，是因为在竞争中，我们具有许多优势。我们有世界一流的无线基础设施。我们的市场极具竞争力，这使得我们能以合理的价格充分选择富有创意的优质无线服务。事实上，我们的企业，尤其是中小企业，以开发新产品所具有良好的企业精神和敏锐的市场触觉而著称。另外，我们的大众成熟，他们有学养，了解无线技术，愿意接受创新产品和服务。所有这些因素使得中国成为无线开发商眼中的一块优秀的试验地，去开发并试验新的无线产品。

女士们、先生们，我刚才勾画了中国在提高亚洲无线技术开发方面所具有的优势。为了充分发挥优势，我们需要与所有相关单位紧密合作，合作方包括政府部门、设备供应商、无线运营商、产品供货商，乃至整个信息技术产业。我们的未来是无线的未来，我期待着和大家一起努力，促进无线业在中国的发展。

中国无线开发中心的成立让我所提到的方方面面进行合作找到了凝聚点。我希望该中心能使无线服务开发方面的所有主要力量之间都能建立成功的合作和联系。我们将积极加快中国无线服务的发展，从而促进其在亚洲和世界的发展。

# 参考译文
## Reference Version

**篇章口译 A**

尊敬的来宾,女士们、先生们:

上午好!我很高兴为"信息安全论坛"致开幕词。对信息科技专业人士和从业人员来说,这是一个在信息安全方面交流专家意见、分享知识和成功经验的重要盛事。

据研究结果表明,由全球因特网终端用户而产生的网络交通流量预计在几年之内每年都将翻番。越来越多的电子服务已经改变了了商业操作的模式,取代了传统的信息传输渠道。上网让用户开心,让商业富有竞争力。然而,计算机用户也同样置身于各种网络攻击的更大的风险面前,比如计算机服务中断、数据贪污、计算机内机密信息的泄露。信息安全实际上是每个人关注的事情。

上网冲浪、电子邮件和在线操作是网络风险的通常来源。大家都知道"网络钓鱼"和非法网站是干什么的,知道他们如何诱使粗心的因特网用户来泄露自己的机密信息,将钱从银行账户中非法转出。更有甚者,如果信息系统含有易受攻击的漏洞,因特网用户即使再警惕,也会成为广告软件、间谍软件或恶意共享软件的牺牲者。为了保护我们的计算机网络和系统免受攻击,非常有必要利用诸如防火墙、防毒软件、侵入识别系统、其他防护机制等多种应用科技去实施安全措施,从而监控、甄别并阻截各种网络攻击。最为重要的是,用户必须确保程序补丁正常应用。

电子邮件已经成为因特网必不可少的一部分,用户用它来与人联系。然而,在我市所收到的邮件中,约60%是垃圾邮件,因特网服务商为垃圾邮件所支出的花费高达一个月600万美元。垃圾邮件是个讨厌的不速之客,侵占个人隐私,破坏因特网安全。垃圾邮件可以被恶意地使用来传播病毒,堵塞网络交通,传输非法内容,并为网络犯罪提供方便。

政府意识到垃圾邮件对社会的伤害之后,采取了一系列行动来打击垃圾邮件。这一系列行动为政府、信息技术产业、电子市场产业和社会在统一战线上的合作提供了基础。另外,我们正在积极推行不同的推广与宣传活动,以提高公众对垃圾邮件问题的意识,我们向他们提供正确有用的信息来应对这种问题。

在彼此沟通的世界里,信息常常跨越界限,在公司内或公司间流动。价值链上的数据流动始终处于保护之下,这点非常重要。近来美国发生了可能是迄今为止规模最大的一起数据安全泄露事件,4000多万信用卡账户置于受诈骗的风险之中,这则消息令人震惊。

现在越来越多的公司和企业开始成立并改进各种安全政策、制度和措施。我们政府率先在政府信息系统上加强了信息技术的安全性能。早在2005年我们就安装了安全管理体系以确保和提高内部因特网的安全。

我们必须在信息安全方面紧跟时代,时刻不放松,同时规范自己,遵循成功的经验,成为网络世界的良好公民。政府已经建立了不同的信息源,让大众和公司能够更加方便地获取信息安全方面的信息和更新资料。一个安全可靠的电子社会的发展需要每个公民的共同努力。

看到许多著名的业内人士为了提高全社会信息技术的安全而共聚一堂,真是鼓舞人心。我希望此次论坛取得巨大成功。

**篇章口译 B**

Distinguished Guests, Ladies and Gentlemen,

It gives me pleasure to attend the China International Wireless Conference. I am particularly grateful to the organizers for bringing together many local and international experts in the field to this conference.

Wireless and mobile technology has been growing at a breath-taking pace in the past decade. This is evident not only in countries where information and communications technology development has reached an advanced stage, but more so in the developing world. Some even predict that wireless and mobile devices could be a more efficient and effective means to bridge the digital divide in the least developed countries.

With an excellent telecommunications infrastructure, one of the highest mobile penetration rates in the world, the roll-out of 3G network services and a high proportion of avid users of mobile applications, China possesses many of the success factors to be a key or even leading player in the development of innovative wireless applications, content and services.

For this reason, the Government has identified wireless technology and services as one of the focus areas for technological development in our Digital 21 Strategy, the blueprint for ICT development in China. A number of initiatives have been launched to support the further development of the industry.

As early as December 2003, the Government funded the establishment and initial operation of the China Wireless Development Center. The CWDC provides a unique multi-operator and multi-vendor platform with connectivity to the wireless network of different standards, impartial to all commercial concerns. Wireless developers can develop and test their applications across different operators and devices, significantly reducing their costs and shortening development cycles.

Last year, the Government set up a task force together with the industry to implement a program of activities covering awareness promotion, applications development and professional training. To take the program forward, a new task force has been established earlier this year comprising representatives from the industry, academia and the Government to drive the adoption and development of innovative applications. The new task force aims to identify matters of common interest among various sectors and resolve issues relating to wireless technology and services.

The Government will continue to play a facilitating and enabling role in the development of wireless technology and applications in China, by putting in place the right infrastructure, regulatory regime and business environment and funding worthwhile initiatives. Notwithstanding the strengths of and exciting prospects for China, the success or otherwise of the wireless industry, as with other industries, depends to a large extent on the innovative capability, entrepreneurial spirit and business acumen of our industry players.

I am glad to note that today's conference will provide excellent opportunities for the participants to exchange views on the future trends of and challenges to the wireless industry. I'm positive that participants will benefit from the fruitful discussions here at the conference.

**口译练习**

**第一项 句子精练**

**A.**

1. 信息技术是不断向前发展的,只有不断创新、投资、给予政策支持,最重要的是,只有所有相关人士共同努力,信息技术产业才能继续发展下去。
2. 我想借此机会感谢所有提出建议的人士,许多人还出席了今天的会议,感谢大家在打击垃圾邮件这个问题上用自己的专业知识向我们提供帮助。
3. 全社会都很关注垃圾邮件引发的信息安全和经济损失问题,因此,我们要更加努力,为电子商务的运行提供一个安全的环境。
4. 对电信营运商,尤其是因特网服务商而言,垃圾邮件增加了营运成本,服务器需要额外容量来管理反垃圾邮件系统,也需要额外资源来应对客户投诉。
5. 最近,政府就信息安全问题成立了一支由业内人士构成的特别任务组,解决具体的信息安全问题,开展一系列的重大活动,以此提高我市的信息安全。

**B.**

1. Not only does Asia contribute to the growth of the mobile population, Asia actually drives the adoption of more advanced use of wireless services, such as data services.
2. In the information age, we need to connect ourselves effectively and efficiently to all our partners in the global system, and use IT to sharpen our competitive edge.
3. For China to remain competitive, we need to continue to enhance our capability in the development of innovative applications, services and contents, and our ability to adopt and apply fruits of IT industry.
4. A good supply of local talent in multimedia content creation and their knowledge of China and international markets further add to China's strengths as a wireless content provider.
5. Different economies around the world have formulated specific strategies that are suitable for their own state of development to exploit fully the potential of IT in an effort to enhance productivity, generate economic growth and improve the quality of life for their citizens.

# 第13单元 信息技术 Information Technology

第二项 段落口译

A.

　　大家都认为,随着科技的进步,垃圾邮件制造者所用的科技只会越来越复杂。垃圾软件的最新发展表明不断升级正是这一问题的本质所在。幸运的是,我们还没有完全走到黑暗的一面来。

　　为了帮助与垃圾邮件作斗争,电脑用户可以安装有效的电子邮件过滤器,规范电子邮件的使用,并采取积极措施打击网上的不速之客或罪犯。现在已经采取了各种反垃圾邮件措施去制止全球的垃圾邮件普遍化发展态势,其中包括成立相关的法规和非法律的措施。

B.

　　Demand for mobile services has caught on in a big way such that we have now more mobile phone subscribers in the world than the number of fixed lines. In 2003, the number of mobile phone subscribers increased by around 230 million to over 1.3 billion. In other words, subscribers were signing up at a spectacular rate of more than 430 per minute! It is estimated that we will pass the 2 billion mark by 2009. The much awaited third generation mobile services, or 3G, has also begun to establish their foothold in various parts of the world. Meanwhile, the world's economy is moving ahead, and we expect demand for wireless communication will pick up further.

第三项 篇章口译

A.

女士们、先生们:

　　正如俗话所说"一年之计在于春"。因此,我很高兴能在新春伊始,告诉大家我们为打击垃圾邮件而定下的"计"之所在。

　　如大家所知,垃圾邮件是影响信息时代几乎每一个人的问题。它的表现形式多样——垃圾传真、垃圾电子邮件、垃圾语音、固定电话,甚至手机上的视频信息。随着科技的发展,它还会以其他形式出现。

　　对个人消费者来说,垃圾邮件是讨厌的侵入者,侵犯个人隐私,用病毒和间谍软件破坏信息技术安全,传输非法内容——色情服务、非法赌博甚至商业诈骗行为。

　　对公司而言,垃圾邮件消耗工作能量,处理垃圾邮件要求公司具备网络升级能力,加大信息安全的投资,耗资巨大。

　　毫无疑问,垃圾邮件已经成为21世纪的主要问题,它不加区别地影响所有的人,其受害人的唯一不同就在于受害程度轻重不一。我们在意识到垃圾邮件对社会造成的危害之后,于去年六月召开了一次磋商会,以弄清问题的严重程度,听取相关人士的建议,了解应对措施。我们共收到42条有用的建议。

　　女士们、先生们,我想我们一定要加快与垃圾邮件斗争的步伐。根据意见书中的观点和近来的发展趋势,我们要选取技术合适的产品,来保护自己免受垃圾邮件大范围的侵袭。对服务商而言,选用这样的产品可以提高对用户的服务水平,减低网络设备的压力。

　　虽然我们不应该强令,也不应该推荐使用某种产品或某条建议,但我们可以提供诸多便利,为该行业、各公司、消费者提供方便,以更多了解最新的发展状况和推出的产品。因此,我们将与该行业合作,召开研讨会和展览会来改善用户的反垃圾邮件的技术。

　　我之前所介绍的方法标志着我们对垃圾邮件的战争刚刚拉开序幕。毫无疑问,这些方法也需要随着时间而不断升级。正如我们永远不可能清除电脑病毒一样,我们也永远不可能根除这个问题。但是我们要尽力将其控制住。在这场战斗中,我们需要来自社会方方面面的努力。我们的计划为政府、信息技术产业、电子市场行业和全社会在同一阵线上的合作提供了问题的背景。在这里,我们的观点一致。大家是我们的盟友,我期望与你们在控制这个 21 世纪的难题上紧密合作。

**B.**
Distinguished Guests, Ladies and Gentlemen,
　　I am delighted to know that today's conference has brought to China the Wireless Development Center's counterparts from Australia, Canada and the United Kingdom to explore further co-operation opportunities.
　　It is, indeed, timely to bring together today vendors, service providers and the developer community of the wireless industry to explore technology sharing, joint product development, funding and marketing.
　　It is not surprising to note that Asia has led the spectacular growth of the wireless industry. At present, Asia alone accounts for over 75 per cent of some 110 million wireless data subscribers worldwide. Many expect that Asia will continue to fuel wireless data services growth given the vibrancy of its wireless markets.
　　China is well placed to promote the further development of wireless services in Asia. Our strength lies particularly in our ability to spearhead the development of wireless applications which constitute the driving force for wireless adoption and revenue growth.
　　My confidence in China's strength on wireless application development is founded on many of our competitive advantages. We have world-class wireless infrastructure. Our market is extremely competitive. This has led to a wide choice of innovative and quality wireless services at very reasonable prices. Indeed, our enterprises, particularly the small and medium ones, are renowned for their entrepreneurial spirit and astute market sense in developing new applications. And our mature and sophisticated wireless-savvy population is always receptive to innovative products and services. All these factors make China an excellent testbed for wireless developers to develop and test new wireless applications.
　　Ladies and gentlemen, I have just outlined China's strengths in promoting wireless development in Asia. To exploit our strengths fully, we need close collaboration of all the relevant actors, and they include government, equipment suppliers, wireless operators, application and content providers, and even the IT industry. Our future is wireless, and I look forward to working with you all to promote wireless development in China.
　　The establishment of the China Wireless Development Center provides a focal point for co-operation of all the actors that I have mentioned. It is my wish that the Center will

foster successful co-operation and ties among all the key players in the development of wireless services. Together, we will seek to accelerate the development of wireless services in China, and in turn, in Asia and in the world.

# 第 14 单元 法律制度

## Law and Legal System

# 篇章口译

## Passage A (E-C)

### Vocabulary Work

Work on the following words and phrases and write the translated version in the space provided.

| | | | |
|---|---|---|---|
| enforced rules | social institution | without regard for | obligation |
| set penalties for | violate | amend | prophecy |
| pretentious | enforceable | administrative | judicial |
| status quo | | | |

### Text Interpreting

**Listen to the tape and interpret the following passage from English into Chinese.**

Ladies and Gentlemen,

Today we'd like to address a simple but very important issue in our lives, that is, what is law?

Law is the set of enforced rules under which a society is governed. Law is one of the most basic social institutions—and one of the most necessary. No society could exist if all people did just as they pleased, without regard for the rights of others. Nor could a society exist if its members did not recognize that they also have certain obligations towards one another. The law thus establishes the rules that defined a person's rights and obligations. The law also set penalties for people who violate these rules, and it states how government shall enforce the rules and penalties. However, the laws enforced by government can be changed. In fact, laws frequently are changed to reflect changes in a society's needs and attitudes.

In most societies, various government bodies, especially police agencies and courts, see that the law be obeyed. Because a person can be penalized for disobeying the law, most people agree that law should be just. Justice is a moral standard that applies to all human conduct. The laws enforced by government have usually had a strong moral element, and so justice has generally been one of the law's guiding principles. But governments can, and sometimes do, enforce laws that many people believe to be unjust. If this belief becomes widespread, people may lose respect for the law and may even disobey it. However, in democratic societies, the law itself provides ways to amend or abolish these unjust laws.

There have been and will continue to be different definitions of law. Aristotle saw law as a rule of conduct. Plato believed that law was a form of social control. Cicero contended

# 第14单元 法律制度 Law and Legal System

that law was the agreement of reason and nature, the distinction between the just and the unjust. The British jurist Sir William Blackstone described law as "a rule of civil conduct prescribed by the supreme power in a state, commanding what is right, and prohibiting what is wrong." In America, the eminent jurist Liver Wendell Holmes, Jr., contended that law was a set of rules that allowed one to predict how a court would resolve a particular dispute: "The prophecies of what the courts will do in fact, and nothing more pretentious, are what I meant by law."

Although these definitions vary in their particulars, all are based on the following general observation: "Law consists of enforceable rules governing relationships among individuals and between individuals and their society. This very broad definition of law implies the following:

1. To have law, there must be established rules, such as constitutions, statutes, administrative agency regulations, and judicial decisions.

2. These rules must be capable of enforcement, that is, law and order must prevail with resolution in a judicial system.

3. The rules must establish approved conduct by which individuals deal with each other and participate in society.

In the next lecture, I'll focus on the functions of the law:
1. Maintaining social control while facilitating social life.
2. Protecting the public order.
3. Resolving disputes.
4. Protecting the status quo.
5. Facilitating orderly change.

## 篇章口译

## Passage B (C-E)

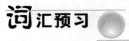 Vocabulary Work

Work on the following words and phrases and write the translated version in the space provided.

| 财产 | 渗透 | 商场盗窃 | 逃税 |
| 恐怖主义 | 婚姻暴力 | 虐待 | 城市化 |
| 腐败 | 可卡因 | 重罪 | 轻罪 |
| 刑期 | 绑架 | 放火 | 重偷盗罪 |
| 小偷小摸 | 殴打 | 公共场所酗酒 | 卖淫 |
| 各种机动车违章行为 | | | |

## 译实践 Text Interpreting

Listen to the tape and interpret the following passage from Chinese into English.

众所周知,在当今世界诸多问题中,没有哪个问题像犯罪那样普遍,那样古老。犯罪的形式多种多样,其中包括对财产、人身和政府的犯罪。各式各样的犯罪渗透到每一个社会阶层,触及到每一个人。你可能从未遭遇过抢劫,但是别人在商店盗物导致商店购买物品价格上涨,你也因之受害;由于他人逃税,你付的税款因此增加。由于你居住的社区犯罪率上升,你的房产的现值也许比前几年降低了;由于你居住的世界的那一个地区恐怖主义活动增加,旅游业衰退,你的生意也许不像过去那样红火。无论你干什么行当,无论你居住何处,无论你是否乐意,无论你是否知晓,你都是犯罪的受害者。

犯罪,尤其是暴力犯罪,已经到了十分严重的地步,许多人不敢在自己的街区单独行走,天黑以后不敢开门。

专家们对于犯罪数量是不是真的增加持有争议。在婚姻暴力以及丈夫、妻子或儿童虐待案中情况尤为如此。在人类历史的大多数时期,家庭暴力和无人照管案件常常不被曝光,世人常常认为家庭事务不过是私事。

其他专家对究竟谁该真正对犯罪行为负责——个人还是社会——争执不一。许多研究人员发现社会中的几个因素会导致犯罪率上升或下降:大规模的城市化进程、失业和贫困、庞大的移民人口群体。而其他一些国家则更多地受到诸多政治、政府腐败和宗教等因素的影响。

显而易见,犯罪是危害社会的行为。我们的法律制度认为犯罪不仅仅是针对特定受害人的违法行为,而且是对整个社会的犯罪。的确,不一定要有具体的受害个体才能说存在犯罪。比如持有可卡因是犯罪,尽管不可能有特定的个人声称因为另外一个人的吸毒而受害。其之所以是一种犯罪,是因为社会通过其管理机关集体断定吸食可卡因是危害公众福利的行为。

最后我们还可以了解一下犯罪的种类。刑法把较为严重的犯罪称作重罪,相对不太严重的犯罪称为轻罪。一般说来,重罪是罪犯可被监禁一年以上的犯罪;而轻罪的刑期不超过一年。重罪通常包括谋杀、强奸、绑架、放火、使用致命武器试图伤害、抢劫以及重偷盗罪。典型的轻罪包括小偷小摸、普通的企图伤害和殴打、公共场所酗酒、妨碍社会治安行为、卖淫、赌博以及各种机动车违章行为。

## 口译讲评

## Notes on the Text

**Passage A**

1. **social institution**:解释"社会制度,社会准则"。Institution:An elementary rule, principle, or practice. 文章中这句话的意思是"法律是最基本的社会准则之一,也是最必

# 第14单元 法律制度 Law and Legal System

需的准则之一。"

2. **obligation**：此处翻译为"义务"；法律英语中"权利"与"义务"的表达便是 rights and obligations。要注意的是来自罗马法的 obligation，通常还翻译为"债"。
3. **... see that the law are obeyed**：这里的 see that 是"保证"的意思。
4. **Aristotle**：亚里士多德，公元前384—公元前332，是古希腊的伟大思想家。
5. **Plato**：柏拉图，公元前427—公元前347，古希腊哲学家，师从苏格拉底(Socrates，公元前469—公元前399)，又是亚里士多德的老师。
6. **Cicero**：西塞罗，全名 Marcus Tullius Cicero，公元前106—公元前43，古罗马政治家和杰出的法律思想家。在法律思想方面，他根据斯多葛学派的观点，首先系统地提出自然法学说。
7. **Sir William Blackstone**：威廉·布莱克斯通公爵许多法律著作中最著名的是《英国法释义》(*Commentaries on the Laws of England*，1765—1976)，以至于读 Blackstone 成为了"读法律"的代名词。
8. **Oliver Wendell Holmes**：奥利佛·温德而·霍姆斯，1841—1935。1902年罗斯福总统任命他为联邦最高法院法官，直到1932年。其传世之作首推《普通法》(*The Common Law*，1881)，著名论文《法律之道》(*The Path of the Law*，1897)，该文于1897年在《哈佛法学评论》(*Harvard Law Review*)上发表。霍姆斯的"实用主义法学"体现在他的"法律预测说"之上。

**Passage B**

1. **犯罪，尤其是暴力犯罪，已经到了十分严重的地步**：这里我们可以使用一个由 point 引导的定语从句，所以此句可译成 Crime, especially violent crime, has risen to a point where...
2. **婚姻暴力**：指的是婚姻内的暴力，也就是发生在夫妻之间的暴力，我们译成 conjugal violence。
3. **丈夫、妻子或儿童虐待**：虐待这里用 abuse，所以译成 the abuse of husbands, wives or children。
4. **重/轻罪**：两个专有法律词汇都有专门的翻译方式，重罪称为 felony，轻罪称为 misdemeanor。
5. **使用致命武器企图伤害罪**：可以译成 assault with a deadly weapon。
6. **重偷盗罪**：不能译成 serious theft，专门的表达方式为 grand larceny，theft 传统的叫法是 larceny。在美国 grand larceny 包括偷盗超过某一具体金额的钱款或物件。
7. **普通的企图伤害和殴打**：可译成 simple assault and battery，这种犯罪并不伴随着和致命武器有关的可加重罪行的因素(aggravating factors)。
8. **妨碍社会治安行为**：可译成 disorderly conduct，conduct 经常会表示"行为"的意思，比如常用语 code of conduct(行为准则)。

## 相关词语  Relevant Words and Expressions

裁决 verdict
传票 summons
在押 behind bars
仲裁 arbitration
代理权 power of attorney
普通法 common law
实际的 de facto
通缉令 wanted order
充公;没收 confiscation
大陪审团 grand jury
法庭判令 decree
犯罪未遂 criminal attempt
共同过失 contributory negligence
立即执行 immediate execution
藐视法庭 contempt of court
审判地点 venue
捏造的证据 fabricated evidence
伪造;伪造文书 forgery
不在犯罪现场证明 alibi
(财产权利的)转让 assignment

# 口译技能
## Interpreting Skills

### 模糊表达

我们已经知道,口译的过程主要由三大步骤组成,即听力理解、短时记忆和译语输出。在实战口译中,译员难免会受到种种因素的影响,有时很难将所有信息无一遗漏地全部传达给听众。譬如讲话人的语篇中有一小部分没有听清或没有听懂、数字没有完全记录下来或者一下子没有反应出来、几个地名或专有名词超出了自己的词汇范围……这时,译员首先要镇定下来,千万不要慌了手脚,然后适当地利用一些口译中的模糊表达技巧来帮助自己渡过难关。

模糊性是所有人类语言的一种客观属性,尤其是在口语中,模糊表达更是屡见不鲜。而口译自身的特点也直接导致口译表达有时无法顾及语言细节。模糊表达方式则可以有效地

# 第14单元 法律制度 Law and Legal System

减少信息的流失、减轻译员的心理压力,从而提高口译效率。一般而言,译员可以在口译实践中利用如下几个模糊表达技巧:

1. 近似法

这一方法主要用于数字的口译。当译员听到一长串的数字却没能全部记录下来时,利用近似法肯定要远远好过将其隐去不译。如"去年我省的贸易额达到了492亿3千9百70万美元"即可用近似法译为 Last year the trade volume in our province reached about 49 billion US dollars。

2. 概括法

即将所听到的内容大意总结出来,而不是将其细节一样一样依次译出。如 Today, the peoples of Europe are celebrating EU enlargement in a series of cultural events from the west coast of Ireland to the eastern border of Poland, and from Valletta in the south to the northern most tip of Finland. 这段话里出现了多个地名,大部分还是大家熟悉的,但 Valletta(瓦莱塔,马耳他首都)就未必是每个译员都知道的,这样口译就遇到了麻烦。这时,译员就可以采用概括法将其"模糊地"译为"今天,欧洲人民正用一系列的文化活动来庆祝欧盟的扩大,整个欧洲的人民都在庆祝这一盛事"。

3. 仿音法

当译员听到一些不熟悉的人名、地名或专有名词,且无法回避时,就可以根据将听到的读音再模仿出来。在大多数情况下,听众还是能够明白的。

4. 意译法

这个方法主要用于习语和引语的口译。译员在平时的学习中,要有意识地积累一些常用的习语和引语,但当碰到的习语或引语不在自己的储备范围之内,而直接翻译又可能引起误解或过于拖沓时,就只能通过意译法传达其内涵了。例如:

1) 良言一句暖三冬,恶语伤人六月寒。A kind word is remembered for a long time, but an abusive language hurts the feelings at once.

2) 千里送鹅毛,礼轻情义重。A present, though trifling, is accompanied with sincere wishes.

3) 老吾老以及人之老,幼吾幼以及人之幼。Expend the respect of the aged in one's family to that of other families; expend the love of the young ones in one's family to that of other families.

5. 忽略法

如前所述,模糊性乃是所有人类语言的一种客观属性,有时并非所有的信息都有必要一一译出,适当的忽略并不会影响到听者的理解。如:"欢迎来自五大洲的年轻选手们"只需译成 Welcome the contestants from all over the world 即可,而没有必要一定要将"五大洲"译为 five continents。另外,在翻译会议名称的时候,有时为了节约时间,也可将忽略会议的名称不译,简单说成 this meeting 即可,通常而言,与会者都应该知道会议名称的。

最后,需要指出的是,上述的种种模糊翻译策略大多是为译员遇到困难时提供的一些解决方法和回避手段,并不是鼓励译员"模糊"对待口译。这一点,想必大家也都是明白的。

## 口译练习 Enhancement Practice

### 第一项 Project 1
#### 句子精练 Sentences in Focus

**A. Interpret the following sentences from English into Chinese.**
1. The principal purpose of a trial is to resolve disputed issues of fact.
2. These 10 amendments were ratified by the States before 1791, and are popularly known as the "Bill of Rights".
3. In other words, however immoral or unjust an act may be thought to be, it is not a crime unless the law says it is.
4. When it comes to a criminal or intentional tort case, litigation may be a more effective process than mediation because it results in a finding of liability or guilt.
5. There are a number of specialized federal courts created by the congress since 1855 that perform certain highly specialized functions that aid the Congress in fulfilling its legislative power.

**B. Interpret the following sentences from Chinese into English.**
1. 对公众健康和自然环境的保护在法律上正受到越来越多的重视。
2. 为制止各类商标侵权行为,以规范市场活动,商标法的修改迫在眉睫。
3. 中国对禁止生产核裂变材料用于制造核武器的条约谈判一贯保持积极态度。
4. 政府注意到滥用海洛因在东欧国家正呈上升趋势,准备在这一地区对与毒品有关的犯罪进行严厉打击。
5. 是否将某一特定行为划为犯罪是一个社会问题,社会价值观念因时而异,我们对犯罪行为的界定也因而随之发生了变化。

### 第二项 Project 2
#### 段落口译 Paragraph Interpreting

**A. Interpret the following paragraph from English into Chinese.**

Law is a pervasive feature of social life that profoundly affects us. Law shapes our lives from our conditions of birth to our conditions of death and everything else in between. Law must be encountered, studied, criticized and changed for people to realize their full capacities as citizens, as productive members of society, and as creators of their identities and of the social institutions through which they make their lives. Law has complex and frequently contradictory effects on our lives. Often law supports our well-being and equal participation in social life.

# 第14单元 法律制度 Law and Legal System

**B. Interpret the following paragraph from Chinese into English.**

为了成为一名合格的辩护人和法律顾问，律师必须了解案情的一切真相。在相互信任和充分交流的基础上，律师担负起为委托人案情辩护的艰巨任务。在民事诉讼案件中，律师与当事人关系往往表现为这种信任和充分的交流。然而，在刑事案件中，两者关系相比之下更常常表现为不信任，甚至对抗。

第三项 Project 3
篇章口译 Passage Interpreting

**A. Listen to the tape and interpret the following passage from English into Chinese.**

Good morning, everyone. I'm David. Today's lecture is about the American law. Americans have always had ambivalent feelings about law. Our rhetoric is full of noble ideals such as "equal justice under law" and the "rule of law." We pride ourselves on having a "government of laws, not men," and on the assertion that no one is above the law."

At the same time, disregard for the rule of law has been part of our political tradition. We are a nation born of violent revolution, and during our frontier period watchman groups often took the law into their own hands. Even in our own time we debate the role of civil disobedience in the civil rights, animal rights, abortion, and antinuclear movements.

In many ways the questions we ask ourselves about the nature of law are the same ones we ask about our political system and about society at large. How do we account for the conflicting attitudes Americans have toward law? How can persons who are law abiding one minute turn into a law-breaker the next? How can a nation founded on the basis of its citizens "inalienable rights" systematically deny those rights to African Americans and other minorities? How can we explain these contradictions? The answers to these questions are not easy, but we can begin to understand the paradox by looking at three approaches to the nature of law. They are natural law approach, positive law approach and sociological approach.

First, natural law theorists believe that the laws that govern relationships among people, like the laws that govern the physical universe, are sown in nature. The second approach, positive law, is the belief that law should simply reflect the will of the majority. Despite the immorality of segregation or colonialism, if a majority wishes to have a segregated society or a colonial policy, then they may have it. Those who disagree with the law can certainly work within the democratic process to change it, but they must accept it as the legitimate reflection of the will of the majority. Finally, the sociological theory of law holds that law represents a reflection of the values, morals, and culture of the society. As the society changes, the law will also change.

**B. Listen to the tape and interpret the following passage from Chinese into English.**

青少年是祖国的未来，正确引导青少年的人生观和培养造就一批21世纪的栋梁之才是立足当前着眼未来的一件千秋大事。

然而,当前青少年违法犯罪率在直线上升,这不仅直接危害了青少年本人及其家庭,给社会治安带来不稳定因素,而且关系到祖国的前途和命运,因此,如何预防青少年违法犯罪,如何创设良好的社会环境就成为摆在我们面前的一项重大课题。

对于青少年法庭以及相关缓刑部门的功能存在着很多的分歧和误解。有人急呼整个程序只会造就那些青少年罪犯,而并非使之减少。有言论称要对那些孩子严厉些,还有一大群人则认为对待那些孩子应该采取更加理解和温和的态度。对于目前现存的相关服务的质疑,从很大程度上来说,应该归结于国家现行的措施的混乱情况。

一方面,青少年法庭隶属于刑事法庭范畴,有责任对某些具体的受指控的个体判定有罪或无罪。另一方面,他们有责任提供一系列的处理、监督以及引导那些失足的青少年,无论他们犯了什么样的罪。这两种相互矛盾的任务必须同时承担,而且要非常恰当的以一种非正式的方式展开,这样才不会在孩子们成长定型的岁月中留下阴影。

青少年违法的主要原因有以下四个方面:
1. 社会原因;
2. 家庭原因;
3. 学校原因;
4. 心理生理原因。

而我们需要做的是:
1. 强化家庭教育功能,明确家庭教育责任。
2. 学校要大力推行素质教育和养成教育,做到教书育人。
3. 加强法制教育,增强自我防范意识。
4. 严厉打击侵害未成年人合法权益的犯罪分子,奖励知法、守法的模范。

# 参考译文

# Reference Version

## 篇章口译 A

女士们、先生们:

今天我要为大家讲一个在我们生活中非常重要的话题,那就是法律,那么,法律是什么呢?

法律是指一系列使社会得以有序治理的强制性规则。法律是最基本的社会准则之一,也是最必要的准则之一。如果人们为所欲为,无视其他人的权利,那么这个社会将无法存在。同样,如果社会成员没有意识到彼此之间的权利和义务,那么这个社会也将荡然无存。因此,法律建立了规则,从而确立了人们的权利和义务。法律也同时制定了对违法之徒的惩罚措施以及政府该如何执行这些规则和措施。然而,由政府制定的法律是可以变更的。事实上,法律会经常性地变更以适时反映社会的需要与态度。

在多数社会中,各种各样的政府部门,特别是警察机构以及法院保证法律得以遵守。由

于犯法将得到制裁,所以大多数的人认为法律应该是公正的。公正这一道德标准是适用于所有的人类活动的。由政府强制执行的法律通常具有很强的道德因素,因此公正便成了法律的指导原则之一。但政府制定的法律有可能,也通常会让人们感到并不公正。当这种认识蔓延开来,人们就会失去对法律的尊重从而不去遵守它。然而,在民主社会里,法律本身会修正那些不公正的法律法规。

对于法为何物,从来就存在着不同的定义,从前是,将来也是。亚里士多德将法看做一种行为准则。柏拉图认为法是社会制约的一种形式。西塞罗则认为法是理性与自然的统一,也是公正与非公正的区别所在。英国著名法学家布莱克斯通将法描述为:"由一国最高权力规定的市民行为准则,命令做正确的事,禁止做错事。"在美国,杰出的法学家奥利佛·温德而·霍姆斯则主张法是允许人们去预测法院将如何解决某一特定纠纷的一整套准则:"对于法院在事实上将如何处理的预测,而绝非其他更虚饰的东西,这便是我所谓的法。"

尽管这些定义在它们各自的特殊之处有所不同,但是所有的这些关于法的定义都是建立在下面这一普遍的判断之上的。即:法是由调整个人与个人以及个人与社会之间关系的强制性规则所组成的。这个对法所下的宽泛的定义包含下列意思:

1. 要有法就必须制定成文的规则,例如宪法、制定法、行政机关规章以及司法判例等。
2. 这些规则必须是可强制执行的,换言之,法律和命令在一司法体系内必须能够坚决占优势地位。
3. 这些规则必须制定一些被认可的行为准则,个人可依此与他人交往或参与社会活动。

在下一讲中,我们会介绍法律的功能:

1. 保持社会管理的同时改进社会活动。
2. 保护公共秩序。
3. 解决纠纷。
4. 保护现状。
5. 促进有秩序的变化。

**篇章口译 B**

As we all know, of the many problems in the world today, none is as widespread, or as old, as crime. Crime has many forms, including crimes against property, person, and government. Crime, in all its forms, penetrates every layer of society and touches every human being. You may never have been robbed, but you suffer the increased cost of store-bought items because of other's shoplifting and you pay higher taxes because of other's tax evasion. Perhaps your house is not worth as much today as it was a few years ago because of the increased crime rate in your neighborhood, or maybe your business is not doing as well as it used to because tourism is down due to increased terrorism in your part of the world. Whatever you do, wherever you live, you are a victim of crime whether you like it or not, whether you know it or not.

Crime, especially violent crime, has risen to a point where many people are afraid to walk alone in their own neighborhoods, afraid to open their doors after dark.

Experts argue whether the number of crimes committed is actually on the rise: This issue is particularly true in cases of conjugal violence, the abuse of husbands, wives or children. Throughout much of history, cases of family violence and neglect often went unreported because of the attitude of society, which considered family matters to be private.

Other experts argue about who is really to blame for criminal behavior: the individual or society. Researchers have identified several factors in society that contribute to the crime rate: massive urbanization, unemployment and poverty, and a large immigrant population. Other countries are more affected by factors such as politics, government corruption, and religion.

Evidently, crime is an injury against society. Our legal system regards crimes not merely as wrongs against particular victims but as offenses against the entire society. Indeed, there does not have to be an individual victim for there to be a crime. For example, it is a crime to possess cocaine, even though it is unlikely that a particular individual will claim to have been victimized by another person's use of the drug. This is a crime because society, through its governing institutions, has made a collective judgment that cocaine use is dangerous to the public welfare.

Finally, we could understand different types of crime. Criminal law distinguishes between serious crimes, known as felonies, and less serious offenses, called misdemeanors. Generally speaking, felonies are offenses for which the offender can be imprisoned for more than one year; misdemeanors carry jail terms of less than one year. Common examples of felonies include murder, rape, kidnapping, arson, assault with a deadly weapon, robbery, and grand larceny. Typical misdemeanors include petit theft, simple assault and battery, public drunkenness, disorderly conduct, prostitution, gambling, and various motor vehicle infractions.

## 口译练习
### 第一项 句子精练
**A.**
1. 审理的主要目的在于解决有争议的事实问题。
2. 这10条修正案在1791年前得到各州的批准和生效,这就是众所周知的《权利法案》。
3. 换言之,无论一个行为可能是多么不道德或不正义,如果法无明文就不为罪。
4. 如果是刑事案件或故意侵权案,诉讼是一种比调解更为有效的程序,因为诉讼会导致有责或有罪的裁决。
5. 自1855年以来,国会创建了一些联邦专门法院,负责行使某些高度专门的职能,从而协助国会实现其立法权。

**B.**
1. The protection of the public health and the preservation of the natural environment are growing to be a major concern of the law.

# 第 14 单元　法律制度　Law and Legal System

2. Amendment to the Trademark Law to check various trademark infringements is urgently needed to standardize market activities.
3. China has all along adopted a positive attitude to the negotiation of a convention that prohibits the production of fissile materials for nuclear weapons purposes.
4. While noting the rise of heroin abuse in Eastern European countries, the government prepared a crackdown on drug-regulated crime in the region.
5. It is a social question whether to classify a given act as criminal. As our social values have changed over time, so have our definitions of criminal conduct.

## 第二项　段落口译

**A.**

　　法在社会生活中无处不在，深刻地影响着我们。我们的生、死以及生命存续期间所发生的一切无一不受法律的规范。我们必须正视法、研究法、评价法、改变法以使人们充分实现作为公民、社会的生产者以及自身身份和赖以生存的社会制度的创造者的权能。法对我们的生活有着复杂而且往往互相矛盾的影响。法常常使我们享有幸福，并能够平等地参与社会生活。

**B.**

　　In order to be an effective advocate and counselor, the lawyer must know all the facts of a case. Based on trust and a full exchange of information, the attorney assumes the difficult task of advocating a client's case. In civil litigation the relationship between lawyer and client is often characterized by such trust and full disclosure. In criminal cases, however, the relationship is more likely to be marked by distrust and hostility.

## 第三项　篇章口译

**A.**

　　大家，早上好。我是大卫，今天的讲座是关于美国的法律。美国人对法一直怀有矛盾的情感。在我们的语言中充满了高尚的理想，如"法律面前人人平等"、"法治"等。我们为拥有一个"法治政府而非人治政府"以及"无人凌驾于法律之上"的主张而自豪。

　　但同时，漠视法治一直是我们政治传统的一部分。我们的国家在暴力革命中诞生，在西部开拓时期治安维持会常常把法操纵在自己手里。甚至在现在这个时代，我们也在争论非暴力反抗在公民权、动物权、堕胎以及反对使用核武器运动中所起的作用。

　　我们对法的本质所提出的问题在许多方面就是我们对政治制度和整个社会所提出的问题。我们如何解决美国人对法的这种自相矛盾的态度？此时守法的人为什么转眼却成了一群违法分子？在公民"不可剥夺的权利"的基础上建立起来的国家为什么却在制度上剥夺了黑人和其他少数民族的那些权利？我们如何解释这些矛盾？对这些问题的回答并不容易，但对三种有关法的本质的观点稍加探究会有助于我们对这一矛盾的理解，他们是自然法学派、社团法学派和社会法学派。

　　首先自然法理论家认为规范人际关系的法律和支配世间万物的规律一样，源于自然。这些法则，正如一切法渊源上帝一样，是永恒的。第二种观点即社团法认为，法应当反映多数人的意志。尽管种族隔离或殖民主义具有不道德性，如果多数人想要一个实行种族隔离的社会或推行殖民政策，那么他们可以如愿以偿。那些反对这种法律的人当然可以通过民主程序对其加以改变，但他们必须承认其为多数人意志的合法反映。最后，社会法学认为，法反映其所在社会的价值观念、风俗习惯和文化，而且随着社会的变化而变化。

B.

Young boys and girls are the future of our country. It is an unremitting task of great significance that we properly guide our youths, educate and train them so that they form a sound outlook of life and become the pillar of the state in the 21century.

However, there has been a sharp increase in juvenile delinquency, which means great harm not only to the youngsters and the families concerned but also to the destiny and prospects of our nation. For this reason, it is a topic of great importance as to how we can create a sound social environment for the young, thus preventing them from committing transgression and crimes.

There are controversies and misunderstandings about the proper functions of juvenile courts and their probation departments. There are cries that the whole process produces delinquents rather than rehabilitates them. There are speeches by the score about 'getting touch' with the kids. Another large group thinks we should be more understanding and gentle with delinquents. This distrust of the services offered can be attributed in large part to the confusion in the use of these services throughout the country.

On the one hand, the juvenile courts are tied to the criminal court system, with an obligation to decide guilt and innocence for offenses specifically stated and formally charged. On the other hand, they have the obligation to provide treatment, supervision and guidance to youngsters in trouble, without respect to the crimes of which they are accused. These two conflicting assignments must be carried out—quite properly—in an informal, private way which will not stigmatize a youngster during his formative years.

What constitutes the four major factors leading to juvenile delinquency? They are:

1. the society,
2. families,
3. schools,
4. the psychological conditions of the youths.

There is really much we can do:

In the first place, we should strengthen the function and responsibility of family education.

Secondly, schools should carry out plans of education for students' all round development with equal attention of teaching and cultivating.

Thirdly, law education and precautionary alertness should be enhanced.

Last but not least, criminals infringing upon the legal rights of the minors should be severely punished and models knowing and abiding by the law awarded.

语言文字 第15单元

Unit 15 Language and Writing

# 篇章口译

## Passage A (E-C)

### Vocabulary Work

Work on the following words and phrases and write the translated version in the space provided.

| | | | |
|---|---|---|---|
| ancestor | transmit | evolve | vocalization |
| external stimulus | chimp | utterance | progression |
| hominid | Homo erectus | Homo sapiens | primate |
| pidgin | Creole | mutation | |

### Text Interpreting

Listen to the tape and interpret the following passage from English into Chinese.

Ladies and gentlemen,

Good morning! It is a pleasure and honor to have this opportunity to talk about the origins of human language.

As we all know, language plays a unique role in our daily life. We are constantly amazed by the variety of human thought, culture, society, and literature expressed in many thousands of languages around the world. We can find out what other people think through their language. We can find out what they thought in the past if we read their written records. We can tell future generations about ourselves if we speak or write to them. If we want other civilizations in space to learn about us we send them messages in our planet's six thousand languages.

Language is so important, but how much do you know about it? Do you know the origins of human language?

Language is a communication system that is unique to humans. In the six million years since apes and humans evolved from a common ancestor, language appears to have emerged only in the human line, along with all the necessary brain structures for encoding thoughts into sounds and transmitting them to other members of the species.

Other animals possess basic systems for perceiving and generating sounds that enable them to communicate with each other. These systems may have been in place before the appearance of language. Are the vocalizations of animals related to human spoken

# 语言文字 Language and Writing

language? According to Chomsky, the most fundamental difference between human language and vocalization of animals is that human language is infinitely creative, free of stimulus control and unlimited in its capacity to express ideas, whereas animal communication consists of a fixed number of signals, each of which is associated on a one-to-one basis with an external stimulus. This view is disputed because some who observed chimps have heard them creating novel utterances.

According to some scholars the progression from animal grunts to full modern human language may have proceeded as follows. The first step by early hominids would be represented by monkeys, who produced different sounds under voluntary control. The sounds they produced were overestimated as language though we are not able to understand the exact meaning or its significance.

During the course of human evolution brain size increased rapidly in a short period, bringing forth a new species. The first was the arrival of Homo erectus about 1.8 million years ago and the next was the existence of Homo sapiens 500,000 years ago. The increase in mental power would have enabled the hominids to increase their vocabulary, and progress from one word statement to two word or even multiple word statements. The level of communication must have been low but possibly intermediate between humans and primates.

The greatest step would have been the progression from the simplified pidgin-like communication to a Creole-like language with all the grammar and syntax of modern languages. Scholars believe that this step could only have been accomplished with some biological change to the brain such as a mutation. It has been found that a gene, named FOXP2, may have undergone a mutation allowing humans to communicate. Evidence shows that this change took place somewhere in Africa around 50,000 years ago, which rapidly brought significant changes in lexicon of the Homo sapiens.

Ultimately there is no full scientific evidence showing the origins of languages, but still there are several assumption which shows that languages evolved with the evolution and development of brain. It is also believed that before any script was developed the humans were able to communicate among themselves. Researches are still doing a lot of investigation in this arena and we are hoping to find more about the birth of languages.

# 篇章口译

## Passage B (C-E)

### Vocabulary Work

Work on the following words and phrases and write the translated version in the space provided.

视角　　　　　字母语言　　　　方块字　　　　　形部
声部　　　　　字母表　　　　　音素　　　　　　音节
音译　　　　　罗马字母　　　　词典编纂者　　　威妥玛—翟理斯拼音法
象形文字　　　表意文字　　　　博大精深

### Text Interpreting

Listen to the tape and interpret the following passage from Chinese into English.

女士们、先生们：

早上好！很高兴看到在座的各位都对中文如此感兴趣，并从这么多不同的国家来到中国学习中文。我教授外国人学习中文已经20多年了，有时我会觉得从一个外国人的视角来看中文也是一件挺有趣的事情。今天，我感到非常荣幸能有这个机会向大家简要介绍一下中文。

我们都知道，中文不是一种字母语言，汉字常常被称作"方块字"。它们似乎非常复杂，也很难学，但中文是世界上使用范围最广的语言之一，当然也是最美丽的语言之一。我敢肯定，大家在日后的学习中会发现这一点。

汉字通常由两部分组成：形部和声部。每个汉字都与中文中一个单一的音节相对应，因此汉字中的声部不像字母表中的字母那样代表着一个音素，而是代表着整个音节。正因为如此，有时人们会说中文有着一个音节表，而不是字母表。然而，这个音节表却并不是非常理想，因为同一个符号往往代表着许多不同的发音，而同样的发音又常常由许多不同的符号来表示。

中文没有真正的字母表，但汉字的发音却可以转写或音译成罗马字母或其他字母。譬如19世纪的两名词典编纂者因为要在自己的汉英词典中教授外国人如何拼读汉字而发明了威妥玛—翟理斯拼音法，至今仍为许多图书馆所使用。1958年，中国内地采用了一套标准的罗马化拼音系统——汉语拼音，以帮助学生学习中文发音。这套拼音系统已经被联合国采用，并日益成为将中文转写成罗马字母的标准系统。

汉字有着悠久的历史。据传说，汉字是历史学家仓颉在4500年前发明的。考古研究则表明，早期的汉字早在8000年前就出现了，并于约3500年前形成了一套完整的书写系统。

在当时使用的书写系统中,只有汉字沿用至今。

经常会有人说,每个汉字都是一幅图画,但事实上只有一部分汉字是真正的象形文字。一些汉字仍可从字形推断出字意,但大部分都很难马上辨明其意了。大部分汉字都是象形文字和简单的表意文字的综合体。

汉语博大精深,因此很难在这么短的时间里对它做出非常全面的介绍。下次我将回答几个我以前的外国学生经常会问到的问题,谢谢大家!

## 口译讲评

## Notes on the Text

**Passage A**

1. **We are constantly amazed by the variety of human thought, culture, society, and literature expressed in many thousands of languages around the world**:这句话若按照原句的语序而翻译成"我们一直惊异于世界上数以千计种语言所呈现出来的形形色色的人类思维、文化、社会以及文学",这样听上去则很不自然,因此可以调整语序,将原句中的起始部分放到最后,推迟译出,例如:"世界上数以千计种语言所呈现出来的形形色色的人类思维、文化、社会以及文学,一直令我们惊异不已。"

2. **..., along with all the necessary brain structures for encoding thoughts into sounds and transmitting them to other members of the species**:这句话比较长,若一口气译出,就会显得拖沓难懂,不如将其分为几个短小的分句:"与此同时,必要的大脑结构也得以发展,使人类能够将思想编码,形成声音,并传送给同类中的其他成员。"

3. **Chomsky**:乔姆斯基(Noam Chomsky, 1928— ),美国语言学家,转换—生成语法的创始人。1928年12月7日出生于美国宾夕法尼亚州的费城。1947年,在哈里斯的影响下他开始研究语言学。1951年在宾夕法尼亚大学完成硕士论文《现代希伯来语语素音位学》,1955年又在该校完成博士论文《转换分析》,获得博士学位。乔姆斯基是一位富有探索精神的语言学家,逐步建立起转换—生成语法,1957年出版的《句法结构》就是这一新方法的标志性著作。后来他又不断丰富和发展了转换—生成语法的理论和方法,相继发表了《句法理论要略》、《深层结构、表层结构和语义解释》、《支配和约束论集》、《管约论》、《自然与语言》、《最简方案》等重要著作,对世界语言学的发展方向产生了巨大的影响。

4. **each of which is associated on a one-to-one basis with an external stimulus**:这里的 on a one-to-one basis 表示"一一对应"。on a...basis 的意思是"以……为基础、以……为根据",如:on a five-day-week basis 按照每周五天工作制;on a 50—50 basis 平分,对等地;on a self-supporting basis 按照自给自足的原则。

5. **who produced different sounds under voluntary control**:此句中的 under voluntary control 只需译成"有意识地"就足够了。

6. **Homo sapiens**:智人,全称"智慧的人",是人类发展史上的第二个阶段。其中又可分为早期智人和晚期智人两个发展阶段。早期智人相当于以前划分的古人阶段。这个时期的人类与现代人更为接近,但仍带有许多原始性质。晚期智人相当于以前划分的新人阶段。这个时期的人类除有某些原始性之外,基本上和现代人相似。文化上已有雕刻和绘画艺术,出现了装饰品。生存年代大约从五万年前开始,直到现代。

7. **pidgin-like communication**:pidgin 即洋泾浜,也叫皮钦语,是临时混合语,常常只是用于在不同的族群之间的临时交际,如经商所需要的彼此之间的沟通,只使用于有限的范围,使用时间通常也不长。词汇比较贫乏,语音和语法都不太规范。
8. **Creole language**:克里奥尔语是正式混合语,一般是从洋泾浜发展而来的。如果洋泾浜因为种种原因得到了发展,语言混合的程度较深,时间较长,词汇不断增加,语法规则不断完善,被有的族群作为母语来学习和使用,或者获得官方语言的地位,就成为克里奥尔语。
9. **It is also believed that before any script was developed**:这句话的中文译文可以适当加入主语"人们还相信……"。
10. **Researches are still doing a lot of investigation in this arena**:investigation 一词按照中文表达习惯,可加上"工作"二字,翻译成"研究工作"。

**Passage B**

1. **汉字通常由两部分组成**:这句话可以有多种表达方式,除了参考译文中的 Chinese characters generally have two parts 以外,还可以说 Chinese characters generally is composed of two parts 或 Chinese characters generally consist of two part。
2. **形部和声部**:英文中没有相应的词汇,因此只能使用解释的翻译手段译成 one of which represents the meaning and the other the sound。
3. **同一个符号往往代表着许多不同的发音**:the same symbols often represent many different sounds。这句话用被动语态翻译亦可,可以译为 the different sounds are often represented by the same symbols。
4. **威妥码—翟理斯拼音法**:the Wade-Giles system。现代书面汉语的拉丁化拼音体系,原为西方读者学习汉字设计的,最初由英国外交官、剑桥大学汉语教授威妥玛(Sir Thomas Francis Wade)提出,再由剑桥大学教授翟理斯(Herbert Allen Giles)予以修正,载于其《华英字典》(1912)中。
5. **汉字有着悠久的历史**:Chinese characters boast a very long history。译文中的 boast 一词有"以拥有……而自豪"的意思,因此用这个词来翻译要比用 has 感情色彩浓厚很多。
6. **一些汉字仍可从字形推断出字意**:Some of these are still interpretable。这里的一个 interpretable 就完全将原文中的意思表达出来了,言简意赅。
7. **汉语博大精深**:"博大精深"通常用 extensive and profound 来表示,有时也会用 broad and profound。
8. **经常会有人说,每个汉字都是一幅图画**:根据英文表达习惯,这句话改换主语,用 it 来引导:It is often said that every Chinese character is a picture。

# 第15单元 语言文字 Language and Writing

## 相关词语  Relevant Words and Expressions

俚语 slang language
手势语 gesture / sign language
书面语 written language
丰富汉语 enrich the Chinese language
日常用语 everyday language
原始语言 primitive language
商业语言 language of commerce
同语族的语言 cognate languages
威胁性的语言 threatening language
通俗语言 popular language
掌握一种语言 master / command a language
下层社会的语言 the underworld language
富于表现力的语言 expressive language
用简明的语言表达 express in clear and simple language
官方文件的呆板语言 the stilted language of official documents
流畅正确地说 speak with ease and accuracy
用明白无误的语言表达一个想法 clothe an idea in unmistakable language
精确而恰当地表达自己的思想 clothe one's thoughts with accurate and appropriate language

## 口译技能
## Interpreting Skills

### 知识习得

总体而言,译员的知识习得是译员口译生涯中一个长期而重要的部分。相对于笔译,一般人们认为口译员的专业知识要求相对要低些,即使口译员在自己的职业生涯中所积累的各种知识比从事其他领域的人要多。那么就翻译的最低知识要求而言,口译与笔译在以下两点上有着重大的区别。其一,口译中对语言的准确性及术语用法的要求相对要低。其二,一般口译时译员可以事先获得一定的相关资料,并且也有机会可以与讲话者进行沟通。

口译中译员虽然不是信息的发布者,但是为了了解讲话者的意图,译员须在口译任务前获得尽可能多的专业知识。当然,无论在理论上还是实际操作过程中,译员不能达到讲话者所具备的专业知识水平,但他们必须拥有与讲话者同等的智力水平。这里的智力水平是指译员能将所获得的信息与存在的知识和经验相结合的能力。因此,译员必须具有超出普通人的知识水平。由此可见，译员必须是通才，能理解所有的信息。那么就口译的知识习得而言，它包括长期的知识习得（knowledge acquisition）和短期的知识习得（short-term knowledge）。

长期的知识积累可以说是贯彻译员的整个职业生涯。他/她须了解人类社会各个领域中的基础知识，并长期储存于自己的知识库中。需要时，译员可随时激活相关的知识。因此，译员在生活中应经常收看各种时事新闻，不断关注周围发生的一切现象，并主动获取各类知识。至于短期的知识积累，一般有以下一些策略。

1. 会议前的准备

译员接受了口译任务后，一般应主动联系主办方，向他们索取相关的文件资料，包括会议的议程、代表的名单、会议的背景资料、讲演稿或发言的提纲、摘要。这些材料对译员非常重要，也是译员在会议前所需大量做的准备。此外，会议前的简介会非常重要。一般主办方会请相关的专家和译员参加简介会，主要向译员介绍会议的流程。译员也可以就会议的内容进行提问以便进一步了解主题背景和有关术语。一般简介会在会议前一天举行，有时也可能在会议前不久举行。一般译员在会议前准备时可以做一个相关术语的词汇表，将参加会议的重要代表做一个中英对照的列表，以免搞错他们的名字和头衔。

2. 会议前最后时刻的准备

由于会议筹备方面的原因，译员经常无法事先得到讲演稿。这主要是一方面主办方比较忙，无法及时将所有相关的文件资料提前交给译员。另一方面，发言者往往也是在会议前不久才定稿，有时甚至只提供大纲。此外，有些发言者不希望发言的内容提前泄漏，经常在会议前那一刻才给译员。因此，译员就只能在会议开始前短短的时间内准备发言的内容。此时译员应抓紧时间快速阅读讲演的内容以获得总体的概念。可能的话，译员应尽量与讲话者进行简短的交流以对一些术语有更好的理解。这种情形在会议口译中经常发生，所以译员对此要有充分的心理准备。

3. 会议中的准备

译员在会议进行的过程中还可以不断习得所需的知识。这对译员来说可以获得更为有利的工作环境。毕竟译员可以从前面代表的发言、讨论及休息时的各种交流中进一步获得相关的知识，以便更好地进行下面的口译任务。根据许多译员的经验，会议中的讨论能让译员更全面了解讲演中的观点，这可以使译员更好地掌握大会的主题知识。其实，译员在整个会议的过程中在边译边学习新的知识，这是个非常自觉的过程。

总之，译员知识水平的提高是一项长期的任务。译员一方面要不断积累，拓宽知识面；另一方面，口译任务前译员对主题背景要尽可能做好充分的准备。即便主办方事先未给讲演内容，译员亦可以通过各种途径查阅与大会主题有关的内容及资料以补充自己在这个领域的知识缺陷。

## Enhancement Practice

第一项 Project 1

句子精练 Sentences in Focus

A. Interpret the following sentences from English into Chinese.

1. Endangered languages are languages that are on the brink of extinction, much like

endangered species of plants or animals.
2. A language is considered to be endangered when parents are no longer teaching it to their children and are not using it actively in everyday life.
3. In ancient times, language also provided a means to engage in communal activities, such as hunting, and to transmit knowledge, such as tool-making.
4. The original official languages of the United Nations were English, Chinese, French and Russian, the languages of the permanent members of the Security Council.
5. English loanwords now appear in many languages, especially in the fields of technology and culture, and international terminology is dominated by English words.

**B. Interpret the following sentences from Chinese into English.**
1. 汉语,连同西藏语、缅甸语及南亚和东南亚地区的众多部族语言,共属于汉藏语系。
2. 大部分中文字典都根据部首来编排汉字,若读者想寻找某个汉字,就必须首先确定其部首。
3. 拼音于1958年被中国内地正式采用,其主要目的是让普通话的推广和汉字的学习更加便利。
4. 最近,中国内地的字典中所收录的部首已经降至178个,因为有一些部首由于汉字的简化而变得过时了。
5. 如今,很少有人从上到下书写汉字了,因为这样书写算术等式的时候就会遇到问题,尤其是当等式的长度超过一行时。

第二项 Project 2
段落口译 Paragraph Interpreting

**A. Interpret the following paragraph from English into Chinese.**
Only 9% of Americans can speak their native language plus another language fluently, as opposed to 53% of Europeans. There is a shortage of language professionals in the US diplomatic corps, military, and intelligence agencies. The national deficiency in language professionals is compromising American security and business interests at home and abroad. Approximately 90% percent of Americans who study foreign languages choose Spanish, French, German and Italian while only 10% choose languages such as Chinese, Arabic, Japanese, Russian and other languages spoken by the overwhelming majority of people around the world.

**B. Interpret the following paragraph from Chinese into English.**
汉字大约有7000个左右,普通人只要认识3000个左右汉字就可以读报纸了。中学教授汉字的数量为5000个左右。作为亚洲占主导地位的语言,中文还极大地影响了邻国语言的书写体系和词汇,如日本语、韩国语、越南语等。据估计,在18世纪以前,世界上印刷书籍中的一半以上都是用中文书写的。

第三项 Project 3
篇章口译 Passage Interpreting

**A. Listen to the tape and interpret the following passage from English into Chinese.**

Thank you for giving me this opportunity to brief you on world languages.

Before I talk about world languages, I'd like to say a few words about Ethnologue. Ethnologue has been a research project for more than fifty years and is regarded as the most comprehensive and authoritative listing of world languages. A new edition is published every four years. The data in my speech are based in large part on Ethnologue.

Ethnologue lists 6,912 living languages in the world today. Keep in mind, however, that the number of languages may never be determined exactly. Languages are not always easily treated as discrete entities with clearly defined boundaries because they represent a continuum of features extending across geographic, political and social boundaries. Not all scholars agree on the criteria that distinguish "language" from "dialect". At the same time, estimates of how many people speak a given language can vary considerably. Some surveys include only native speakers; others include both first and second language speakers.

As a result of such indeterminacy, some mutually intelligible varieties such as German and Dutch are considered to be separate languages because they are spoken in different countries, while mutually unintelligible Mandarin and Cantonese are considered to be varieties of Chinese because they are spoken in one country, and share a common writing system. In addition, some languages are poorly studied. As a result, it has not been possible to establish whether they are separate languages or dialects of other languages.

Most countries in the world have more than one spoken language. With 311 languages, the United States is the fifth most linguistically diverse country in the world. Its diversity comes from both indigenous and immigrant sources: the 311 languages spoken in the United States are divided between 162 indigenous and 149 immigrant languages. On the other hand, Papua New Guinea's 820 languages are all indigenous.

According to Ethnologue, Asia has the largest number of languages and the largest number of speakers, accounting for 61% of all language speakers in the world. Africa has the second largest number of languages after Asia but it accounts for only 11.8% of all language speakers in the world. Europe has the smallest number of languages and the second largest number of speakers after Asia, accounting for 26.4% of all language speakers in the world.

The world faces enormous challenges in maintaining language diversity. Of the 6,912 languages, half may be in danger of disappearing in the next several decades, although this figure cannot be verified.

Wouldn't the world be simpler if there were fewer languages? The truth is that a people's identity and culture are intimately tied to their language. Each language is unique. No one knows what riches may be hidden within an endangered language. The wholesale loss of languages will greatly restrict how much we can learn about human culture, human cognition and the nature of language. Wouldn't that be a pity?

**B. Listen to the tape and interpret the following passage from Chinese into English.**

很高兴再次见到大家！

我的许多外国学生都对中文非常好奇，问了我许多问题。今天我想借此机会回答两个问得最多的问题。

很多外国人都觉得很难记住这么多不同的汉字，所以他们经常问我为什么汉字会如此复杂。没错，与其他一些书写系统相比，人们的确常常觉得汉字过于繁复。其中的原因之一是汉字中包含着很多不同的信息。大量的汉字有着相同的发音，但意思却并不相同。

汉字过于复杂的另一个原因也许是在过去，学习中文很困难，这使得那些受过良好教育的人们能够脱颖而出，他们选择了一种难度很大的书写方式，以此来炫耀自己的技能。中国历史上长期的科举制度也许加剧了这一问题。

1949年新中国成立之后，政府决定淘汰一些过于复杂的汉字。1956年的第一份简化字表淘汰了29个汉字，并改写了486个。1964年又公布了2238个简化后的汉字。这些简化字的重点在于减少字的笔画，而不是加强其语音和语义信息。

我以前的外国学生经常问我的另外一个问题就是，要如何用中文来写外国的名字。中文在翻译外国单词时常常是翻译其概念，但这种做法在翻译外国国名和人名时就遇到了问题，因为名字中隐含的意义往往并不明确，即便是在其母语当中。

于是，在翻译国家名字时就采用了一些不同的方法。当意思非常清楚时，就将其所表达的概念翻译出来，如Iceland被翻译成"冰岛"。当意思完全不明时，就采取音译的方法，如Italy被译成"意大利"。还有一些国家的名字是用汉字书写的，如日本，在中文中就直接使用这些汉字，并采用中文的读音。外国的人名很少会有明显的意义，因此它们往往完全根据读音来音译。

最后，我真诚地希望大家能够喜欢在这里学习中文。

# 参考译文

## Reference Version

**篇章口译 A**

女士们，先生们：

早上好！我很高兴，也很荣幸能有这个机会谈一下人类语言的起源问题。

大家都知道，语言在我们的日常生活中发挥着独特的作用。世界上数以千计种语言所呈现出来的形形色色的人类思维、文化、社会以及文学，一直令我们惊异不已。从语言中我们可以得知其他人的想法；我们可以从书面记录中得知他们过去在想些什么；我们可以通过说或写的方式告诉后代关于我们自己的事情；如果我们想让太空中的其他文明了解我们，我们会通过我们星球上的6000种语言来向他们发送信息。

语言如此之重要，但是你们对语言的了解又有多少呢？你们知道人类语言的起源吗？

语言是人类所独有的沟通体系。在过去的600万年里，自从类人猿与人类从共同的祖先进化开始，语言似乎就只出现在人类的这条进化线上，与此同时，必要的大脑结构也得以发展，使人类能够将思想编码，形成声音，并传送给同类中的其他成员。

　　其他动物拥有着领会声音含义和发出声音的基本机制，使得它们能够彼此沟通。这些系统在语言出现之前也许起到了适当的作用。动物的叫声与人类的口语有关系吗？乔姆斯基认为，人类语言与动物叫声之间最本质的差别在于，人类语言有着无限的创造力，不受刺激物的控制，而且表达想法的能力无穷无尽；而动物之间的沟通则由一些固定数量的信号组成，每个信号都与一个外部刺激一一对应。这一观点也引起了异议，因为一些黑猩猩的观察人员曾听到它们发出了前所未有的声音。

　　一些学者认为，从动物叫声发展到完备的现代人类语言也许经历了如下几个阶段：第一阶段的早期人类以猴子为代表，它们可以有意识地发出不同的声音。但若将它们的声音视为语言，则显得评价过高，虽然我们并不能理解其确切含义或其重要性。

　　在人类的进化过程中，大脑容量在短期内迅速增加，于是出现了一个新的物种。最初是180万年前的直立人，接着是50万年前的智人。智力的增强使得原始人类的词汇量有所增加，并从一个单词的语句发展到两个单词，甚至是多个单词的语句。当时的沟通水平一定不高，也许介于人类和灵长类动物之间。

　　最大的飞跃即从简化的洋泾浜式的交流发展到一种类似于克里奥尔语的语言，并有着现代语言所具有的全部语法和句法。学者认为，这一步的完成只可能是因为大脑发生了突变等生物变化。目前已发现，基因FOXP2就可能经历了突变，使得人类能够彼此交流。有证据表明，这一变化发生在约5万年前的非洲某地，并迅速为智人的词汇带来了重大变化。

　　最终并没有充足的科学证据来告诉我们语言的起源，但仍有一些假设表明，语言的演变是与大脑的进化和发展同步的。人们还相信，在任何书面记录出现之前，人类就已经能够彼此交流了。研究者们仍在这一领域做着大量的研究工作，我们希望对语言起源这个问题能够了解得更多。

## 篇章口译 B

Ladies and gentlemen,

　　Good morning! I'm very happy to see that all of you here are so interested in Chinese language, and have come from so many different countries to China to learn Chinese. I've been teaching foreigners Chinese language for over twenty years, and sometimes I found it very interesting to look at it from the angle of a foreigner. Today I'm very honored to have this opportunity to make a brief introduction of Chinese language.

　　As we know, Chinese is not an alphabetic language, and the Chinese characters are very often called "squared characters". They seem very complicated and hard to learn. But Chinese is one of the most commonly used languages in the world and certainly one of the most beautiful languages. I'm sure you will find it later in your study.

　　Chinese characters generally have two parts, one of which represents the meaning and the other the sound. Every character corresponds to a single syllable in Chinese, so the part which represents the sound does not represent a phoneme like a letter in an alphabet but rather represents a whole syllable. For this reason, it is sometimes said that Chinese has a syllabary rather than alphabet. However, this syllabary is not a very ideal one, since the same symbols often represent many different sounds and the same sounds are often represented by many different symbols.

While Chinese does not have a real alphabet, the sounds of Chinese characters can be transcribed or transliterated into Roman alphabet or other alphabets. For instance, the Wade-Giles system, which is still used in many libraries, was created by two 19th century lexicographers who needed to show foreigners how to pronounce the characters in their Chinese-English dictionaries. In 1958, a standard Romanization system, Pinyin, was adopted by mainland China to help students learn Chinese pronunciation. This Pinyin system has been adopted by the United Nations and is increasingly the standard system for transcribing Chinese into the Roman alphabet.

Chinese characters boast a very long history. According to legend, Chinese characters were invented by the historian Cang Jie about 4,500 years ago. Archeological research indicates that precursors of Chinese characters appeared as early as 8,000 years ago and that Chinese characters formed a complete system of writing by about 3,500 years ago. Among the writing systems in use at that time, only Chinese characters are still used.

It is often said that every Chinese character is a picture, but the fact is that only some of them are actual pictographs. Some of these are still interpretable, but most are now written in a way that is hard to immediately discern their meanings. Most Chinese characters are combinations of these pictographs and simple ideographs.

Chinese language is both extensive and profound, so it is very difficult to give a comprehensive knowledge of it in such a short time. Next time I will answer some questions which were frequently asked by my former foreign students. Thank you!

口译练习

第一项 句子精练

A.

1. 濒危语言即那些濒临灭绝的语言,正如濒临灭绝的植物与动物那样。
2. 当父母不再教授孩子某种语言,也不在日常生活中积极地使用它时,这种语言就被视为濒危语言。
3. 在古代,语言也提供了一种手段,使人们能够参与狩猎等集体活动,并传达工具制作等方面的知识。
4. 联合国最初的官方语言是英语、汉语、法语和俄语,即安理会常任理事国所使用的语言。
5. 现在,英语外来词出现在许多语言中,尤其是技术和文化领域,国际上的术语也是由英文单词来主导的。

B.

1. Chinese, together with Tibetan, Burmese and many tribal languages of South and

Southeast Asia, belongs to the Sino-Tibetan family of languages.
2. Most Chinese dictionaries arrange characters according to their radicals. If a reader wants to find a character he must first determine which part of it is the radical.
3. Pinyin was officially adopted by Mainland China in 1958, and its main aim is to facilitate the spread of Putonghua and the learning of Chinese characters.
4. The number of radicals used in dictionaries in Mainland China has recently been reduced to 178, since a few radicals were eliminated which became obsolete with the simplification of characters.
5. Nowadays Chinese characters are very seldom written vertically, since problems may arise with mathematical equations, especially when the equations run more than one line.

## 第二项 段落口译

**A.**

只有9%的美国人可以流利地讲自己的母语外加一门外语,而53%的欧洲人能够做到这点。美国的外交使团、军事机构、及情报机构都缺少外语专业人才。国家外语专业人才的缺乏危害了美国的国家安全,同时也损害了美国在国内外的商业利益。学习外语的美国人中,将近90%的人选择了西班牙语、法语、德语和意大利语,而只有10%的人选择了世界上绝大多数人所使用的中文、阿拉伯语、日语、俄语及其他语言。

**B.**

There are roughly 70,000 Chinese characters. An average person has to know about 3,000 characters to be able to read the newspaper. In secondary schools the number of characters taught is around 5,000. As the dominant language of East Asia, Chinese has greatly influenced the writing systems and vocabularies of neighboring languages, such as Japanese, Korean, and Vietnamese. It has been estimated that until the 18th century more than half of the world's printed books were Chinese.

## 第三项 篇章口译

**A.**

谢谢,很高兴有这个机会向大家简单介绍一下世界上的语言。

在谈论世界上的语言之前,我想先简要介绍一下Ethnologue。Ethnologue是一个已经延续了50余年的研究项目,被视为收录世界语言的最全面、最权威的一览表,每4年发布一个新的版本。我讲话中的大部分数据都来源于Ethnologue。

Ethnologue列出了6912种当今世界上正在使用的语言。但是,请记住,语言的确切数量是永远都不可能确定的。语言并不总是能够被简单地视为有着明确界限的离散实体,因为它们代表的是跨越地理、政治及社会界限的一系列特点。并非所有的学者都赞同区分"语言"与"方言"的标准。同时,对多少人在讲某一特定语言的估计也会千差万别。一些调查只包括母语使用者,还有一些调查则既包括母语使用者,也包括第二种语言使用者。

# 第15单元 语言文字 Language and Writing

正是由于这种不确定型,一些彼此能够理解的语言,如德语和荷兰语,被视为两种独立的语言,因为它们在不同的国家使用,而彼此无法理解的中国普通话和粤语则被视为同属于中国话,因为它们在一个国家使用,并有着相同的书写体系。此外,对一些语言的研究也是少而又少,于是也就无法确定它们是独立的语言还是其他语言的方言。

世界上大多数国家有一种以上的口语。美国有311种语言,是世界上第五大语言多样化的国家。其形形色色的语言中既有本土固有的,也有移民带入的:美国的311种语言中,162种为本土所固有,149种为移民的语言。而巴布亚新几内亚的820种语言则全部为本土所固有。

据Ethnologue统计,亚洲有着最多的语言及语言使用者,占世界上全部语言使用者的61%。非洲的语言种类仅次于亚洲,居世界第二,但其语言使用者的人数只占世界总人数的11.8%。欧洲的语言种类最少,但语言使用者的人数却居世界第二位,仅次于亚洲,占世界总人数的26.4%。

如何保持语言的多样性?世界正面临着巨大的挑战。在6912种语言里,有一半可能会在未来的几十年中消失,虽然这个数字并无法核实。

语言少一些,世界不就能简单一些了吗?事实上,一个民族的身份和文化与其语言密不可分。每种语言都是独一无二的。没有人知道一种濒临灭绝的语言里会蕴藏着什么宝藏。语言的大批消失将会严重地限制住我们对人类文化、人类认知以及语言本质的了解。这难道不是一种遗憾吗?

B.

Very happy to see you again!

Many of my foreign students are very curious about Chinese language and asked me a lot of questions. Today I'd like to take this opportunity to answer several most frequently asked ones.

Many foreigners find it very difficult to memorize so many different Chinese characters, so they often ask me why Chinese characters are so complicated. Yes, it's true that Chinese characters are often considered to be too complex compared with other writing systems. One reason for the added complexity is the different information content of the characters. There is a huge number of characters in Chinese which sound the same but have different meanings.

Another reason for the excess complexity in Chinese characters may be that in the past the difficulty of learning Chinese allows those well-educated people to distinguish themselves from their peers, and they try to show off their skills by choosing to write in a difficult way. The long imperial civil examination system in China's history has perhaps aggravated the problem.

After the proclamation of New China in 1949, the government decided to eliminate some over-complicated characters. The first list of simplifications in 1956 eliminated 29 characters and altered 486 of them, and then in 1964 a new list of 2,238 simplified characters was announced. The emphasis in all these cases was on reducing the number of strokes, not on strengthening the phonetic and semantic information in the characters.

The other question my former foreign students always asked me was the way foreign names were written in Chinese. Foreign words are usually imported by translating the concept into Chinese, but it runs into a problem when foreign country names and personal names are imported because the underlying meanings of the names are often obscure, even in the original foreign language.

Therefore, a number of different patterns are applied in the translation of the names of countries. In cases where the meaning is blatantly apparent the concept is usually translated. For instance, "Iceland" becomes 冰岛. When the meaning is completely unclear the sound is transliterated. For instance, "Italy" becomes 意大利. In cases where foreign countries have their own names which use Chinese characters, such as Japan, these characters are also used in Chinese and they are pronounced according to Chinese pronunciation. Since personal names of foreigners rarely have much meaning that is apparent, they are almost always transcribed according to their pronunciations alone.

Finally I sincerely hope that all of you will enjoy your study of Chinese language here.

# 第16单元 外交政策

 **Foreign Policy**

# 篇章口译

## Passage A (E-C)

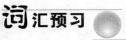 **Vocabulary Work**

Work on the following words and phrases and write the translated version in the space provided.

| | |
|---|---|
| EU (European Union) | external policy |
| international arena | regional group |
| intensify | Maastricht Treaty |
| Common Foreign and Security Policy (CSFP) | at stake |
| illegal immigration | Mediterranean |
| crisis zone | Afghanistan |
| the Palestinian Territories | the Democratic Republic of Congo |
| the Horn of Africa | hallmark |
| cornerstone | span |
| grapple with | demographic shift |

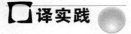 **Text Interpreting**

Listen to the tape and interpret the following passage from English into Chinese.

Distinguished Colleagues, Ladies and Gentlemen,

Today I'm very happy to have this opportunity to talk about EU's external policy and its role in the international arena.

Since its birth in the 1950s, the European Union has been developing relations with the rest of the world through a common policy on trade, development assistance and formal trade and cooperation agreements with individual countries or regional groups. The idea that a strong Europe should act as one on the world stage has encouraged member countries to work together to achieve a coherent approach to foreign policy.

In the last 15 years, the Union has intensified efforts to play an international political and security role more in line with its economic status. The EU's agreements with its partners around the globe cover not only trade and traditional financial and technical assistance but also economic and other reforms as well as support for infrastructure and health and education programs. Moreover, in 2003 the EU decided that all new agreements must include a clause in which its partners commit themselves to the non-proliferation of weapons of mass destruction.

Since 1993, under the Maastricht Treaty, the EU has been developing a Common Foreign and Security Policy (CFSP), which becomes the heart of the EU external policy, to enable it to take joint action when the interests of the Union as a whole are at stake. Defence is becoming an important aspect of the CFSP as the EU seeks to promote and maintain stability around the world. As it deals with terror, international crime, drug trafficking, illegal immigration and global issues like the environment, the Union also works closely with other countries and international organizations.

The EU's common trade policy operates at two levels. Firstly, within the World Trade Organization (WTO), the European Union is actively involved in setting the rules for the multilateral system of global trade. Secondly, the EU negotiates its own bilateral trade agreements with countries or regional groups of countries. The EU has become a key player in the successive rounds of multilateral negotiations aimed at opening up world trade. The European Union is the world's biggest trader, accounting for 20% of global imports and exports. The EU believes that globalization can bring economic benefits to all, including the developing countries. The EU also seeks to help developing countries by giving them better access to its market in the short term, while allowing them more time to open their own markets to European products.

The EU's trade policy is closely linked to its development policy. The two come together as the Union assumes its share of responsibility to help developing countries fight poverty and integrate into the global economy. Development assistance and cooperation, originally concentrated in Africa, was extended to Asia, Latin America and the southern and eastern Mediterranean countries in the mid-1970s.

The European Union has also made human rights and democracy a central aspect of its external relations. The EU has confronted serious crises in more than 100 countries around the world, getting essential equipment and emergency supplies to the victims as quickly as possible. The EU is active in all major crisis zones including Afghanistan, the Palestinian Territories, Darfur, the Democratic Republic of Congo and the Horn of Africa.

Effective multilateralism is the hallmark of the European Union's external policy. The United Nations system is its cornerstone. Relations between the EU and the United Nations have developed over time into a rich and diverse network of co-operation and interaction, spanning virtually the entire range of EU external relations. The main areas in which the UN is active today, such as promoting international peace and security, promoting respect for human rights, protecting the environment, fighting disease, fostering development and reducing poverty, are also priorities for the European Union. Also, EU, together with other member states, seeks to rebuild the UN and to make it capable of meeting the challenges of the 21st century.

Ladies and gentlemen, Europe is not the same place it was 50 years ago, and nor is the rest of the world. In a constantly changing, ever more interconnected world, Europe is grappling with new issues: globalization, demographic shifts, climate change, the need for sustainable energy sources and new security threats. These are the challenges facing Europe and the world in the 21st century. Let's work together even more closely than before to jointly meet these challenges!

Thank you.

# 篇章口译

## Passage B (C-E)

### Vocabulary Work

Work on the following words and phrases and write the translated version in the space provided.

| 深刻的变化 | 曲折发展 | 独立自主的和平外交政策 | 和平共处五项原则 |
| 始终不渝 | 奉行 | 结盟 | 领土完整 |
| 军备竞赛 | 霸权主义 | 诉诸武力 | 内政 |
| 睦邻友好政策 | 朝鲜半岛 | 东盟 | 全方位的对外开放政策 |
| 军控、裁军与防扩散 | | | |

### Text Interpreting

Listen to the tape and interpret the following passage from Chinese into English.

尊敬的主席先生,女士们、先生们:

自新世纪的来临,国际形势发生了深刻的变化。世界多极化和经济全球化的趋势在曲折发展。和平与发展仍然是我们这个时代的主题。世界还很不安宁,人类依旧面临诸多严峻的挑战。中国致力于全面建设小康社会,为中国的改革开放和现代化建设创造一个良好的国际环境。中国将一如既往奉行独立自主的和平外交政策,同世界各国一起在和平共处五项原则基础上维护世界和平,谋求共同发展,建设美好的和谐世界。

中国对外政策的根本目标是始终不渝地奉行独立自主的原则,维护中国的独立、主权和领土完整,促进世界的和平与发展。中国不同任何大国或国家集团结盟,不参加军备竞赛。中国反对霸权主义,认为世界上国家不分大小、强弱、贫富,都是国际社会的平等一员。国与国之间应通过和平协商解决彼此的纠纷和争端,不应诉诸武力或以武力相威胁。中国积极推动建立公正、合理的国际政治经济新秩序,主张国际新秩序应该以和平共处五项原则和其他公认的国际关系准则为基础。中国尊重世界的多样性,主张世界的多样性不应成为国与国之间交往的障碍。

## 第16单元　外交政策　Foreign Policy

　　中国愿意在互相尊重主权和领土完整、互不侵犯、互不干涉内政、平等互利、和平共处五项原则的基础上，同所有国家建立和发展友好合作关系。中国一贯奉行睦邻友好政策，加强同广大发展中国家的团结与合作，重视改善和发展同发达国家的关系。我们在维护朝鲜半岛及东北亚地区的和平与稳定做出了积极的贡献。我们还积极发展与东南亚各国的友好合作，与东盟建立面向二十一世纪的战略伙伴关系。

　　中国实行全方位的对外开放政策，愿意在平等互利原则的基础上，同世界各国和地区广泛开展贸易往来、经济技术合作和科学文化交流，促进共同繁荣。中国同广大亚、非、拉发展中国家在政治领域里的合作和协调不断加强。中国积极致力于推进国际军控、裁军与防扩散。中国愿意与国际社会加强合作，共同对付人类发展面临的环境恶化、资源匮乏、贫困、失业、人口膨胀、疾病流行、毒品泛滥、国际犯罪等全球性问题。

　　主席先生，新世纪，世界充满希望，也面临严峻挑战。要和平、求合作、促发展是各国人民的共同愿望。中国将一如既往地坚持独立自主的和平外交政策，发展和加强与世界各国的友好合作关系，并将为维护世界和平与人类的共同发展做出自己应有的贡献。

　　谢谢各位。

## 口译讲评

# Notes on the Text

**Passage A**

1. **external policy**：这里表示"对外政策"或"外交政策"。external policy 与 foreign policy 表达的意思一样，只是用词不同而已。"法国外交部长"英语的表达为 the French External Relations Minister，而"中国外交部长"的英语则为 the Chinese Foreign Minister。类似的例子还有，"中国总理"的英语为 the Chinese Premier，"德国总理"的英语则是 the German Chancellor，而"澳大利亚总理"的英语却是 the Australian Prime Minister。由此可见，同一个概念，中、英文中都可以有不同的表达。作为译员，不能只知其一，不知其二。

2. **in the international arena**：中文表示"在国际舞台上"，另一个英语的表达为 on the world stage。口译时虽然时间紧迫，但译员也一定要注意词语的不同搭配。

3. **The EU's agreements with its partners around the globe cover not only trade and traditional financial and technical assistance but also economic and other reforms as well as support for infrastructure and health and education programs**：这是个长句，记忆理解，尤其是笔记时要抓住几个转折词：not only, but also 和 as well as，以帮助记忆这三个不同层次的内容。

4. **Maastricht Treaty**：《马城条约》，其正名为《欧盟条约》(the Treaty on European Union)，是 1992 年 2 月 7 日由当时欧洲共同体 12 个成员国于荷兰马斯特里赫特签署的条约，1993 年 11 月 1 日开始生效。该条约催生了欧洲联盟（欧盟），赋予新的政治和社会责任，以取代欧洲共同体，并为成员国加入欧洲经济货币联盟（EMU）确定了条件以及时间表。

5. **the European Union is actively involved in setting the rules for the multilateral system of global trade**：multilateral system 即"多边贸易体系"，也称 global trading system，是 WTO 的核心。虽然 WTO 在 1995 年 1 月 1 日才建立，但多边贸易体系已有 50 年的历史了。自 1948 年起，关税与贸易总协定（GATT）就已为多边贸易体制制定了规则。大多数国家，包括世界上几乎所有主要贸易国，都是该体制的成员，但仍有一些国家不是。因此使用"多边"一词，而不用"全球"或"世界"等词。

6. **The EU has become a key player in the successive rounds of multilateral negotiations aimed at opening up world trade**：successive rounds of multilateral negotiations 表示"连续回合的多边贸易谈判"。"多边贸易谈判"是经历了许多不同回合的谈判，其中最新一轮的谈判称作"多哈回合贸易谈判"。口译时背景知识掌握得越多，理解就越容易，产出也越顺利。

7. **The EU is active in all major crisis zones including Afghanistan, the Palestinian Territories, Darfur, the Democratic Republic of Congo and the Horn of Africa**：这里的 the Horn of Africa 表示"非洲之角"，有时按照其地理位置，又称"东北非洲"。非洲之角位于非洲东北部，是东非的一个半岛，它是非洲大陆最东的地区。作为一个更大的地区概念，"非洲之角"包括了吉布提、埃塞俄比亚、厄立特里亚和索马里等国家。

8. **The main areas in which the UN is active today, such as promoting international peace and security, promoting respect for human rights, protecting the environment, fighting disease, fostering development and reducing poverty, are also priorities for the European Union**：这句句子中虽然有不少列举的内容，但它们都是国际事务中经常出现的话题。如果译员平时常看国际新闻，那么口译时记忆自然就容易多了。

## Passage B

1. **世界多极化和经济全球化的趋势在曲折发展**："曲折发展"口译时其英语表达可以是 to develop amid twists and turns。"曲折"在英语中有等值的表达，即 twists and turns（复杂的状况），但不是 zigzag（弯弯曲曲）。

2. **中国致力于全面建设小康社会**："小康社会"是具有中国特色的词汇，在英语中无等值对应。因此这里采用解释性的翻译，译为 a well-off society in an all-round way。由于这个词汇已有官方的译文，口译时最好采用现有的表达。至于具有中国特色的词汇，译员平时应该通过经常阅读《中国日报》来进行积累。

3. **中国将一如既往奉行独立自主的和平外交政策，同世界各国一起在和平共处五项原则基础上维护世界和平，谋求共同发展**：这句的内容是中国外交政策的核心。译前准备时要熟知中国外交政策的基本内容及中、英文的准确表达，因为许多涉及政治性主题的表达基本上都是官方固定的，如句中的"独立自主的和平外交政策"（independent foreign policy of peace），"和平共处五项原则"（the Five Principles of Peaceful Co-existence）。

4. **中国不同任何大国或国家集团结盟，不参加军备竞赛**：这里的"大国"口译成英语时用 big power 而不是 big country，又如"超级大国"（superpower）。

5. **国与国之间应通过和平协商解决彼此的纠纷和争端，不应诉诸武力或以武力相威胁**：这里的"纠纷和争端"是两个概念，应分别译成 dispute 和 conflict。"武力"习惯上用 force，前面就不用再加 military 了。

# 第16单元 外交政策 Foreign Policy

6. **我们还积极发展与东南亚各国的友好合作,与东盟建立面向 21 世纪的战略伙伴关系**:"东盟"是"东南亚国家联盟"的简称,是亚洲的一个区域组织。其英语全称为 Association of Southeast Asian Nations（ASEAN）。成立几十年来,"东盟"已日益成为东南亚地区以经济合作为基础的政治、经济、安全一体化合作组织,并建立起一系列的合作机制。"面向 21 世纪的战略伙伴关系"是中国外交政策中的最新术语,其英语为 strategic partnership in the 21st century。

7. **中国积极致力于推进国际军控、裁军与防扩散**:"国际军控、裁军与防扩散"分别是国际政治中的术语,口译时应分别译成 international arms control, disarmament and non-proliferation。

8. **中国愿与国际社会加强合作,共同对付人类发展面临的环境恶化、资源匮乏、贫困、失业、人口膨胀、疾病流行、毒品泛滥、国际犯罪等全球性问题**:口译这句时要对目前国际上的一些主要问题有比较全面的了解,这样可以提高笔记、记忆的效果。

## 相关词语  Relevant Words and Expressions

两岸关系 Cross-Straits relations
全球行动 global action
台海问题 Cross-Straits issue
外交安全 diplomatic security
防扩散组织 non-proliferation regime
经济一体化 economic integration
贸易自由化 trade liberalization
政治多元性 political pluralism
中美联合公报 Sino-US Joint Communique
发展和民主进程 development and democratization process
祖国的和平统一 peaceful reunification of the motherland
开放、坦诚的关系 relationship of openness and candor
有利于和平与稳定 be conducive to peace and stability
糟糕的全球环境治理 poor global environmental governance
建设性、战略合作伙伴 constructive strategic partnership
通过外交途径进行谈判 negotiate through diplomatic channels
完全获取市场准入机会 fully exploit market access opportunities
国际与地区人权保护框架 international and regional framework for the protection of human rights
将自己国家的社会制度和意识形态强加于他国 impose its social system and ideology upon others
向千百万难民和冲突中的受害者提供维持生活的救济 life-sustaining relief for millions of refugees and victims of conflict

# 口译技能
# Interpreting Skills

## 语言提高

国际会议口译员协会(AIIC)将口译中的工作语言分成三种：

1. A语言：指译员所掌握的纯正母语(native language)。口译中要求译员能流畅地用母语将外语信息的意思表达出来。

2. B语言：指积极语言(active language)，即译员能掌握的目的语。

3. C语言：指消极语言(passive language)，即理论上讲译员能如母语般掌握它，但不用将其作为目的语。

要成为一名合格的译员，他/她必须熟练掌握两种工作语言。然而在实际工作中，译员还是会碰到与语言各个层面相关的问题，包括语音、词汇、语法、语义等等。口译中译员对两种语言的掌握是指其能完全运用语言来进行成功的交际。广义上讲是译员能将语言知识与其他认知知识的结合。在语言提高方面译员应注意以下几点：

1. 译员首先自己必须掌握外语的正确发音，不能影响听众的理解。此外，译员还须会辨析各种口音，并且不受发言人的发音和语调的影响。毕竟，在实际的工作场合中，讲话者并非全来自英语国家。无论是母语讲话者还是非母语讲话者，他们的口音始终会影响译员对源语信息理解的程度。就母语为英语而言，它也有美国英语、英国英语、澳大利亚英语、新西兰英语等。美国境内还分南、北口音；英国境内有苏格兰口音。中文讲话者亦如此，不是每个人都能讲标准的普通话。因此，译员平时应不断通过收听、收看各类的外语广播和电视节目以熟悉不同的口音。在口译教学中，教员应特别选用一些由不同国家讲话者讲同一种语言的材料对学员进行专门训练。学员自己课后也应找类似的材料进行大量的操练。

2. 译员除了掌握应该达到的词汇量外，还应具备尽可能多的近义词，积累有关各行业的词汇、新词及具有文化承载意义的词汇。人类社会中词汇量的不断扩大可以说是无止境的。随着时代的不断变化和发展，时刻都会有各类新词出现，如"和谐社会"(harmonious society)；"八耻八荣"(eight disgraces and eight honors)；"建设信息化军队"(build computerized armed forces)；niche market(利基市场)。美国自9·11之后便有了Homeland Security(国土安全部)和Counter-terrorist Unit (CTU:反恐小组)。还有，现在有术语表示"因手机铃声而导致焦虑"，其英语是ringxiet(铃声焦虑症)。此外，有些词会随着时代的变化而消失，被新的词汇所代替。韩国的首都Seoul原来中文为"汉城"，而现在则改成了"首尔"；印度的"孟买"原来英文是Bombay，而现在则为Mumbai。因此，学员平时练习口译时要有意识地积累各类同义词、反义词和新词。毕竟，词汇量的大小会最终影响译员的听力理解。

3. 至于语法，汉语中的动词没有明显的时态、单复数的标志；也没有定冠词与不定冠词之分。这与英语中的情况截然不同。因此，汉译英时译员必须时时意识到这些不同，并能准确运用时态、单复数、定冠词及不定冠词。还有，中英句子结构也非常不同。中文结构是左悬式(left-branching)，而英语则是右悬式(right-branching)。口译时这种差异会给译员增加记忆的负荷。因此，学员平时训练时须充分掌握中、英修饰语位置的不同，从而在双语转换时选择有效的句型。从下面中、英句子中下划线部分我们可以看出两种语言在结构上的差异：

斐济是南太平洋的重要国家。独立以来，在马拉总理的领导下，斐济<u>在维护国家主权，加强国内民族团结，发展国民经济和提高人们生活水平方面进行了坚持不懈的</u>努力并取得了显著的成绩。Fiji is an important country in the South Pacific. Since its independence, Fiji has, under the leadership of Prime Minister Mara, made unremitting efforts and scored remarkable achievements <u>in safeguarding state sovereignty, strengthening the unity of all ethnic groups, developing national economy and improving people's living standard</u>.

总之，学员应多掌握中、英文中的一些基本、常用句型，包括主动、被动句之间的转化、双重否定的运用等，以便在真实的口译场合可以实现快速转换，从而有更充分的时间来获取和分析不断接听到的信息。学员平时训练时除了记忆、模仿，还可以采用一句多译的方法，以便口译时能采用灵活多样的句型。

4. 在特定的上下文中选择正确的词义对现场工作的译员来说是一项巨大的挑战。译员虽然掌握了相当的词汇量，但实际口译中一种语言向另一种语言的过渡并非是简单的词汇到词汇的过渡。人类生活最基本的经验中产生的词汇一般在另一种语言中可以找到对应词，如中文里的"吃、喝、睡、工作、休息、玩"在英语中分别是 eat、drink、sleep、work、rest、play。然而，由于各民族间的文化差异，同一概念在两种语言中的表达会不同，如中文的"公共卫生"，英语中对应的不是 public sanitation 而是 public health。这里应将"卫生"理解成"卫生健康"，而非"清洁卫生"。又如"基层"，英语中为 grass-roots 而不是 basic level。英语中的 dry town 表示"禁酒的城市"，而非"干旱的城市"。

总之，译员需要不断提高自己中、外文的应用水平。平时训练时，应时时注意两种语言的比较。至于外语，译员应多听、多看外语讲话的材料。而对自己的母语，译员平时也应不断听、看各类材料，尤其要多积累两种文化中特有现象的词汇表达。由此可见，在口译教学中，教员应时刻提醒学员课后要不断进修语言，以避免口译课堂教学变成语言提高的课程，而非口译技能训练的课程。

# 译练习  Enhancement Practice

第一项 Project 1
句子精练 Sentences in Focus

A. Interpret the following sentences from English into Chinese.
1. The EU has to make sure that the different aspects of its external policies are consistent with each other and convey a clear overall message.
2. The EU humanitarian aid is unconditional and its aim is to get help to victims as quickly as possible, irrespective of race, religion or the political convictions of their government.

3. As early as 1971, the EU began reducing or removing tariffs and quotas on its imports from developing countries. In 2001, the Union grants the 49 least-developed countries free access to the EU market for all their products, except weapons.
4. In the past, environmental issues were seen as a barrier to development. Today, they are an integral component of the sustainable model of development. The EU actively supports the preservation of the environment and natural resources.
5. The discovery of weapons of mass destruction (WMD) developments and the frequent terrorist attacks have given a new dimension to the issue of non-proliferation and disarmament. The EU keeps a global approach, which insists on the respect, development and effective implementation of international multilateral treaties and conventions to ban or to minimize the development of WMD.

**B. Interpret the following sentences from Chinese into English.**
1. 中国将坚定不移地走和平发展的道路,不参与军备竞赛并且永不称霸。
2. 中国将坚定不移地坚持双赢的开放政策,兼顾其他国家的合法利益,尤其是其他发展中国家的利益。
3. 中国支持国际社会为帮助发展中国家提高独立发展的能力、改善人民生活、缩小南北差距而做出的努力。
4. 和平发展是中国政府和人民的一个战略选择,中国主张和平解决国际争端和热点问题,促进国际与地区的安全与合作,反对任何形式的恐怖主义。
5. 中国积极参与多边外交活动,是维护世界和平和地区稳定的坚定力量。中国是安理会的常任理事国,积极参与政治解决地区热点问题。

## 第二项 Project 2
### 段落口译 Paragraph Interpreting

**A. Interpret the following paragraph from English into Chinese.**

For the moment the EU-US relationship is still at heart of the international system. Our combined economic and political weight on the world stage gives us a privileged role in global affairs. We are a strategic partner for issues as varied as international terrorism, climate change, AIDS, and resolving the world's most entrenched conflicts. Today we dominate the global economy. Together the EU and the US generate 57% of world economic output and around 40% of world trade, with exchanges worth over 1.7 billion a day. In the area of climate and energy security, we have agreed to cut our carbon-dioxide emissions by 20% and to raise the share of renewable energy sources also to 20%.

**B. Interpret the following paragraph from Chinese into English.**

过去一年中国—东盟之间的关系有了新的发展。政治上,双方保持了高层的接触,并进行了各个级别富有成果的对话与协商。经济上,我们双方的贸易保持稳步增长。中国—东盟在其他领域的合作也在稳步发展。目前,中国和东盟都进入了一个新的历史发展时期。

# 第16单元 外交政策 Foreign Policy

未来我们应加强和提升中国—东盟的战略伙伴关系,将中国—东盟的经济关系和贸易上升到一个新的高度,争取双赢和共同发展。

第三项 Project 3
篇章口译 Passage Interpreting

**A. Listen to the tape and interpret the following passage from English into Chinese.**

Dear Friends, Ladies and Gentlemen,

Today I'd like to talk about the EU-China relations in the new century. The current relationship between the EU and China is stronger than before. Two sides have put in place a mechanism of annual meetings between the leaders, established a comprehensive strategic partnership.

EU-China relations are based on a solid foundation. Two sides share much in common as both believe in multilateralism, pursue democracy in international relations and work to safeguard the authority of the United Nations. In October 2006, the European Commission set out its strategy towards China, which is "EU-China: Closer partners, growing responsibilities". It signals the EU's wish to continue and further intensify its comprehensive engagement with China.

To meet the challenge of sustainable development, the EU and China must work together to ensure clean, secure and sustainable energy supplies, to combat climate change and improve the environment, to promote more balanced growth and development, to improve coordination on development, to establish sustainable economic growth.

The EU is China's largest trading partner, representing about 19% of its external trade. The emerging middle class in China is a growing market for EU exports and European consumers benefit from competitively priced inputs and consumer goods. Openness brings benefits to both the EU and China. While encouraging China to implement fully its commitments to the World Trade Organization (WTO) to guarantee reciprocal and fair trade relations, the EU will encourage China to further open its market and provide better access for European investors and exporters to the Chinese markets.

Bilateral cooperation is already extensive in the form of exchanges of views and experience or technical assistance. The cooperation covers all areas even if priority must be given to flagship areas such as cooperation in science and technology, the development of people-to-people links and cultural exchanges.

The EU and China both have an interest in promoting international peace and security through a multilateral system like that provided by the United Nations or through a regional system. Both sides must strengthen their cooperation and conduct a structured dialogue covering the regions of the world. China could play a fundamental role in reconciling the interests of developing and developed countries, and in promoting peace and stability in Asia. The EU will further enhance consultations with China on the ASEAN Regional Forum (ARF) to reinforce the ARF's role on regional security issues.

The EU and China should conduct more frequent dialogues on global governance issues, the promotion of a coordinated approach and of joint EU-China initiatives, the promotion of multilateralism, security, non-proliferation and disarmament issues, strengthened dialogues on counter-terrorism, and collaboration in the face of global environmental challenges.

The new maturity of the EU-China relationship in the 21st century is based on closer coordination. In the current climate, there is undeniable interest in acting as strategic partners, particularly with regard to the essential role of organizations and multilateral systems. It is the common responsibility and mission for EU and China to lay out strategic plans for further developing bilateral ties and jointly shape a better future for both sides.

Thank you.

**B. Listen to the tape and interpret the following passage from Chinese into English.**

女士们、先生们,朋友们:

今天我想借此机会回顾一下中美两国的关系。过去几年,中美双方在许多领域的双边合作取得了重大的进展。双边各级别的高层对话与接触增加了。中美目前已建立了二十多个战略、功能对话机制,涉及贸易、军事领域以及健康、文化等非传统领域。

中美两国领导人高度重视双边关系,并同意进一步加强两国在重大国际问题上的对话与合作。紧密的双边合作符合中美两国和人民的基本利益。双方一致认为,中美作为联合国安理会的常任理事国,应该继续共同努力促进世界和亚太地区的和平与稳定。双方应在六方会谈框架内共同致力于通过外交途径解决朝核问题。

中美两国经贸关系继续快速发展。中国扩大内需以及确保快速、平衡的经济社会发展的战略将给两国的经贸合作带来更多的机遇。胡锦涛主席访问美国时曾指出:"中国鼓励中美的大中小企业建立牢固的商业联系,开拓新的合作机会。"同时他还指出:"两国应加强经济战略对话,妥善处理双边的经贸摩擦。互利、双赢的经贸合作有利于中美两国人民。"

台湾问题是中美关系的核心问题。中国政府高度赞赏美国政府坚持一个中国的政策。维护台海和平的现状符合中美双方的利益。

中国将高举和平、发展与合作的旗帜,奉行独立自主的和平外交政策,致力于和平发展。在中美关系未来的发展过程中,双方不仅要捍卫两国及人民的共同利益,而且还要促进亚太乃至世界的和平、稳定与繁荣。由于全球和平与安全面对新的挑战,双方应在互利的基础上在打击国际恐怖主义、保护环境与人类生存环境、打击跨国犯罪等方面加强合作。

朋友们,我们所处的时代是一个充满机遇和挑战的时代。为此,中方愿意同美方加强对话,增进互信,深化合作。中国也愿意与美国一起共同维护世界和平与安全,并将进一步加强两国建设性的战略合作伙伴关系。

谢谢。

# 第 16 单元 外交政策 Foreign Policy

# 参考译文

## Reference Version

**篇章口译 A**

尊敬的同事们、女士们、先生们：

今天我很高兴有机会和大家谈谈欧盟的对外政策以及欧盟在国际舞台上所扮演的角色。

欧盟自20世纪90年代成立以来，便通过采取贸易、发展援助及与各国和地区组织之间签订正式贸易与合作协议的共同政策与世界各国发展关系。一个强大的欧洲可以在世界舞台上作为一个集体的理念促使所有成员国同心协力，实现外交政策的一致性。

过去15年间，欧盟加强努力，在国际政治和安全方面扮演着与其经济地位更为一致的角色。欧盟与其全球合作伙伴签署的协议不仅仅包括贸易以及传统意义上的经济和技术援助，还包括经济和其他方面的改革以及支持基础设施、健康和教育项目。此外，2003年欧盟决定所有新的协议必须包括一项内容，那就是欧盟的合作伙伴要致力于防止大规模杀伤性武器的扩散。

自1993年来，根据《欧盟条约》，欧盟已经发展了一项"共同外交与安全"政策，这项政策成为欧盟对外政策的核心，使欧盟在其整体利益处于危机时采取集体行动。由于欧盟谋求促进和维护世界的稳定，国防正在成为"共同外交与安全"政策的一个重要的方面。就在应对恐怖主义活动、国际犯罪、毒品走私、非法移民和像环境等全球性的问题时，欧盟也与其他国家和国际组织紧密合作。

欧盟的共同贸易政策在两个层面上展开。首先，在世界贸易组织内，欧盟积极参与全球多边贸易体系规则的制定。其次，欧盟与其他国家及区域国家组织展开有关自己的双边贸易谈判。欧盟在针对开放世界贸易的多边谈判的连续回合中已扮演着重要的角色。欧盟是世界上最大的贸易体，占全球进出口贸易的20%。欧盟深信全球化可以给世界上所有国家，包括发展中国家，带来益处。欧盟在允许给予发展中国家更多时间向欧洲产品开放他们市场的同时，也谋求帮助发展中国家，给予他们短期的市场准入。

欧盟的贸易政策与其发展政策是紧密相连的。这两项政策在欧盟担负起其应有的责任帮助发展中国家消除贫困，融入全球经济中发挥着同样的作用。发展援助与合作项目最早集中在非洲，到20世纪70年代中期扩展到亚洲，拉丁美洲和地中海南部及东部国家。

欧盟还将人权与民主定为其对外关系的主要内容。欧盟应对了世界上100多个国家发生的严重危机，并以最快速度向受害者提供基本的设施和紧急救援物资。欧盟积极参与所有主要发生危机地区的援助工作，包括阿富汗、巴勒斯坦地区、达富尔夫地区、刚果民主共和国以及非洲之角。

有效的多边主义是欧盟对外政策的核心。联合国是实施多边主义的基石。欧盟与联合国的关系多年来已发展成一个丰富而有多样的合作与交往的网络体系，这个网络体系最终贯穿于欧盟对外关系的整个范围。联合国积极参与的主要项目，如促进国际和平与安全、尊重人权、保护环境、抗击疾病、促进发展和消除贫困，也是欧盟优先关注的问题。欧盟也与其他成员国一起谋求重建联合国,使其能应对21世纪的挑战。

女士们、先生们,欧洲不再是50年前的欧洲了,世界也今非昔比了。在这个不断变化和越来越相互依赖的世界,欧洲正在努力解决新出现的问题:全球化、人口迁移、气候变化、满足能源的持续需求以及新的安全威胁。这些是21世纪面对欧洲和整个世界的挑战。让我们比以往更加紧密地合作,共同应对这些挑战!

谢谢。

**篇章口译 B**

Respected Mr. Chairman, Ladies and Gentlemen,

The international situation has been undergoing profound changes since the advent of the new century. The trend towards world multipolarity and economic globalization is developing amid twists and turns. Peace and development are the themes of our times. The world is hardly a tranquil place and mankind is still confronted with many serious challenges. China is committed to turning herself into a well-off society in an all-round way and aspires for a favorable international environment. China will as always pursue its independent foreign policy of peace and work closely with other countries to promote democracy in international relations, maintain world peace, pursue common development and build a beautiful harmonious world on the basis of the Five Principles of Peaceful Co-existence.

The fundamental goal of China's foreign policy is to persist consistently in the principle of independence, safeguard its state sovereignty and territorial integrity, and promote world peace and development. China will never form allies with any big power or group of countries and will never join in the arms race. China opposes hegemonism and holds that all countries are equal members of the international community whether they are big or small, strong or weak, rich or poor. All countries should settle their disputes and conflicts through peaceful consultations instead of resorting to force or the threat of force. China actively promotes the establishment of a just and rational new international political and economic order. China advocates that such international new order should be based on the Five Principles of Peaceful Co-Existence and other universally acknowledged norms of international relations. China respects the diversity of the world and holds that the diversity of the world should not be a barrier to the development of relations among various countries.

China is willing to establish and develop friendly relations and cooperation with all the countries on the basis of the Five Principles of Peaceful Co-Existence, namely, mutual respect for territorial integrity and sovereignty, mutual non-aggression, non-interference in each other's internal affairs, equality and mutual benefit, and peaceful co-existence. China persists in developing friendly relations with our neighbouring countries, strengthens cooperation with developing nations and attaches more importance to improving relations with developed nations. We have made positive contributions to maintaining peace and stability on the Korean Peninsular and in North-East Asia. We have actively fostered friendly cooperation with South-East Asian nations and has established strategic partnership with ASEAN in the 21st century.

China carries out an all-round policy of opening up and is willing to conduct trade, economic and technical cooperation, scientific and cultural exchanges with all the countries and regions in the world on the basis of the principle of equality and mutual benefit, to promote common prosperity. China has consolidated the cooperation and coordination with Asian, African and Latin American nations in politics. China also actively commits itself into international arms control, disarmament and non-proliferation. China is willing to work closely with the international community to deal with global issues facing human development such as environmental degradation, insufficient natural resources, poverty, unemployment, population growth, spread of diseases, drug abuse and international crimes.

Mr. Chairman, the world is filled with hope and also faces tough challenges in the new century. It is the common aspiration of the world countries to seek peace, cooperation and promote development. China will as always persist in independent foreign policy of peace, develop and intensify friendly cooperative relations with world countries and will make its due contributions to maintaining world peace and promoting the common development of mankind.

Thank you.

**口译练习**

第一项 句子精练

**A.**
1. 欧盟必须确保其对外政策的各个方面是一致的,并传递明确的主旨。
2. 欧盟的人道主义援助是无条件的,其目的是让受害者,无论其种族、宗教及对他们政府的政治信仰,能及时得到援助。
3. 早在1971年,欧盟开始降低从发展中国家进口货物的关税,并取消了进口配额。2001年,欧盟允许49个最不发达国家的所有产品,除了武器,自由准入欧洲市场。
4. 过去,环境问题被视为发展的障碍。今天,它们成为可持续发展模式中不可分割的一部分。欧盟积极支持环境和自然资源的保护。
5. 发展大规模杀伤性武器的发现及恐怖袭击的频繁发生使我们更加关注防扩散及裁军问题。欧盟对此采取全球性的方针,也就是坚持尊重、发展和有效贯彻多边条约和公约来禁止和尽可能减少大规模杀伤性武器的发展。

**B.**
1. China unswervingly follows the path to peaceful development and will not engage in arms race and will never seek hegemony.
2. China will persist in a win-win strategy of opening up and will accommodate the

legitimate concerns of other countries, especially other developing countries.
3. China supports international efforts to help developing countries enhance their capacity for independent development, improve the lives of their peoples and narrow the North-South gap.
4. Peaceful development is a strategic choice for the Chinese government and people, and China advocates peaceful settlement of international disputes and hotspot issues, promotes international and regional security and cooperation, and opposes terrorism in any manifestation.
5. China actively engages in multilateral diplomacy and is the major force for keeping world peace and regional stability. As a permanent member of the UN Security Council, China actively engages in resolving regional hotspot issues through political means.

## 第二项 段落口译

**A.**

目前,欧盟—美国的关系依旧是国际体系的中心。我们在国际舞台上拥有的经济与政治力量使我们在国际事务中有着举足轻重的地位。我们现在在许多诸如国际恐怖主义、气候变化、艾滋病以及在解决世界上最根深蒂固冲突的问题上是战略伙伴。今天,欧盟与美国在全球经济中占据主导地位。我们占世界经济产量的57%,世界贸易的40%,一天的交易量达到17亿欧元。在气候和能源方面,我们同意将二氧化碳的排放量降低20%,并将可再生能源的比例提高20%。

**B.**

China-ASEAN relations have witnessed new progress in the past one year. Politically, two sides have maintained close high-level contact and conducted fruitful dialogues and consultations at various level. Economically, our trade has maintained steady growth. China-ASEAN cooperation in other fields is also making steady progress. We've both have entered a new historical period of development. In the coming years, we should strengthen and upgrade China-ASEAN strategic partnership, bring China-ASEAN economic relations and trade to a new high and achieve win-win results and common development.

## 第三项 篇章口译

**A.**

朋友们,女士们、先生们:

今天我想谈谈新世纪欧盟—中国的关系。目前欧盟—中国的关系比以往更加牢固。双方建立了领导人之间每年会晤的机制,建立了全面的战略伙伴关系。

欧盟—中国的关系建立在牢固的基础上。由于双方坚信多边主义,追求国际关系民主化,努力捍卫联合国的威信,彼此间有着许多共同之处。2006年10月,欧洲委员会制定了对华战略,也就是"欧盟—中国:更加紧密的伙伴,不断增强的责任"。这表明了欧盟愿意继续进一步加强与中国的全面交往。

# 第 16 单元　外交政策　Foreign Policy

　　为迎接可持续发展的挑战，欧盟必须与中国一起努力，确保清洁、安全、可持续的能源供应来应对气候变化，改善环境，促进更加平衡的发展，改进关于发展的协调工作，保持可持续的经济发展。

　　欧盟是中国最大的贸易伙伴，占其外贸的 19%。中国新兴的中产阶级为欧盟的出口提供了不断增长的市场，并且欧洲消费者也受益于具有价格竞争力的来自中国的消费品。市场开放同时有利于欧盟和中国。在鼓励中国完全履行其对世贸组织的义务，以保证互惠、公平贸易关系的同时，欧盟将鼓励中国继续开放其市场，并向欧洲投资者和出口商进入中国市场提供良好的途径。

　　双边合作已以互相交换意见、经验和技术帮助的形式广泛展开。即使必须优先考虑一些重要方面的合作，如科技、人与人交往的发展和文化交流，双方的合作还是涵盖了各个领域。

　　欧盟和中国都致力于通过像由联合国提供的多边体系或区域体系来促进国际和平与安全。双方必须加强合作，并就世界各地区的问题进行结构性的对话。中国在协调发展中国家与发达国家之间的利益，促进亚洲的和平与稳定方面可以起重要的作用。欧盟将就东盟地区论坛进一步增进与中国的协商，以增强东盟地区论坛在地区安全问题上所起的作用。

　　欧盟与中国应该就全球治理问题，促进采用协调的方法以及欧盟—中国的共同行动，促进多边体系、安全、防扩散和裁军问题进行更多的对话，并就反恐、面对全球环境挑战方面的合作加强对话。

　　欧盟—中国关系在 21 世纪要达到新的成熟阶段基于双方的紧密合作。在现有的条件下，欧盟与中国作为战略伙伴对双方都具有不可否认的益处，尤其是鉴于双方在地区和多边体系中起的重要作用。因此，欧盟与中国肩负着共同的责任和使命，为发展双边关系和共同创造更加美好的未来构筑战略计划。

　　谢谢各位。

**B.**

Ladies and Gentlemen, Distinguished Friends,

　　Today I would like take this opportunity to review Sino-US relations. In the past few years, China and the United States have made positive progress in the bilateral cooperation in many areas. China and the United States have so far established more than 20 strategic and functional dialogue mechanisms, covering fields of trade, military affairs and non-traditional fields such as health and culture.

　　Sino-US leaders both attach great importance to bilateral relations and have agreed to strengthen dialogues and cooperation on major international issues. Closer bilateral cooperation serves the fundamental interests of the two countries and the peoples. Both sides hold that China and the United States, as the permanent member of the UN Security Council, should continue to work together to promote peace and stability in the Asia-Pacific Region and the world as a whole. Both sides should jointly work for resolving North-Korea nuclear issue through diplomatic means within the framework of Six-party Talks.

Sino-US economic and trade ties continue to grow fast. China's strategy of boosting domestic demand and ensuring fast and balanced economic and social development will create more opportunities for economic cooperation and trade between the two countries.

President Hu Jintao pointed out in his visit to the United States that China encourages Chinese and American companies, large, medium-sized and small ones alike, to build strong business ties and explore new opportunities for cooperation. He also pointed out that China and the United States should strengthen strategic economic dialogues and properly address bilateral trade frictions. A mutually beneficial and win-win economic and trade cooperation between China and the US would benefit the two peoples.

Taiwan issue is at the heart of Sino-US relations. The Chinese government highly appreciates the US government for reaffirming their one-China policy. Maintaining the status-quo of the Cross-Straits peace brings benefits to both China and the United States.

China will hold high the banner of peace, development and cooperation, pursue an independent foreign policy of peace, and commit itself to peaceful development. In the future development of Sino-US relations, both sides should not only safeguard the common interests of the two nations and two peoples, but also promote peace, stability and prosperity in the Asia-Pacific Region and the whole world. As the global peace and security face new challenges, both sides should intensify their cooperation in fighting against international terrorism, preventing the environment and human habitat and combating transnational crimes.

Dear Friends, we are now living in an era with more opportunities and challenges. In this regard, China is willing to promote dialogue, improve mutual-trust, and advance cooperation with the United States. China is also willing to work together with the U.S. to promote world peace and prosperity, and further strengthen our constructive strategic partnership relations.

Thank you.